Labour's Apprentices: Working-class Lads in Late Victorian and Edwardian England

The three decades before the First World War witnessed significant changes in the working life, home life and social life of adolescent English males. In *Labour's Apprentices*, Michael Childs suggests that the study of such age-specific experiences provides vital clues to the evolving structure and fortunes of the working class as a whole and helps to explain subsequent development in English history.

Beginning with home life, Childs discusses the life cycle of the working-class family and considers the changes that becoming a wage-earner and a contributor to the family economy made to a youth's status. He explores the significance of publicly provided education for the working class and analyses the labour market for young males, focusing on the role of apprenticeship, the impact of different types of labour on future job prospects, the activities of trade unions, and wage levels. Childs makes a detailed investigation of the patterns of labour available to boys at that time, including street selling, half-time labour, and apprenticed labour versus "free" labour. He argues that such changes were a major factor in the creation of a semi-skilled adult workforce. Childs then examines the choices that working-class youths made in the area of their greatest freedom: leisure activities. He looks at street culture, commercial entertainments, and youth groups and movements and finds that each influenced the emergence of a more cohesive and class-conscious working class during the period up to the First World War.

MICHAEL J. CHILDS is an assistant professor in the Department of History, Bishop's University.

Labour's Apprentices

Working-Class Lads in Late Victorian and Edwardian England

MICHAEL J. CHILDS

McGill-Queen's University Press
Montreal & Kingston • London • Buffalo

© McGill-Queen's University Press 1992
ISBN 0-7735-0915-1

Legal deposit fourth quarter 1992
Bibliothèque nationale du Québec

Printed in Canada on acid-free paper

Canadian Cataloguing in Publication Data

Childs, Michael James, 1956–
    Labour's apprentices
    Includes bibliographical references and index.
    ISBN 0-7735-0915-1
    1. Youth – England – History – 19th century.
    2. Working class – England – History – 19th century.
    3. Youth – England – History – 20th century. 4. Working class – England – History – 20th century.
    5 England – Social life and customs – 19th century.
    6. England – Social life and customs – 20th century.
    I. Title.
    HQ799.G7C48 1992   305.23'5'094209   C92-090232-4

Published simultaneously in the United Kingdom by
The Hambledon Press.

This book was typeset by Typo Litho composition inc.
in 10/12 Palatino.

To Danielle

Contents

Tables and Figure

Preface

Although the research and writing of this study often seemed to be a solitary endeavour, it could not have been either attempted or accomplished without the advice, aid, encouragement, and support of many individuals and institutions.

A large debt of gratitude is due to Professor Paul Thompson of the University of Essex and to Dr Elizabeth Roberts of the Centre for North-West Regional Studies at the University of Lancaster, for allowing me access to their superb oral history archives. The material contained within these archives was both fascinating to read and central to the composition of this work. Elsewhere in England, the Public Record Office at Kew, the British Newspaper Library, the British Library, and the British Library of Political and Economic Science at the London School of Economics all deserve thanks for their efficiency and their openness to visiting scholars.

Financial aid from various bodies allowed me to undertake and to complete this study, which began life as a doctoral thesis at McGill University. I would like to thank McGill University for the award of a McConnell Memorial Fellowship in 1983–84 and for a Graduate Faculty Research Grant in 1985. My grateful acknowledgments are also owed to the Social Sciences and Humanities Research Council of Canada for the award of a Doctoral Fellowship for 1984–85 and 1985–86. The Senate Research Committee of Bishop's University also provided funding for a further research trip in 1989.

This book has been published with the help of a grant from the Social Science Federation of Canada, using funds provided by the Social Sciences and Humanities Research Council of Canada. An additional grant was made by the Publications Committee of Bishop's University. Both institutions deserve my sincere thanks.

Additional debts of a more personal nature must also be acknowledged. Professor Martin Petter, who introduced me to modern British history in a graduate seminar, was of great help in the preparation of the thesis upon which this book is based. His knowledge, critical sense, and interest are much appreciated. Professor James Epstein of Vanderbilt University provided pertinent criticisms of certain sections of the work, as did my colleagues in the Department of History and the Division of Humanities at Bishop's University. I would like to record the kindness and hospitality of those friends who put me up (and put up with me) in England, particularly the Donovans and Tim Lintott. I also thank my family for their encouragement during my interminable years as a student. Finally, I must give lasting and heartfelt acknowledgment to Danielle St-Vincent, whose friendship, love, and support have been of inestimable value to me for over a dozen years.

Introduction

One historical constant is the tendency of all societies to agonize over the state of their youth – will they be ready and willing to act as fit guardians of the traditions of the past and the values of the present, and will they take this precious cargo into the future? In its relationship with its youth, every society faces a fundamental human dilemma: how does ephemeral and mortal humanity construct and maintain an enduring culture and civilization? The day we stop worrying about youth will be the day the human experiment declares bankruptcy.

These fears may be a constant, but the specific ways in which they manifest themselves change over time and are historically conditioned by the forces at work in any particular era: class conflicts, economic changes, political developments, and foreign threats. At various periods, as well, these fears rise above the usual chronic fretfulness and assume nightmarish proportions; a crisis about the state of youth usually runs parallel to a concomitant crisis within the larger society's value system. Age relations are thus particularly fit subjects for historical analysis; by a study of the views and the fears about youth in past eras, the historian may not only hold up a mirror to that society's values but also gaze with it into a crystal ball to see what *its* vision of the future was. It was, of course, usually bleak. But beyond this, and in addition to the usual dynamism contained within history, arising from the sheer sequentiality of its subject matter, the study of youth adds another dynamic element – an extra joker to the pack – because the young do not stay young, but pass into adulthood profoundly affected and shaped by their earlier experiences. They do this not in a mechanical, deterministic way, but as a result of their own responses to their upbringing, their own assessment of their environment, and their own needs and desires. In the end, it is these factors that are decisive, since the young have time on their side. Yet the role of succeeding generations of youths, who grow up and pass into adulthood, gradually reshaping their society in the process, is relatively ignored. Perhaps one of the least understood factors of historical change is the one contained within the simple process of growing up and into adulthood.

This world of youth, long a favoured preserve of the poet and the novelist, has, in fact, only recently become the subject of serious study by the historian. In this work, conscious of following in the footsteps of such pioneers as John Gillis, J.O. Springhall, and Stephen Humphries, I seek to add to their findings by investigating youth in a specific time and place. I seek to present, in as complete a degree as possible, the world of late Victorian and Edwardian working-class adolescents, to examine the factors affecting their world and the actions they took in response, and to estimate the consequences of such responses on the larger society. This is attempted through a combination of oral history and of documentary material, so that, having once reconstructed the "objective" world of the late Victorian and Edwardian youth, we can, as far as possible, hear him tell us what he thought about this world and why he acted as he did. Convinced that the proper way to understand a person's or group's actions is to understand the environment in which those choices are made, I am using a global approach, which, in turn, examines a series of sites of experience – the home, school, work, the street, and so on – which correspond in a rough way to the chronological phases of a youth's life. In each of these areas, I seek a sense of change over time, as well as industrial and regional variations.

In this study, "youth" will be taken to mean the group of males between the school-leaving age and, roughly, twenty to twenty-one. The school-leaving age itself varied over the years covered in this work, but may be generally taken to be about twelve in the 1880s and fourteen by the beginning of World War I. As will become clear, this six to eight year period corresponded in large measure to a definite period in the life of a member of England's working class. No longer a schoolchild, not yet a recognized member of the adult workforce, the working-class youth was rather a member of a special category – that of boy labourer, or learner, or apprentice – each with its own traditions, responsibilities, and pressures, in both the workplace and the home. It was during this period, as well, that youths engaged in leisure behaviour distinct in many ways from that of either children or adults. The consequences of these relatively autonomous experiences at home, at work, or on the street must be delineated if we want to understand both what it meant to be a working youth in this period and the creation of adult working-class attitudes in the early twentieth century.

This work limits itself to males, except in the case of specific relationships, such as those of the mother, sisters, or girlfriends, where the interactions between the sexes within the family, on the street, or in the workplace is clearly of importance to the subjects of the study. To limit the work to a study of males is perhaps to incur the charge of sexism, but this decision was based primarily upon the recognition of the all-pervading sex-based differentiation of the period. Quite simply, the life experiences and life expectations of working-class girls were too different from those of boys for both to be usefully encompassed within the same study. Female work at the time was ghettoized to a high degree, largely confined to industries such as domestic service and home work, where earning capacity was both low and (more importantly) static. In textiles, the one industry in which boys, girls, and women could be found in large numbers, the tasks and eventual destinations of each were sharply different. Questions that were vital and central to the working-class boy, and that particularly interested me when I came to this field, such as apprenticeship, the gaining of a secure place in the workforce, and a viable skill, or the possible responses to the blandishments of organized youth movements, were either largely irrelevant to females, or else, given the very different sexual roles assigned to them, required strategies and responses that need to be examined independently. The world of working-class girls and women is an important topic that merits study in its own right, as the work of scholars who have explored "a woman's place" confirms.

Likewise, I deal with the urbanized and industrialized areas of England and Wales to the exclusion of both rural and semi-rural areas and, for the most part, Scotland. Within the industrial areas themselves, I have treated differences due to geographical, industrial, or social disparities, but to give such coverage to all of areas and regions of Britain would require these disparities to take up an inordinate amount of space and would preclude the possibility of formulating viable generalizations about urban youth and change over time. Evidence from the urbanized and industrial areas of Scotland has been used on occasion, in cases where this evidence seems compatible with the rest of Britain and where objective factors are clearly similar to those being explored elsewhere.

To turn from "youth" to "working class" is to move from a relatively straightforward category to one much more complicated and controversial. In this study, the working class is generally taken to be the group of manual workers and their families in urban and industrial England and Wales. It is by no means held that only such people are working class, since the rural working class has been left out, but that the working class in its characteristic form was to be found most often in the urban environment, drawing its sustenance from pursuits in which a large degree of mechanization and concentration had taken place. Nonetheless, since in this study I am dealing with social and cultural, as well as economic forces, it has seemed more suitable to use information from a broader group of people where warranted. Thus, information from oral respondents from the small shopkeeper class has been used in cases where the locale was a recognizably "working-class" quarter. The example of such authors as Robert Roberts should remind us of both this group's potential for acute social awareness and their often deep family and social ties to the class among whom they lived.

Based as it is in considerable part on the recollections of individual working people, the treatment of class will be descriptive and empirical rather than theoretical, with whatever dynamic elements presented being the result of observation. Here, the work of E.P. Thompson has proved useful, particularly his view that class is not a theoretical construct, but a lived experience, "something that in fact happens ... in human relationship."[1] In this view, class is not only or even primarily the sum total of the objective differences that separate one group of people from another, but also the result of the assumptions and actions taken by people who find themselves in a certain social situation distinct from others in the community. Class is thus as much a product of conscious human thought and action as it is of impersonal economic or social factors, and, for many, the recognition of class comes by an identification with a group through common experiences, events, and symbols.[2] For working-class youth, the period was one of a growing similarity in life experiences across the regional and industrial spectrum, while one vital ingredient of class consciousness – another class – was increasingly introduced into young people's lives in the form of educational authorities and youth movement leaders. How working-class youth reacted to these factors owes nothing to theory and everything to their own judgment of their needs and their hopes. As Thompson also reminds us, "Class is defined by men as they live their own history, and, in the end, this is its only definition."[3] The historian's task, when dealing with class, is to delineate that definition and to trace the pattern of its development.

To describe an era as a "crucial period" or "turning point" is to lapse into the use of rather tired historical clichés. Nonetheless, with regard to working-class youths, such claims are far from being without value. The years from 1870 to World War I witnessed a long-term and vigorous movement to educate, socialize, and "civilize" the nation's young, to fit them for efficient and productive activity in the industrial life of the nation, and to train them in the proper social and political attitudes, a task made more urgent with each successive widening of the franchise. Political and social motives melded with economic ones, as Britain began to feel the first real threats from its continental rivals, to produce in these years an almost obsessive interest in the condition of the young of the working class. "National efficiency," "race suicide," and other pseudo-scientific concepts began to replace the religious metaphors of sin and depravity that previously had shaped the apprehensions of the élites about social stability.

Parallel to this offensive of social reform was widespread change in the industrial structure of the nation, which saw a gradual reduction of artisan-labourer barriers, resulting from the introduction of a host of mechanical and organizational innovations. Central to this process was the abandonment throughout many industries of a formal apprenticeship system and its substitution by a much more open and less structured method of trade recruitment. The recognition on the part of workers and of the middle class that this was occurring, coupled with the growing awareness of the problems of unemployment, led to widespread fears of growing industrial indiscipline and of the creation of a "residuum" to rival ancient Rome's in the heart of the new empire. Two of the major trends of the late Victorian and Edwardian period thus found a common focus in the working-class adolescent, whose education, vocational training, and social conditioning were increasingly seen by many in the upper classes to be crucial to the future well-being of the nation.

One result of this identification was the spate of studies of social problems that appeared from the 1890s to World War I and that provide one of the main sources for this work. Many deal solely or largely with the special questions of "boy labour" or "The Boy," while the larger studies such as Booth's *Life and Labour of the People of London* or Rowntree's *Poverty: A Study of Town Life*, also provide a good deal of information on working-class youth. Less anecdotal than previous investigations of "Darkest England," such studies looked toward a new era of social inquiry, in which statistics and a search for economic and social causes took the forefront. In the field of working-class adolescents, the work of writers and reformers such as C.E.B. Russell, A. Paterson, and A. Freeman provide a wealth of information for the researcher, but there are problems associated with their use that must be borne in mind. Many are exercises in advertising a problem and proposing a solution, and both the extent of the perceived danger arising from lawless and untrained youth and the effectiveness of the proposed remedy are apt to be exaggerated. Fortunately, these aims and motives are usually in plain sight, and the critical difficulties associated with these types of sources are no different from those to be found in any comparable historical source. Handled with care, they may furnish a great deal of data useful in the re-creation of the life of working-class youth in these years.

Government documents, both published and unpublished, form another major source of information. Some statistics relating to wage levels, hours of work, and educational patterns are available throughout this period, and they provide important data on the general patterns to be found in these areas. Unfortunately, too often the categories used change from one inquiry or census to the next, making the search for development over time much more difficult than it would otherwise be. At other times, the categories provided are unhelpful to a specific investigation of youth.[4] Within these limits, however, such statistics can be useful in marking out the limits and the norms of working-class youth life.

Of greater help are the numerous governmental committees and royal commissions set up in this era to investigate and report on various perceived problems. Among the more important royal commissions for the present work are the royal commissions on labour in the early 1890s, on elementary education in the late 1880s, on militia and volunteers in 1903–4, and on the poor laws in 1909, while governmental committees on the employment of schoolchildren, on physical deterioration, and on continuing education are also revealing. Besides statistical and scientific evidence, such inquiries, in their minutes of evidence, present the researcher with the opportunity to enter the debates of the period and to become conversant with the opposing or divergent points of view among policy makers.

A further primary source comprises the memoirs, autobiographies, and biographies of working-class people. Some of these fall into the "workhouse to Westminster" category and as such are often more concerned with later careers than with early experiences, while their writers are often possessed of a strong political and social philosophy. Those memoirs that are the product of more ordinary people are preferable as sources, being both inherently less coloured with polemical intent and more concerned with day-to-day realities. The collections compiled by J. Burnett have been extremely useful in this regard.

One obvious gap in the record is that of first-hand evidence from working-class youths themselves, except in isolated and highly anecdotal fragments found in the works of the middle-class authors. We therefore possess virtually no direct account by youths of their feelings, opinions, and desires. This gap, however, is to a large extent remedied by the use of oral history material collected by Paul Thompson at the University of Essex and by Elizabeth Roberts at the University of Lancaster. In these archives, the ordinary person has been given a chance to recount the circumstances of daily life in the years before and during World War I, and to explain opinions and actions that previously had been the subject of speculation (and often condemnation) by middle-class observers and reformers. It is rare for social historians to be able to get the other side of the story in so direct a fashion – to gain access, even at the remove of many decades, to the daily life of ordinary people as they themselves experienced and remembered it. As the present study developed, I began to place an increasingly important emphasis on such material, because at an early date it became apparent that on numerous topics, such as family life and attitudes to school, work, and leisure, oral history revealed a different, more consistent, and more convincing explanation for the attitudes and behaviour of working-class teenagers than that to be found in any other contemporary source. Its importance to the social historian therefore cannot be exaggerated, and it would be safe to say that any social history of the late nineteenth or twentieth century that ignores oral history material is incomplete.

The problems associated with the use of oral history sources are certainly no greater than those of other types of evidence with regard to veracity and accuracy.[5] Nonetheless, to be truly useful, the interviews must be read carefully with great attention to chronological sequence and social situation. It is important to get the "feel" of each respondent's family circumstances and industrial experiences, while at the same time remaining aware of the appropriate historical and geographical context. An additional problem with the transcripts is that they reproduce the exact phrasing and sentence structure of the interview. I have taken the liberty of smoothing out the text and removing stutters, repetitions, and confusing structures in order to make the transcripts easier to read. Keeping the sense of the respondent's answer has been the main priority in this process; readers who would like the full response are referred to the original transcripts. With these caveats in mind, oral history can prove to be an extremely rich source for researchers interested in social, political, and cultural change.

The last two decades have seen a remarkable growth in the field of social history, and a great deal of interesting and thought-provoking work has been produced. Many of these works have proved invaluable in the present study, by providing evidence and information, by elucidating approaches to the various fields that any history of youth must deal with, and by proposing models of explanation. The debt I owe to recent scholars is evident in the endnotes and bibliography.

During these years, historians have tended to turn away from a prior interest in working-class organizations, both political and industrial, to begin examining other, less structured aspects of working-class life, such as the family and leisure. Along with, and complementary to, this development has come an interest in inter-class relationships outside the workplace, especially in the fields of popular culture, the educational system, and organized youth movements. In these areas, scholars have often used such explanatory concepts as "social control," the process by which ruling élites develop mechanisms to inculcate the working class with their own attitudes and behaviour, and "cultural hegemony," a more subtle model of how a ruling élite's guardianship of the very terms of political and economic debate tends to perpetuate their dominance. Arising from the work of Talcott Parsons, but finding its most welcome home on the Left, the concept of social control has been used in the exploration of areas of conflict and control such as leisure and religion, but it has been the bureaucratic administration of the state school system that has leant itself to the most developed exposition of the theory. The aim of the school system from its inception, according to this theory, was the deliberate and wholesale destruction of working-class modes of thought and ways of life and their replacement by a subordinate version of the dominant culture.[6] Perhaps the most complete examination of this theme with regard to children and youth is Stephen Humphries' work.[7] Drawing on social theory of the day and on oral history testimony, Humphries shows that the battle for control in the school, in reformatories, and on the streets was not an easy one, that the working class fought back against cultural domination, and that behind the seemingly chaotic behaviour of youths and children there often lay a rational basis of resistance.

Humphries' work has performed a valuable service, by insisting that the aspirations and the opinions of youth be considered in any history of reformist and educational agencies and by making us more aware of the hidden motives behind schemes of social amelioration when these are directed by one class toward another. Nevertheless, by concentrating almost exclusively on incidences of friction and areas of class conflict, Humphries tends to ignore or downplay other significant aspects of the life of the working-class child or youth, such as family relations, hobbies, and commercial entertainment. Above all, the topic of youth in the workplace has been neglected by virtually every modern writer on working-class adolescents. By omitting this topic, a central feature of working-class life is ignored, while one of the mechanisms whereby youth fought or evaded authoritarian structures is passed over. This is doubly surprising, since contemporary middle-class observers identified the position of the boy labourer as the crucial factor that allowed him to evade discipline and control from family, employers, and social agencies. In this study I will explore the male youth in the workplace and will attempt to relate his experiences there to his actions and opinions. I will also attempt to elucidate the effect of changes in the nature of the boy labour market on the working class as a whole.

Beyond this, in order to estimate with any accuracy the impact of socializing agencies and institutions, one must take a universalist approach, by investigating other potential areas of experience that may well have been more significant. While revealing, the emphasis on areas of conflict tends to obscure much that went on in the daily lives of working-class youth, which had little immediate bearing on inter-class relationships but which, over time, came to have an important, thought diffuse, impact on the attitudes and self image of this group. An example is the experience of the youth in the music hall, where the assertion of class was quite pronounced, but where overt class hostility was generally lacking. An understanding of such areas as family, work, and commercial entertainment, in short, might make the pattern of class conflict, where it occurs, more intelligible by revealing areas of strength and weakness on the part of youth in their struggle for autonomy and self-expression. It might also reveal areas in which collaboration or compromise was possible. Finally, such an investigation might reveal other, non-class relationships that have intrinsic interest for the historian in their own right. Studies that investigate the culture of workers in its own terms rightly tend to emphasize the "dynamic and shifting" nature of the hegemony exercised by the elites.[8] An awareness that class relations work in both directions, and that they draw upon the very real values and strength of the subordinate culture, is necessary if we are to understand both the working class and its relationship with other social groups.

Although Humphries' work is certainly the most complete history of working-class youth in our period, various other scholars have studied topics in these years that involved or concerned youths. One of these topics is the emergence of the organized, and often uniformed, youth movements. Paul Wilkinson was perhaps the first historian, two decades ago, to draw attention to the many youth movements of the twentieth century and to suggest that an investigation of their similarities and differences might yield interesting information on past theories of child-rearing and socialization, as well as wider concerns about national efficiency, juvenile crime, and industrial competitiveness.[9] J.O. Springhall has studied the various boys' brigades and the Boy Scouts in their formative years, seeing in them a paradigm of the socializing agency, a highly effective means whereby dominant cultural and social values were spread among the nation at large.[10] Both of these studies contain information useful for this work. Both, however, deal largely with movements that begin virtually as the present study ends and, in large part, with youth of other classes. In this study, I will look at the boys' clubs – the archetypical working-class youth organizations – in greater detail and will investigate their effectiveness among the mass of working-class boys from oral material and from the writings of the club organizers. It is only by an examination of the whole age group that one can estimate, with any degree of accuracy, the final influence of such movements.

The place of youth in the wider working-class world also needs to be discussed, in an effort to understand the interaction of age relations with those of class. For these reasons, some specific, empirical information will be provided on concrete relationships between the young and their elders, particularly parents, teachers, and employers. The larger and more dynamic question referred to earlier remains, however, because the young grow up, becoming in their turn what historians traditionally see as the whole of "society." In this sense, the question is how far the experiences of youth in these years contributed to perceived longer-term changes within the working class as a whole. In a seminal article, G. Stedman Jones noted the paradox, in this era, of a working class becoming at once more conservative and more class conscious, while S. Meacham has taken this hypothesis and located its operative factors in the social and economic changes of the day.[11] It is one of the theses of this study that these changes were first felt by, and operated through, successive generations of youths who, undergoing increasingly common experiences in school, on the job, and in their leisure hours, became adults with a heightened intra-class cohesiveness compared with their mid-century peers. In this way, age relationships, and the changing nature of generational experiences and attitudes, are inextricably bound up with the patterns of class relationships. To understand the processes of one requires an awareness and understanding of the other.

To provide a definitive solution to such questions, or to propose an enduring model of the role of generational differences in historical change, must be the work of many social scientists and many more years of research. In this work, I claim to do neither. Rather, my goal is to offer some additional information and analysis to the continuing debate and to provide another building block, however small, for the historical reconstruction of modern English society.

Labour's Apprentices

CHAPTER ONE

Youths and Working-Class Families

Since the primary source of identity and security for the working-class youths of late Victorian and Edwardian England was their families, any discussion of this group must begin with an examination of their home life – at once one of the most important and one of the most opaque subjects for social historians. The role of the family as an agency of nurture, protection, and socialization cannot be ignored if we want to understand the values and customs of the working class teenager. It was mainly within the home that the young child learned the realities of working-class life, that behavioural norms were created and enforced, and that skills and attitudes necessary for adaptation to the larger world were taught. Family life, in short, provided the earliest and probably the most important formative influence on the individual child, one that intimately coloured and influenced his subsequent options, behaviour, and outlook.

No family, of course, exists in isolation. The working-class family of the period was especially affected by social and economic pressures from the larger society, and a good deal of the family's time, effort, and resources were directed toward strategies designed effectively to counteract these forces. The working-class family has, in fact, come under increasing scrutiny in the last two decades by researchers anxious to uncover the links between the structure and functions of the family and economic, technological, cultural, and political change.[1] These exterior factors and internal responses had, in turn, an effect on children and youths, and they help explain the working-class youth as a product of and actor upon his environment. A brief overview of the working-class family and the challenges it faced is, therefore, necessary before discussing the place of the adolescent male within society.

The general problem facing the working-class family in these years was poverty, exacerbated by a chronic instability of income, poor housing, and inappropriate feeding or undernourishment. The findings of the pioneering social investigators of the two decades before World War I allow us to delineate with some accuracy the social and economic constraints against which the working-class family struggled. In the 1890s, Charles Booth's London investigators confirmed what many social agitators had long held – that the continuing industrialization of England had not resulted in the disappearance, or probably even the reduction, of the portion of society living in poverty. He found that 30.7 per cent of London's population lived in poverty and that these unfortunates were neither confined to Dickensian "rookeries" nor recruited solely from the ranks of beggars and criminals.[2] On the contrary, he found, pockets of misery existed throughout the metropolis, often close to wealthy areas, and were populated largely by casual unskilled workers.[3] His findings for the capital at the end of the nineteenth-century Depression (hereafter referred to as the Great Depression) might have been taken as exceptional had not Seebohm Rowntree's study in York resulted in remarkably similar figures. Using a diet followed in Scottish prisons, a price list furnished by the poor law guardians, and local rental rates, Rowntree constructed a basic "living wage," below which real physical want began. His conclusion that 27.8 per cent of York's population (43.4 per cent of its working class) lived in either primary or secondary poverty revealed the widespread nature of the problem in this period.[4] After a decade of slowly falling real wages, Bowley and Burnett-Hurst's investigation of four towns in 1912–13 showed that poverty extended through the industrial spectrum. The collated results for Northampton (boot and shoe industry), Stanley (mining), Warrington (iron and tanning industries), and Reading (boot and shoe industry and food processing) gave a primary poverty figure of 16 per cent of the population.[5] As this figure was twice that of Rowntree's, it is unlikely that the combined figure for primary and secondary poverty would have been less than 30 per cent, had the latter been calculated.

More important, however, than the bare statistics of poverty was the fact that poverty was not permanently confined to a lower third of the population, who could thus be identified and perhaps dealt with. Children were a primary cause and were thus primarily affected by poverty; in 71 per cent of poor households, the reason for this condition was that the wage earner did not make enough to support his three or four children.[6] When these same children began to earn, though, the family raised itself above the poverty line, and

Figure 1
The Family Income Cycle

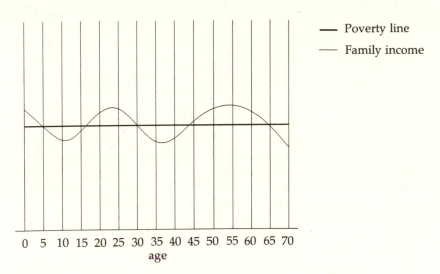

— Poverty line

— Family income

0 5 10 15 20 25 30 35 40 45 50 55 60 65 70

age

Source: Rowntree, *Poverty*, 137.

some years of relative affluence would follow. The grown child, once married with a family, would then once more find himself living in poverty until his children began to earn. A final return to poverty would often occur in the worker's last years, when he became too old to work. Rowntree's diagram graphically expressed this sine curve of relative plenty and absolute want.

In fact, then, although at any given time nearly one-third of the total population lived in poverty, a large percentage of working-class children could expect to experience its effects at some time in their early years, especially those children whose fathers were labourers rather than artisans. Even in a family whose income was relatively high, the years when the children were young were likely to witness hardship. For the working class, "the really difficult time in the family history is in the ten years or so when the eldest child is growing from 4 to 14."[7] The essentially rhythmic nature of the working-class family economy must be borne in mind when we come to discuss the family with earning adolescent offspring; this economy was not fixed but fluid, and the experience of an individual family changed quite dramatically over time.

Although having children could result in poverty, the effects of a large family could at least be foreseen by the working class. Financial disaster of either temporary or permanent duration could, however, descend upon a family without warning. Illness, death, accident, the slackening of trade, or a strike could plunge a family from relative comfort into a precarious hand-to-mouth existence. A Staffordshire boy, whose family suffered four deaths in six months, remembers, "Me mother's life was one large worry from the time me father died until the end of her days."[8] Another family was reduced from the comforts of the lower middle class to penury by the death of the breadwinner, a master sweep. With six children to rear, the mother was forced into the casual labour market of the metropolis when she went out to cook.[9] A foreman's son from Nottingham remembers that when his father died, leaving a wife and five young children, his relatively well-off family was forced to go to the local guardians, who insisted that they sell everything of value before aid was given. "I don't think I have ever got over it."[10] A Londoner notes of his navvy father, "Oh, out of work very often. Well they couldn't work in the winter ... in those days ... we just existed."[11] Life for many working-class families was led either in poverty or on its edge, and no family in this class, from the highly paid "labour aristocracy" to the marginalized and casual unskilled, could afford to be complacent about its prospects or security. In such a situation, children who had earlier been a drain on household funds could well prove to be a family's economic salvation, and many couples were willing to endure poverty induced by children in order to obtain the only security they were likely to possess – working offspring.

Overcrowding of the home was another problem for many working-class families. Middle-class writers made much of this condition in their appeals for more social or religious work among the poor, drawing a direct link between overcrowding and such evils as drink and immorality. In *The Bitter Cry of Outcast London*, the Reverend Andrew Mearns depicted London's slums as "a vast mass of moral corruption, of heart-breaking misery and absolute godlessness," made plain with capital letters his conviction that "THIS TERRIBLE FLOOD OF SIN AND MISERY IS GAINING UPON US," and intimated that incest was common.[12] Another writer alleged that the mother would often pawn the clothes of "the shivering children" for drink, in order to go home "so besotted that the wretchedness, the anguish, the degradation that await her there have lost their grip."[13]

Figures from this period bear out the prevalence of overcrowding throughout the working class, if not its supposed moral consequences. In the Whitechapel and Limehouse relocation scheme of 1878, 2,368 people were found living in 730 one-room dwellings (an average of 3.24 persons per room), while 115 two-room dwellings held 533 people (an average of 2.32 persons per room).[14] In London in 1891, 166,048 dwellings contained more than two people per room, for a total of a least 480,000 people.[15] Two years before World War I, researchers found overcrowding in four towns to range from a low of 8.7 per cent of the population in Northampton to 50 per cent in the Durham mining town of Stanley, where tied cottages, built and owned by the collieries, were the norm.[16] In 1901 16 per cent of London's population lived in overcrowded premises (35.2 per cent in Finsbury alone), while such northern cities as Newcastle-upon-Tyne and Gateshead packed one-third of their population into overcrowded houses and tenements.[17] Moreover, these statistics represent a very rigid definition of overcrowding – one that a three-room house containing four adults, four children, and numerous babies would escape. While not perhaps living in officially overcrowded premises, most working-class children spent their early years in a cramped, cheek-by-jowl existence, whether in the tenement flats common in the metropolis or in the monotonous "two up, two down" cottages that were so much a feature of urbanized England. This premium on space made it difficult for the working-class family to construct and maintain the physical and spiritual sanctuary that the middle class saw in their mythologized conception of the home. This shifted the locus of the home from realty to personality; in many working-class households the family sentiment resided directly in the members themselves rather than in the delapidated collection of bricks and mortar that they were, often enough, forced to evacuate by moonlight.

The final major preoccupation of the working-class family was getting enough to eat and making sure that available food was put to the best use. Booth's and Rowntree's figures show that this must have been a difficult, if not impossible, task for almost one-third of the populace at any given time, and a constant struggle for the rest. Although one writer suggested that the working class could buy much cheaper at Saturday night markets than could the poor law guardians, whose budget was used by Rowntree,[18] this advantage was usually obviated by the need to buy in small quantities through the rest of the week.[19]

Improper feeding or positive undernourishment, for whatever reason, was certainly widespread among sections of the working class, including the unskilled generally and women and children in particular. One report noted that many children did not have the physical energy to play games in the schoolyard;[20] another report suggested that perhaps 16 per cent of London schoolchildren suffered from malnutrition.[21] A study of diets from 1887–1901 revealed that for families living on 18 shillings per week and under, the mean calorific intake per person was only 1,578 kCal per day, while for those in the 21–30 shilling bracket, it was 2,113 kCal. The majority of this went to adult men, whose mean intake was 3,321 kCal per day, the little that remained going to the women and children.[22]

The effects of undernourishment were seen most strikingly in the physique of schoolchildren of different classes. In 1883, thirteen year old males from labouring families were, on average, 3.27 inches shorter and 12.6 pounds lighter than their counterparts in the professional classes.[23] In 1910 in southwest Surrey, the gap between thirteen year olds was even greater, with a difference of nearly 28 pounds between the lowest categories and those whose family incomes exceeded 25 shillings per week.[24] Given this constant dearth, it is not surprising that children were often preoccupied with the thought of food and the means of getting it (sometimes begging at factory gates),[25] or that the local ghost in a Yorkshire mill town was "Breakfast Mary," a phantom who stole the bread from unwary half-timers as they trudged to work in the morning.[26]

The working-class family, then, was faced with an array of problems arising from its lack of economic and social power. Social investigators of the Mearns type believed that, in poverty, the working-class family as an institution had virtually disintegrated under the pressure of these difficulties, leaving the child with little or no social guidance, love, or discipline. As we shall see, even those investigators most closely identified with youth asserted that family ties among the working class as a whole were extremely loose and that a dysfunctional family, per se, was part of the perceived problem of an anomic and feckless working-class youth.

Oral evidence from this period, however, strongly belies this interpretation, showing that the family as an institution had a great deal of vigour among the working class and that families had developed strategies to cope with their problems in a pragmatic and realistic way. Family life among the working class was different in many respects from that experienced by people in easier circumstances, yet it was highly adaptive to its environment and reflected to perhaps a greater degree the cooperation, love, and mutual support that have traditionally been taken as characteristic of the family.

The major responses of the working-class family to its economic environment in the late nineteenth and early twentieth centuries were a gradual reduction in the family size and the practice of regarding the family as a cooperative (though still structured) economic unit. In such a unit, both children and youths were functioning, integral parts of the family, and they assumed roles of support that were often essential to the well-being of the whole. The offspring of the working class were made aware at an early age of the struggle for life and of their responsibilities within it.

The major work on family planning in the nineteenth century suggests that the idea of a smaller family did not "percolate down" to the working class in the late nineteenth century, but rather that birth control techniques were known from the late eighteenth century and were practised where appropriate.[27] In the early nineteenth century, reduced family size made most sense in the textile towns, where working wives were often vital to the family economy and where mill women therefore often practised methods of birth control and abortion.[28] Nonetheless, throughout most of the English industrial landscape, married women's work was either rare or very poorly paid, thus making a large family an obvious solution to the chronic economic pressures besetting the working-class household. From the 1870s on, however, a host of changes gradually lessened the value and necessity of large numbers of children beyond the boundaries of the textile areas, and the restriction of family size began to make sense to a wider section of the working class than before. Compulsory schooling and more stringent factory acts increased the period of dependence of children, while rising real wages over the period, increased state resources, and expanding trade union and friendly society membership began to lessen parental dependence on their offspring in times of need. One effect of these trends was that "by the turn of the century it was clear that a sizeable proportion of the working classes was practising family planning."[29] The birth rate in England began to fall, from 35.5 per 1,000 in 1870–72 to 30.8 in 1890–92 and 24.5 in 1910–12, while the mean ultimate family size contracted from 5.62 for those married in 1876 to 4.13 in 1890–99 and 2.64 in 1910–19.[30] All other things being equal, the effect of this over time would be to flatten out Rowntree's curve; while the upswing of prosperity due to earning offspring would be smaller, the disastrous years of poverty might be considerably softened.

It is not clear exactly how workers went about this reduction in fecundity. One scholar emphatically states that "there can be no doubt that both the fall in illegitimacy and the fall in the number of children born within marriage from the mid nineteenth century was achieved by restraint," rather than through contraceptive techniques. "Edwardian adults, whether married or not, were having less sexual intercourse."[31] Speaking more directly for the working class, however, Thomas Wright ("A Journeyman Engineer") noted at the beginning of our period that abortion was being practised to a wide and growing extent among workers, and Robert Roberts holds that "the fall in the bastardy rate seems to have been due more to newly acquired skills than to moral restraint or fear of father," intimating that these skills were widely known among workers.[32] The more common methods included the use of such birth-control devices as condoms, pessaries, and douches. As a last resort, abortifacients were used or abortion was practised; in the mill towns, a liberal use of Glauber's or Epsom salts was the preferred method,[33] while elsewhere the treatment was "massive doses of penny-royal syrup, and the right application of hot, very soapy water."[34] Whether the fall in the number of children was accomplished by restraint, various birth control methods, or a combination of the two, family planning seems to have come to the working class by the end of the century.

The fall in the birth rate was one sign that the working-class family was evolving slowly into the smaller, home-based configuration of the early to mid twentieth century. So, too, was the appearance of the idea of the "family wage," earned by the male head of household but sufficient for dependent wife and children – an idea that skilled workers began to enunciate in the early nineteenth century, whenever the use of women and children threatened to undercut their bargaining power, and an idea that gradually spread, at least as an ideal, throughout the working class.[35] Nonetheless, despite the statistical evidence of change, the late Victorian and Edwardian working-class family continued to have more in common with past family structures than with those of the future. The Thompson and Roberts interviews examined for this work, for instance, reveal a combined average of 5.87 surviving siblings per family: 5.68 among the families of the skilled, 5.83 among the semi-skilled, and 6.33 among unskilled labourers' families, with higher averages in areas such as London (6.69 surviving siblings per family) where casual labour was prevalent. The pressure of low wages throughout this period and the unstable nature of much adult employment ensured that children would continue to be viewed as important economic assets, whose long-term welfare and ultimate life options were often subordinated to pressing family needs. Children were expected to contribute to the family exchequer, to help out in the home, and to bow to a hierarchy based largely on sex, age, and earning power.

How was this hierarchy shaped? Research conducted during the last decade reveals both a common structure and, within it, important differences through the industrial and regional spectrum. By and large, throughout England, the home and its associated activities – cleaning, cooking, child-rearing, shopping, rent payment, and so on – was unquestionably a "woman's place," as Elizabeth Roberts has shown us. Yet this place and this position, was, as Roberts also shows, not necessarily one of powerlessness.[36] Rather, the parental roles, in some regions at least, though exercised in sharply different spheres, were regarded as being of equal value and importance for the welfare of the family. The mother was the keeper of the household accounts and was responsible for the management of an often limited budget so that the entire family could be adequately fed, clothed, and housed. This was the virtually universal working-class pattern, the only major exception occurring in the textile areas, where large numbers of women worked full time outside of the home and where domestic responsibilities tended to be more equally shared between the husband and wife.[37] In other words, the spheres of adult males and females, with some important exceptions, tended to be quite distinct, and their boundaries were reinforced with an authentic working-class domestic ideology that saw the home as the natural and undisputed arena of the wife and mother.

If the primary responsibility of the working-class wife was the household, the primary responsibility of the husband was to earn enough income, and to pass enough of this on to his wife, to allow her to perform her functions adequately. It is in this area that diversity among the working classes emerges, because often there was an important tension between the perceived duty of the man to provide and his ability or willingness to do so. In northwest Lancashire the responsibility of the wife translated into genuine power; wives in this region were the most important figures in the working-class home and usually had absolute control over the family's income and expenditure. Not only working children, but husbands as well, handed over their wages and received back spending money according to the changing needs of the family. Domestic violence and conflict in this area appears to have been rare, as the roles and power of the spouses were well understood. In London, by contrast, domestic violence was relatively more common, because many husbands in the casual labour market of the capital failed in their duty to provide sufficient income for their families.[38] Because "the economic basis of men's power was highly precarious for perhaps as many as one-half of London's working husbands," the division of roles and responsibilities became an area of conflict and tension, with wives and children on one side and adult males on the other.[39] The ideology of roles underpinning the wife-husband relationship was similar, in other words, throughout most of the working class – males were the providers, females the spenders. Conflict did not revolve around the roles that husband and wife were to play in the family economy, but rather over how well they played these roles.

The gap, large or small, between implicitly understood roles and the ability or willingness to carry them out varied among individual families, regions, and industries, producing variances between a settled and stable division of tasks and power at one end of the spectrum, and constant friction between spouses, at the other.

The mother, then, was the presiding genie of the home, and, in a real sense, the children were hers. Working-class children tended to have a clear understanding of this fundamental division. The comment of a Preston native, eldest of the four offspring of a railway labourer and a former weaver, sums up dispassionately yet fairly the major duties of a mother. "I think my mother was passive; that is, she took life as it came and she sort of made the best of it without having the pretence of any knowledge or intelligence. She just took life as it came and made the best of it. It was a good best as far as we kids were concerned. Although we didn't get any what you might call maternal love in the way of fondling or anything of that sort, we were well looked after physically. There was enough to eat, and we were kept fairly warm in bed and so forth. So as compared with the average of the time, I can tell you that we were pretty well off."[40]

A Barrow respondent says simply of his mother, "She was a good manager and she was a wonderful woman."[41] Each of these men simply assumed that child-rearing and the upkeep of the household were women's tasks, sharply separate from those of adult males. Both praise their fathers, on the other hand, for alternative qualities; though they were labourers earning only £1 per week while the children were young, both were steady men who did not drink and who kept garden allotments – a clearly male sphere – to supplement the family diet.

An additional reason mothers were the dominant parental figure in the early life of the child was quite simply that the father was at home so little of the time. A Guildford boy remembers the schedule of his father, a toolman on the railway; after working from six in the morning to six at night, his father would come home about 6:20 P.M., "have a cup of tea and up the garden ... after he came back from the garden he'd come in and put his tools away, go down the pub and have a pint of beer and then ... about half past nine he'd come home."[42] The son of a coachman for a Yorkshire mill-owner notes that his father did very little housework or child-rearing because of his long hours. "He were out with – carriage until midnight and had to be down at stable again by six or seven o'clock on a morning. Well – he hadn't time to help at home really."[43] The son of a carman for a London coal company would see his father regularly during the summer, when coal deliveries were slack, but in winter the situation was quite different. Often, "we didn't see him for about a week," because then "he didn't used to get in 'til quite late of a night and he'd be up very early in the morning, you know."[44] A Preston dock labourer's son also remembers that "I didn't see much of my father because he was always working, and they had to work. He worked all day and he would take his lunch with him."[45] Nor was it only transport workers whose job kept them out of the home most of the day. The largely Jewish workers who inhabited the Rothschild Buildings in Stepney often did not see their children from one weekend to the next.[46] A skilled iron moulder from Barrow was on the road during half of one respondent's childhood, and he would send his wife £1 per week for the upkeep of the home.[47]

Although in recent years historians of the family have been concerned to establish a truer and more empowered picture of the position of the working-class wife and mother, this should not obscure the equally critical role and central position of the husband and father. For one thing, while in certain areas the mother may have demanded, and received, control over all income, as well as expenditure, this was not the universal pattern. In many working-class families, the male breadwinner would hand over to his wife what he considered to be a sufficient amount to maintain the household.[48] In other words, the clear division of labour within the family did not always lead to an equal division of power. In many working-class families, there seems little doubt that the father, as the main or sole breadwinner, was usually the most powerful figure in the house while the children were young. Among poorer families, this system was apparently most common, the economic justification being reinforced by psychological considerations. "In compensation, perhaps, for the slights of the outside world, a labourer often played king at home."[49] Indeed, the position of the father often veered toward the despotic. One respondent remembers, "There was only father mattered in those days. The father was the head of the house and he had a clean collar and ... his shoes cleaned to go out."[50] Another remembers of his father, "He was that strict, I'll tell you, he used to sit there reading the paper with his feet on the oven door and if [we] wanted to pass to go to the cupboard we had to climb underneath his legs."[51] Children were often expected to remain silent at meal times and to leave the father in peace when he came home from work. Perhaps most obviously, the father's position was shown by the fact that he ate much better than others, a custom noted by many respondents and one that can be found throughout the working class, even among skilled workers with small families.

"He was a big man – he worked pretty hard, you know, but he didn't want it but he always had it ...," explains one, while another notes, "With him being the breadwinner of course, he ... had to be looked after."[52] The son of a London carman remembers his father's breakfast as steak or fish or egg and ham, while the rest of the family enjoyed a cooked breakfast on Sundays alone.[53] A Manchester man notes that his father (a well paid mule spinner) "always got the biggest helping ... he was the worker."[54] In one family, the father had meat every day, the rest twice a week. Children in another worked their way through a cold tea, while the father dined on a steak or a chop.[55] This bias in food distribution was understandable, since for many years the family fortunes rode on the health and employability of the father as wage earner. In these circumstances, the welfare of the breadwinner was a major preoccupation of working-class homes, a welfare all were expected to promote and maintain.

The family structure, then, was based largely on sex, age, and earning power, each variable associated with its own power (or lack thereof) and responsibilities. While among adults the major determinant in the division of tasks was their sex, the position of children appears to have depended more on their age and their lack of earning power. Children below working age moved within "female" space, as subordinate members of that portion of the household whose tasks centred on the provision of comforts to the wage-earners. Children "belonged" to the mother, and their duties essentially consisted of "helping mother" – so much so that in cases where the father kept a garden, the male child would never or only rarely help.[56] Yet, within the broad area of helping mother, sex-based differences can be noted. Boys were usually given household jobs separate from those of their sisters. It seems clear that the larger part of domestic labour, such as laundry, cooking, sewing, and cleaning, fell upon the females of the family.[57] Boys, when young, tended to be responsible for such tasks as cleaning windows, blacking the fireplace, chopping wood, cleaning boots, sweeping the yard, and polishing cutlery.[58] An almost universal task was running errands for the mother.

Exceptions to the general rule can, however, be found, usually in exceptional circumstances. When a Preston respondent's mother went out charring to augment her husband's low wages, he and his sister took over the washing and cleaning for the entire household.[59] A similar but more extreme case can be cited in a case from Wolstanton in the Potteries. The male respondent's mother, a widow, was, until her remarriage, a full-time charwoman, and the home was also dependent on an elder brother's wages. "My elder brother started to work of course; he was eight years older than me, and he worked at the brickyard. I'd have to come home and get him a bit of dinner ready. I used to cook a bit of bacon and cheese, or bacon and egg, take it in and come back again. Me sister was two years older than me, when she started to work of course I had to do ... the housework, take her place ..."[60] When these boys began earning themselves, their household tasks usually ceased, to be picked up by younger siblings or the mother. In the last case mentioned, the boy's tasks changed dramatically when he began to work. With her marriage to a miner and three children now working, his mother reverted to her "normal" role, "and we did, perhaps errands or something like that, but very very little afterwards."[61]

Beyond helping out in the house, children were also expected to keep their eyes peeled for any opportunity to earn, since every penny counted. As one man states, "If you could earn a copper anytime, then you ought to earn a copper, and of course when you came home you turned it up."[62] These earnings could be the yield of chance jobs, such as running an errand for someone to make a penny,[63] but more usually the money was the result of a part-time job. Milkrounds,[64] selling papers,[65] cleaning knives door to door,[66] or acting as a lather boy were the more usual, and very common employments, but such exotic occupations as selling birdseed and leading a blind man about for sixpence a week have also been reported.[67] Occasionally, money would come in unexpected ways, as when one boy found a half sovereign, which he turned over to his mother. "Oh, she kissed me all over. Oh, a wonderful son. Yes, I give it to her ... She soon went and spent most of it anyway, food for the children and meself and Dad."[68]

Children rarely felt that money earned in these ways was theirs alone, and if they did they were quickly disabused of the notion. It was understood that all gains would be given to the mother as the keeper of the household accounts, and that money would be spent according to family priority rather than individual whim. Most of the time, however, the mother would return a portion as pocket money, or, if the amount was small, would allow the child to keep it on the understanding that no further pocket money would be given. In these ways, the working-class child was forcibly taught that the economic health of the family required a corporate effort in which selfishness had little place. In times of crisis, even a child's own savings were likely to be requisitioned for the good of the whole.[69] Such occasions were seen as a necessary hardship by children inured to desperate measures. "Then, when [the box] was full, my poor old mother opened the box and had ... to buy food for us, but I really wasn't disappointed, I just expected it ... it was my money but I never forgot ... Makes me laugh now, and nearly cry."[70]

The constant pressure on family resources ensured that almost all working-class children did their best to help the family whenever and however possible, whether this was in the home or as an earner. A respondent from London succinctly states the general rule: "in a working class family in those days, children were the source of income ... If you had children, you had to go out to work, fetch money – fetch mum in some money."[71] The ethic in this regard was quite clear. It was almost sinful "being idle and not being occupied. For a working person not to be working was wrong. It wouldn't be wasting time as we understand it; it was time not being filled with work."[72] This necessity to work could take on political as well as moral overtones. A Liverpool labourer, says his son, "used to look down on anybody who lived without working. From the King downwards. If a person was able to work and didn't, then he was a parasite."[73] Of all the elements of socialization that the working-class family provided, this necessity to work was perhaps the strongest.

It was when the school-leaving age was reached, though, that the youth became a real economic asset to the household. Taken in total, male supplementary earners in York (almost all youths, since lodgers were excluded from the computation) earned 13.2 per cent of all income. In families in which youths worked, they earned on average 14s.3d. each per week, or 52 per cent of the average wage of a male head of household.[74] In London south of the Thames, the father in many cases contributed only one-half of the weekly income, the other half coming from his children and occasionally his wife.[75] In families that for years had lived in poverty or skirted its edges, the coming of age of a child, and his transformation from an economic liability into an asset, was a major occurrence. "The tears I saw in my mother's eyes when I gave her my first pay packet I shall never forget," wrote the son of a Forest of Dean miner.[76] This transformation signalled a considerable upswing in the family's fortunes, which could improve dramatically as successive children went out to work. The youngest son of a widowed shirt factory worker from London remembers the first few years after his father's death as exceedingly difficult, with the children living largely on church breakfasts and dinners and on guardian charity, with his mother often going without. But "soon after, me eldest brother started, and he fetched in a few bob so we got on a bit." As early as possible, the boy took the Labour Exam, allowing him to leave school, and he was quickly earning 14s. per week in the shoe trade. By this time the family as a whole was well above the poverty line.[77] A Barrow railway labourer's family struggled along on £1 per week with ten offspring, but by the time the respondent – the fifth child – was working, the family income was double this amount.[78] A Preston native notes, "When we started working we had to tip our wages up, and then as they all came along they had to do the same. Later on when we were all working we were well off ..."[79] Another man remembers that "life wasn't very difficult when father, two sisters and m'brother were all working."[80]

A family with working children could also look with something like equanimity at the prospect of the illness or unemployment of the father, and could often afford to relieve the mother of some of her burdens. One mother went charring whenever her husband was laid off, but when the children began to work she stayed home regardless.[81] An artisan's family began employing a neighbour to clean the house when several children went into the labour force.[82] In short, a few working adolescents provided a much needed cushion for the family and often enabled the whole household to enjoy services and goods that had been unobtainable before.

At this stage of a youth's life, parents often exerted considerable sway over the choice of employment. For an artisan's family, an insistence on learning a trade was often paramount. In poorer families, the parents usually insisted on a maximization of immediate income rather than allow their children to follow inclinations that would lead to lower wages. A Liverpool tramdriver's son notes that "it wasn't a matter of what [your parents] hoped you'd grow up to be ... there was never too much money and they could always do with a bit more so as soon as you ... came fourteen ... They weren't very interested in ... where you worked so long as you had a job."[83] Or, as another states, "As soon as you were able to leave school, well, you had to think about earning something. That was a natural outcome. And it wasn't ... 'would you like to be so and so' ... If there was a suitable situation came along, well that was it."[84] For many, the choice of employment was virtually predestined. "You was destined ... for the mill when you ... finished school, you know. That was your object in life more or less."[85] One boy found himself reluctantly learning mule spinning. "One chap says to my father, 'I don't think your Bill likes spinning, Dick!' My father said, 'It's not what he likes, it's what he has to do!'"[86] Another remembers his weaving career. "I wasn't considered in the matter. The 2s.9d. was a useful addition to the family income and I just had to go."[87] In other towns and families, choices were not much more numerous.

In Adlington near Bolton, a boy "had a choice of four things: a bleach works, a dye works, a weaving and spinning mill, and ... a winding mill in Higher Adlington."[88]

In some cases, a boy's stated ambition was frustrated by parents who refused him the chance of establishing a career at initially lower wages. One youth, the eldest of four children, could have obtained a job as an office boy with the railway, "but it would have meant a drop in wages of about 4s. a week and the money was wanted at home so I stayed on at the mill."[89] Another remembers, "The headmaster was Mr Barrow. He twice visited my mother to ask if I could become a pupil teacher. She refused because she dreaded having to keep me."[30] A Durham youth became a miner instead of a trainee newsagent for the sake of the extra 1s.6d. a week his father was unwilling to forgo.[91] The insistence of parents on their teenage sons having a job is shown by a mother in the Potteries who barred her son from the house when he lost his job. "'Get out, and another job ... before you come home,' and you can believe me, I dared not come home." He walked to Chesterton and found a job in a brickyard the same afternoon.[92]

This insistence was particularly marked when it came to eldest sons. A carpenter's son notes, "I should have stayed on [at school but] they needed the wage. We needed everything and me being the eldest, and at that time there were eight children ..."[93] The eldest son of a Preston dock cranedriver found his first job as a furniture restorer at 5s. per week, but after a year switched to the docks. "I went for the money actually. We were hard up so I had to go for more pay."[94] Another, eldest of four, remembers, "The only thing I think that my mother was thinking about was me getting old enough to get out to work and earn some money to help keep the house. I can't remember her ever thinking about me being any special occupation."[95] Meanwhile, noted one author, "It is curiously often the youngest son – the Benjamin of the family – who turns out badly ... he will hang on at home, a curious perversion of the ancient custom by which the youngest son remained at home to support his parents in their declining years."[96] With some years of comfort behind them, with the father often at the peak of his earning power and without a household of children to support, parents were more likely to behave indulgently towards the younger children than toward the eldest sibling.

Younger sons, indeed, often recognized the special position they occupied. The last of three children of a low-paid Guildford railwayman remembers that, when it came the household chores, his parents "didn't press me like they did the elder ones. I almost done as I liked – played a lot of football in me young days ... I never had to clean no knives and forks like a lot of people did." When he left school as well, his parents succeeded in getting him an apprenticeship and were able to afford the loss of wages this entailed. "My brother and sister were both earning bringing money into the home then ... Makes a lot of difference – I was very, very lucky,"[97] Perhaps as telling is the view from the other side, that of a boy who had to forgo better chances in life because he was the elder son. Although his father was a skilled ironmoulder, this youth from Bolton was sent out to work as soon as his elementary schooling was finished. "When I left school I would have liked to have gone and been a reporter on the local paper but I hadn't a secondary school education and that barred me, and when my brother finished his secondary school career he went and got the job I always hankered after and he became a cub reporter on the *Bolton Evening News*, and I used to envy him. I was really jealous about this ... And this was when I really missed my secondary school education."[98]

Although the necessity to curtail ambitions and reduce possible expectations in life seems harsh, there is little evidence that young teenagers felt any general resentment against their parents. Most recognized that parents had an obligation toward the whole family and that money was often urgently needed to keep the household afloat. From an early age, children had been expected to contribute to the family unit according to their capabilities. Schooled in hardship and the need for self-sacrifice, school leavers were rarely surprised when the need for immediate income was put before the chance of a career or the possibility of further education. By the time a youth was thirteen or fourteen, the responsibility to pay one's way had become internalized and rarely had to be imposed by parents.

This internalization provided considerable comfort and some compensation for working lads fresh from school. The sense of contribution was important to many. "I was able to assist with the housekeeping and have a shilling or two in my pocket – not that I had very much, but I remember I did feel quite the ... lad."[99] Another recalls the pride he felt whenever he took home his wages.[100] "Everyone wanted to go to work you know," states another, "boys wanted to be men."[101] The relationship with younger siblings changed radically once a boy was earning regularly. "Oh I felt mighty important I tell you. Course I had a brother older than me working. Of course I couldn't have all the say; he was bringing his wages in as well, but the others were younger than me. They ... had nothing to say because they weren't bringing any cash in."[102] A London boy, eldest of five, was "master of the house" as far as the other children were concerned, on the strength of his job in a rubber ring factory.[103] Household jobs were usually no longer required of working boys, "their contribution to the family's well-being now appearing in the tangible form of shillings."[104] Conversely, because of these benefits from wage-earning, there were good incentives for younger siblings to move into the working world as soon as possible. A Preston native looked forward to becoming a half-timer in a local mill at eleven years of age so as to equalize the position between himself and his elder brother. "He got more spending money than I did, he got a penny and I got ha'penny, so it was a question of I came up to him."[105] Meanwhile, a Londoner, apprenticed as a clicker in the boot and shoe trade, remembers, "You knocked off little jobs ... I used to clean me older brother's shoes for a penny or something like that. Of course when you started work you knock that off, don't you, as above – your dignity, you didn't do them sort of jobs, you got more on a level with 'em I suppose."[106]

Thus, the need to earn at a young age was softened considerably by a new respect from siblings and greater importance in the home. There was also a sense of paying one's dues to the parents, a feeling that had a long tradition and conventional morality behind it. Children, it was felt, "should compensate parents for all the 'kept' years of childhood,"[107] and most children gladly bent to this custom. "I wanted to tell the world I was now a man, working and helping my mother."[108] Perhaps the most telling evidence of the strength of this cultural norm was its enshrinment in a music hall song.

> Mother, I love you, I love you I do,
> Don't let those tears run down your cheeks,
> I'll bring my wages to you every week,
> You've worked for me a long, long time,
> And now I must work for you.[109]

While the children were young, then, the father was accorded a great deal of respect, and as far as possible his nutritional and recreative needs were catered to. The mother, as the chief manager and sustainer of the household, was also a figure of considerable prestige and power, around which, as music hall songs suggest and oral evidence confirms, a good deal of the family's sentiment gathered. The parents stood well at the top of the family hierarchy. Yet this hierarchy, based as it was partly on age and earning power, was liable to change as these variables themselves changed. A major watershed in this process was reached when the youth began, between the ages of twelve and fourteen, to contribute steadily to the family budget.

Before this, within the home, the child was under considerable restraint from the parents. Even in the poorest homes, rigid table manners were enforced. Talking at table was often forbidden, and the child was expected to sit straight, eat what was on the plate, and ask to be excused. Throughout the working class, with very few exceptions, profanity within the home was expressly forbidden, transgressions usually resulting quickly in "a clout side of the ear."[110] When it came to swearing, as Robert Roberts points out, there was one language for street, factory, and schoolyard and another, more decorous one for the family home.[111] Certain types of reading material, especially the Sunday papers, were often the subjects of a general taboo. One man remembers his father's attitude to the *News of the World*. "No – you were not to look at the scandal that was in, ... and – if we were caught reading it – paper wasn't touched."[112] This prohibition was widespread, sometimes as the result of religious convictions,[113] but often applying even when the parents were avid readers themselves.[114] The memory of a Salford respondent illustrates what appears to have been a common urge to shield children from immoral or vulgar information. "One paper came in on a Sunday, but we never read the papers, only my mother and father. My father'd read the paper and hand it to my mother and he'd say, 'Now when you've read that paper tear it up so that the children won't read what's inside.'"[115] It was a rare home that did not also have a rigid bedtime for the pre-teen child and severe retribution for disobedience in this matter.

When boys began to work, however, many of these strictures were relaxed. The working boy might well be on a schedule that excluded him from family meals and thus the discipline of the table. As often as not, Sunday school, "a place 'only fit for kids,'"[116] which parents had earlier insisted be attended, was dropped, to be replaced by football, cycling, walking or sleeping in.[117] In general, boys now had much more say in their choice of leisure pursuits and were also able to make their own decisions about other matters. One boy stood up to his mother on the question of continuation classes. "I wasn't prepared to go to night school because none of me pals went to night school and I wasn't prepared to go."[118] More latitude was also shown with regard to bedtime. Many boys, some time between the ages of fourteen and sixteen, would pass from the strict bedtime of their childhood to almost complete autonomy, usually telling their parents where they were going and what time to expect them back.[119] "After [sixteen]," said one, "I used to do what I liked."[120]

Observers of youth were aware of this transformation in the parent-son relationship and generally deplored it. The working boy, said one author, "becomes more or less independent of parental control and is free to spend his evenings as he thinks fit. So long as he pays his mother a fixed sum weekly he may regard his home as a sort of mere hotel, simply a convenient place for sleep and meals."[121] Another writer noted of the working boy, "He now buys his own clothes (to a large extent), spends his holidays according to his own taste, is allowed to remain out at night till ten or eleven o'clock, and begins to pass outside the jurisdiction of parental punishment."[122] They noted how even the boy's relationship with the revered mother changed. "Up to the age of ten he is devotedly attached to her, then, by degrees, as his need of her becomes less urgent, this feeling is replaced by one of kindly and genial patronage, touched perhaps with contempt; – a feeling which vigorously resents any interference of a woman in his affairs."[123] These writers were usually searching for effect and doing their best to arouse the public to what they saw as the dangers of an undisciplined and aimless youth. Nonetheless, they identified some undeniable facets of this new modus vivendi within the working-class family. At the heart of this change was the fact that the compelling factor of the child-parent relationship – that of dependence of the former on the latter – became increasingly attenuated in the years of adolescence. In some cases, and especially among poorer families, it was even reversed. Through a father's unemployment or illness, a youth of sixteen or so might become the chief earner in the family,[124] in which case, said one author, the boy "will, without comment, expect and receive two kippers for tea, while his unemployed father will make the most of bread and butter."[125] Even without such a drastic reorientation of the family around a newly important member, changes in status were unavoidable. A schoolchild who had previously finished the day with a cold tea would, when working, end it with a cooked supper. A steady diet of bread and jam for another was replaced by a bloater or kipper for supper.[126] Boys now had greater freedom and could demand "immunity from control and the right to be consulted in the politics of the home."[127] With his shillings now often making the difference between relative comfort and renewed penny pinching, the youth now found himself "a person of consequence,"[128] "rather in the position of a favoured lodger ... who must be treated well for fear he should give notice."[129]

This access of independence, however, was far from as sudden as the works of middle-class contemporaries would lead us to believe. In fact, there was a fundamental misunderstanding among these authors of the process at work between working youths and their parents. It was, in truth, not independence that the working youth expected, but rather a new status within the family hierarchy that recognized his position as a young man bringing in wages. There was, as noted, a genuine desire among most youth to help their families, especially the mother with her Sisyphean task of balancing the budget. Family discipline still held good in the majority of cases, and the ties of home still counted for much. Rather, the gaining of a voice on the home and the winning of greater freedom proceeded in stages. In this process, the boy, "with the usual amount of give-and-take, presumption and snubbing ... takes his place as one of the props of the family."[130] In essence, the boy, while recognizing his obligations, wanted the rules he grew up with to continue to apply. As he had done housework, made and delivered lunch to working siblings, or watched the chops and kippers go to the breadwinners, so now as a worker himself he expected to spend his Saturdays free from chores (and his Sundays free from church school), to gain a limited control over younger siblings, and to be given a greater portion of the family's commons. This is largely what he got.

Perhaps in no other matter can the slowly evolving position of the youth be better seen than in the question of pocket money. As a child, the boy was expected to hand over any and all money earned, and spending money rarely amounted to more than a few pennies a week. The working boy, up to the age of sixteen or so, continued to hand over all his wages to his mother, who usually returned a fixed sum[131] or, as was also common, a penny for every shilling earned.[132] After sixteen, however, the youth was usually making over ten shillings a week and was no longer content with a tenpence or shilling return on his investment of labour. It was at about this age that the practice reversed itself; the boy now gave his contribution for bed and board – from eight to ten shillings[133] – and kept the rest, unless the family urgently needed more. It was felt, said Booth, that the parents should not make an unfair profit from the boy.[134] Thus, the older youth's contribution often reflected the local market rate for lodging rather than some arbitrary sum imposed by parents.[135] As his wage grew, so too did his discretionary income, which was the measure and gauge of his status as a man. A teenager of eighteen or so might command an expenditure for leisure uses of eight to ten shillings a week after his familial obligations had been met.[136] Usually the only extra charge on his income was a new requirement to keep himself in clothes, and this was often an opportunity to assert one's individuality rather than a burden; one working lad took the chance to indulge his love of finery by strolling down East End streets as the "Duke of Kent," complete with fancy suit and bowler hat.[137]

The youth's earning power did not translate into a carte blanche inside the home. He was still expected to conform to the standards of the household, but was much less likely to be disciplined when these norms were transgressed. The youth was, as well, still willing to pitch in when necessary, and the idea of cooperation was not forgotten, especially when the father was unable to provide.[138] Yet the parents had much less leverage to use against a recalcitrant adolescent beyond the drastic expedient of expulsion from the family home, which was rarely used. Outside the home, where the youth now spent most of his time, he was usually unfettered in his choice of pursuits. "I could go out," said one, "on my own without – sort of – explaining where I was going or getting permission ... and I could go to the cinema without – sort of – explaining."[139] As we shall see in later chapters, the growing freedom of the adolescent was more likely to be expressed outside of the home than in wars of independence within.

Not all working-class adolescents, however, found their existence to be as unfettered. Exceptions to the overall trend can be found, usually on a geographic, religious, or occupational basis. Although difficult to quantify, it appears that, in general, parents in the north were stricter than those in the south, especially when textile or engineering towns are compared with a great metropolitan centre such as London, where low adult male wages were more common.[140] In addition, parents who were regular church or chapel goers and who had invested much in the struggle for respectability tended to keep their offspring on a tighter rein.[141] Finally, boys who found themselves apprenticed to a skilled trade were usually under greater parental control than others were. Their wages were smaller than those of boy labourers (and their generally skilled fathers not reliant on a youth's earnings), they often had night school after work, and very often they worked under the direct supervision of a relative or friend of the family.[142] In these circumstances, and emphasized by the learning environment at work, an apprentice was not encouraged to consider himself a man until he had completed his time. In the north, these various strands were often conflated; the greater incidence of skilled apprenticeships, the stronger presence of nonconformity, and the lingering self-help traditions of the mid-century artisan culture all conspired to blunt the ability of the youth to free himself from parental control.

For most boys, however, the teenage years were ones of a gradual move from the female-dominated sphere of childhood to the male world of work and wage-earning. This move also involved a major change in the role and power of the youth within the family – from a position of support and subordination to a position in which his primary responsibility was not to perform household tasks but to bring money into the home. It has been noted that "the fact that children through the early teens moved within 'female' space creates special problems of interpretation in the case of boys, who would have to move from the 'woman's' to the 'man's' world sometime in their late teens."[143] The problem lies in part in locating the point where the boundary was crossed and, more important, in identifying the salient preconditions of this transition. While this passage would be different for each individual, a general pattern can be defined. Household chores usually were the first duty of childhood to go; the boy began to expect more and better food and, by the age of sixteen or seventeen, often took on the usual adult male practice of contributing a fixed and "fair" amount of money to the family economy. By this time, the working boy had usually moved decisively into the male orbit, from which his age and lack of earning power had previously debarred him. In this process, it was the youths themselves who usually took the initiative. They decided whether or not to continue Sunday or other schooling, when to come to bed, how to spend their free time, and after age sixteen or so, how much to contribute to the household. It was the adolescent who often unilaterally set the bounds of household chores or the amount of discipline which he would submit. A Lancaster youth remembers standing up to his father on the issue of errand running. "When I was about sixteen I refused to go anymore and my father didn't argue."[144] A poor London family furnishes an example of what was virtually a palace coup against a bullying father by a seventeen-year-old son. "I squared up to him and I told him, 'I'm going to have a showdown with you now. We've had enough of being knocked about just when you thought fit or when you'd had a drink ...' And after that, he was a bit quieter."[145]

Conflicts with parents usually arose because of the parents' unwillingness to recognize the new situation and relax discipline. One boy, raised by parents who had "the Bible in one hand and the big stick in the other," began to think at eighteen that "your parents are showing and ruling you with all them ideas and that, that their parents had and the consequence was there was no progress." Eventually the boy left home because his parents "wouldn't give me a key and wouldn't trust [me] in anything."[146] In a similar situation an artisan's son left home to "make a better life" for himself.[147] A woman remembers four sisters leaving home at a young age because of her father's repressive attitude, while her brother ran away to the army because "he wasn't treated like a man."[148] On the other hand, those who stayed in the family home well into their twenties usually had a good understanding with, and were trusted by, their parents. A Nottingham hosiery trimmer lived with his parents until he was twenty-seven; the fact that he had a house key from the early age of fourteen probably had much to do with this. A Barrow respondent continued to live at home until he married at twenty-four, and, in common with his father, he handed over all his wages to his mother. He did very little housework as an adolescent, had an active leisure life, and remembers that he was "never short of pocket money."[149] The continued presence of a young man in the family home did not therefore necessarily indicate dependence on his part, but often, rather, a settled understanding of the proper roles and relationships between members of the household.

More usually, then, leaving home was the result of a young man's marriage or, in the case of artisans, the necessity for a time-expired apprentice to "go on the tramp." Parents often did their best to delay or obstruct courtship and thus prolong the period when the youth contributed earnings to the home, but without a great deal of success. As will be seen in chapter 5, the marriage market lay largely outside the control of parents, and their strategy of making the possible mate unwelcome often had the converse effect of depriving them of any effective say in the choice of spouse. The timing of marriage was usually influenced more by the youth's or young man's earnings than by the strength of parental discipline, which had few real sanctions by this stage. With the securing of a mate and a man's wage, the newly mature youth left the family home to establish the cycle anew.

Working-class adolescents in this era, then, were often conscious actors in their own right. While they were hardly the undisciplined and unruly youngsters that middle-class authors portrayed, using their home as a hotel and obtaining their freedom by threatening to withdraw their wages, neither can it be said that they lived in a "world in which adult authority generally prevailed" and "the older generation sought to impose its authority with some vigour."[150] It would be truer to say that most youths occupied an intermediate position between these two extremes. That they possessed considerable bargaining power with parents is undeniable; their wages often did make the difference between comfort and poverty, and, at little extra cost and as a last resort, they could wander off to lodgings where, in a buoyant boy labour market, they would have little trouble maintaining themselves. Few were required to do this, however, precisely because of their parents' willingness to bend in matters of independence and to recognize the changing roles and privileges of their offspring. Fewer still wanted to do this, because of a genuine desire to help the family, to pay their debts to their parents and to remain in contact with an entity that continued to represent security and love to the youths. The willingness to turn over wages and to continue to pay one's share as manhood approached was not the result of the parents' exactions but rather of the long example and remembrance of shared striving within the family. In a very real sense, as well, this ability and willingness to make a significant contribution to the family coffers was a major part of what the working class meant by manhood or masculinity, and it fit in well with the definition of an adult male that was an intrinsic part of the domestic ideal shared by most of the English working class. It was only when these contributions – which signified this new status as a man – were met with undue discipline and meddling that conflict arose. In such cases the parents usually backed down, or, if they were unwilling, the youth left to strike out on his own.

In any case, the arenas of the youth were no longer the home. Instead, he was now spending about one-third of his time at work and most of his leisure time outside. With an ever-increasing amount of discretionary income, with a consciousness of his own importance, and with little restraint from parents, the working youth, unlike his richer counterpart, was able to a great extent to indulge the urge for freedom associated with the years of adolescence.

CHAPTER TWO

Education and Working-Class Youths

Since the school years of a member of the working class in this period properly fall outside the scope of this study, it may be argued that education is an unnecessary topic to explore. The youth's earlier experiences of education, however, had wide repercussions on his subsequent career, particularly when he came to decide whether or not to continue into secondary or higher grade education or to attend the evening schools. Moreover, the uses of schooling in this period had a direct and increasing influence on the type of society that was produced in the years preceding World War I. The construction of the national educational system, and its underlying aims and ideals, finally, are topics that have attracted a great deal of interest and debate from historians and sociologists, who interpret these in widely different ways – from liberal humanitarianism in action to a tool of bourgeois social control. In these circumstances, an examination of the immediate end product – youth – is warranted, in order to determine how the youths themselves perceived and reacted to the educational system and its opportunities. The focus of this chapter will be, then, to establish what schooling meant to working-class youths, rather than minutely to explore institutional changes or to examine overt class conflicts, except in cases where these are relevant to the main theme. An overview of the national educational system is necessary, however, in order to set these responses in context.

The education acts of 1870, which laid the administrative and legal foundation for universal state education, also laid the foundation for its subsequent ethos and attitude toward its charges. In the debate between those such as Ruskin and Mill who saw universal education as a genuine response to growing democratic ideals, those such as Lowe who saw the necessity of "educating our new masters," and those such as Forster who saw the need of a trained industrial workforce, it was largely the last option that was favoured.[1] This led to a utilitarian idea of education as training, the opposite of the upper class ideal of liberal studies, which was contemporaneously being institutionalized in the large-scale development of the public schools.[2] The destruction of the indigenous "dame schools," which had provided private and self-directed education for working-class children, was accomplished in these same years. Elementary education was henceforth to be provided for the working class on Whitehall's terms.[3] By this process, education in England was severed into distinct systems separated by a gulf only tenuously spanned by the endowed grammar schools. Education, which was to prove perhaps the most effective consolidator of the élites of the nation, was to act as perhaps the most insidious class barrier among the population at large.

While the 1870 act did not make education compulsory, it did enable local school boards to do so. An act of 1876 made it difficult for boards not to exercise this power, while the 1880 act put education up to at least the age of ten on the statute book. By 1900, in London, education was compulsory until fourteen years of age except for those who had passed all seven standards.[4] Most school boards in large towns (except in the half-time areas) tended to have similar by-laws, but a host of exemption clauses, based on age, financial need, or attendances, often let children out one or two years earlier.

The end of the century witnessed an administrative overhauling of the entire state school system, consolidated in the 1902 education act. The school boards and school attendance committees were abolished, and county, borough, and urban district councils were made the local educational authorities for elementary education. Voluntary schools (usually Church of England) were to be supported from the rates and, except in religious matters, brought under the control of elected authorities. In addition, local education authorities were allowed to provide secondary education and to tax for this purpose.[5]

The local councils, outside of Wales and London, were usually controlled by the Tories, while school boards since 1870 increasingly had been strongholds of radicals and labourites.[6] Beyond this, local councils were usually vulnerable to criticism on the issue of economy, as the provision of services at the lowest possible cost was the yardstick by which many would judge them during elections.[7] Education was thus placed, after 1902, in the hands of the party least sympathetic to a broad interpretation of its needs and was made the responsibility of bodies with many other claims on their resources. One consequence of the act was the absorption and transformation of the higher grade board schools, which had been set up by the more progressive boards in order to continue the work of the elementary schools at little or no cost to the student. The Cockerton Judgement of December 1900 declared expenditure on such schools illegal, and the government, despite vigorous representations, declined to regularize their position. The 1902 act was followed by the 1904 Secondary School Regulations, which emphasized an academic rather than a scientific or technical curriculum. As a result of these developments, the higher grade schools absorbed into the system quickly became almost indistinguishable from the older grammar schools in curricula and clientele,[8] as "the recognition of the higher grade schools could only be obtained at the cost of separation from elementary teaching and the raising of fees."[9] Their student body was now mainly lower middle class and fee-paying. A child going from an elementary school to a secondary school found himself in an environment where curriculum and teaching methods differed in kind as well as intensity and where the composition of the student body was often radically different. In short, the 1902 act ensured that secondary schooling, by and large, was to accord as closely as possible with the existing grammar and public school ideal, and that few indeed would be the working-class children drawn into these institutions. The "broad highway" to secondary education that the progressive educators and working-class leaders wished to construct was replaced by the élitist concept of a "scholarship ladder" favoured by the middle class, the board of education mandarins, and such promotors of "national efficiency" as the Webbs. A chance to create a wide network of secondary schools responsive to the needs and experience of the working class as a whole were ignored, while the foundations of such a system, gradually built up by the urban school boards since 1870, were destroyed.[10]

From the beginning, however, state education for the masses had suffered from other than just administrative and institutional difficulties. These other difficulties came in the main from the attitude toward education of certain sections of the working class, from local resistance on the part of "economic" parties, and from the unwillingness on the part of the judiciary to uphold by-laws made by the school boards. The building of a national school system was in many ways an uphill task against lethargy and suspicion on one side and positive ill will on the other.

The poorer sections of the working class were often unconvinced of the benefits of education or were more cognizant of the immediate need of income derived from their children.[11] In 1886, fourteen years after compulsory education had been established in London, 272,000 children were away from school every day.[12] This was equivalent to a rate of absenteeism of 28.8 per cent,[13] while in districts such as Lambeth, the average rate was 38.5 per cent.[14] In the country as a while, in 1891, "one-fourth of the children are always away," a fraction made up by about three-quarters making a generally good attendance and about one-quarter who were persistent truants.[15]

In the face of this chronic absenteeism, the school authorities could do little. In the slum areas, the essential support of the parents was lacking; indifference or hostility were the norms. In the Nichol area of London (Arthur Morrison's "Jago"), a school attendance officer found that when he "tried to tell them what an excellent thing [education] was, the parents would stand at the street door and threaten and abuse me in the most dreadful language, and nearly all the people in the street would come out and see what was the matter and sympathize in their view."[16] Educators themselves were divided on the issue of compulsion; while very keen on the principle, they were often loath to prosecute the very poor parents who were the most common offenders.[17] For their part, magistrates knew where they stood: squarely with the parents against the interfering busybodies of the school boards. One London magistrate, in direct contravention of the by-laws, refused to fine for nonattendance whenever the child had passed Standard IV. When the school board hired a solicitor to argue a case, the magistrate bowed to the letter of the law and fined 6d. without costs, leaving the board with the option either to surrender or to continue with ruinously expensive prosecutions.[18] Numerous memorials from school boards to the education department complained of the magistrates' laxity, their abuse of discretionary powers, and of the "almost insuperable difficulties of enforcing the payment of fines under the Summary Jurisdiction Act."[19] In any case, as a result of understaffing among attendance officers, seven out of ten attendances by children effectively protected the parents from prosecution, and the working class were not slow to realize this.[20] It was observed, in addition, that some school boards were themselves lax in regard to truancy and child labour and "that when members of those bodies are interested in juvenile labour, the law is evaded, and the employers are never summoned."[21] For all these reasons, it was admitted that "however adequate an instrument compulsion has proved for getting children on to the school register, it is confessedly much less effectual in increasing the regularity of attendance."[22] In fact, even getting children onto the register posed problems. In the poorer parts of London, the turnover among students was usually at least fifty per cent and went as high as one hundred per cent per year. A child whose parents often moved was usually able to escape the administrative net for some time.[23]

The more progressive school boards also had to face a constant barrage of criticism from "economic" parties. Certain sections of the middle and upper classes had always instinctively opposed the education of working-class children past "their station," taking the view, claimed one of their critics, that "the born serf is to be trained as a serf."[24] Such people were ready at all times to criticize the school boards on the subject of expenditures. A series of memorials presented to the education department from 1885 to 1890 bears witness to the anger with which municipal unions and vestries viewed the use of the school rate for science classes, the training of pupil teachers, or such "extravagances" as pianos, which became symbols around which the 1891 School Board for London election was largely fought. According to these guardians of fiscal responsibility, the 1870 act provided solely for the teaching of the three Rs, and they viewed with amazement the temerity of the London school board in going beyond these bounds.[25]

Perhaps the biggest obstacle of all to the provision of a true education was the method of payment and oversight used by the education department until 1895. This was the Lowe Revised Code, implemented in 1862 following the recommendation of a royal commission. Schools seeking a government grant had to submit their pupils to a uniform examination administered by inspectors, the size of the school's grant being determined by the success rate of its students. In this way "payment by results," so dear to the liberal economist's heart, was ensured, but the system had a great many defects from the point of view of progressive educators. The state, through the code, imposed a uniform syllabus on the country, without regard for personal or local preference or need, and concentrated on the three Rs to the exclusion of nearly everything else. It did all the thinking for the teacher, whose value (and often salary)[26] hinged upon his or her ability to push the maximum number of pupils through the examination. Mechanical drills and learning by rote took the place of the encouragement of thinking and the development of mental powers. In effect both teachers and pupils were turned into robots performing to a rigid and inescapable tune. One critic, himself a former chief inspector of schools, noted of the Lowe Revised Code that "as an ingenious instrument for arresting the mental growth of a child, and deadening all his higher faculties, it has never had, and I hope never will have, a rival."[27] What the Revised Code did do, no doubt to the satisfaction of its framers, was to make the child "blindly obedient, mechanically industrious and (within very narrow limits) accurate and thorough"[28] – qualities desired by England's industrialists in their prospective employees.

The Revised Code was abolished in 1895, to be replaced by a system of unannounced inspections and impromptu examinations by which the efficiency of the school was tested. The examination ethos continued, however, to affect the schools; the winning of scholarships and admission to higher grade or secondary schools were contingent upon examination success, rather than on the record of the past years' achievements. For any teacher or pupil who took education seriously, examinations were still an important part of school life, and rote-learning continued to dominate the classroom. Taking the larger strain off the teachers led not to a change in the type of education given but to a change in its intensity. Both pupil and teacher remained for the most part in the old rut of mechanical drills, but were now noticeably slacker, except for those students being fattened like geese for the examination halls.[29] In many schools, the abolition of payment by results merely made a bad situation worse, by reducing the need for even such a dubious virtue as mechanically instilled efficiency.

Working-class children thus found themselves in a school system in which initiative and individualism were at a discount. The tone of the school and a realistic appraisal of the chances of real advancement made it plain to children that they were to be instructed in a manner befitting their station in life rather than to be given an opportunity to exercise their talents to the fullest. As the *Board Teacher* commented in 1886, "Every shrewd man has long seen that the education given under the Code tended to produce a semicultured race of unskilled labourers."[30] Boys understood this in a vague way, believing that "teachers were only allowed to teach you the 3 Rs because if you got too important – learnt too much – you [would] rebel against it, you understand ..."[31] It was, said one respondent, "more of a bread and butter education you got in those days, and the teacher used to know that ... it's no good teaching a child who was going out to work as soon as he was fourteen anything extra."[32]

Beyond the three Rs, the subjects taught reflected the utilitarian concept behind the school system. History consisted of "the Anglo-Saxons upwards, dates and Kings and Queens and all that sort of thing which – of course – is really a waste of time. I can't never remember all the dates now ..."[33] A Yorkshire boy remembered that his "school stood in a district abounding with religious, historic and commercial associations. Yet we were told little or nothing about such interesting things."[34] Instead, schoolchildren were fed a diet of imperial propaganda and recitals of the military and naval glories of England.[35] A school history text of 1911, for example, passes by the Chartists in four sentences and the corn laws in one paragraph, while its social philosophy is illustrated by constant references to "loafers," "idlers," and "agitators."[36] Summing up, a leftist wrote that "the essence of all the teaching … [was] to give me a knowledge of the three Rs, a little history without understanding, a little geography, and above all to make me a good Christian boy who would be ready and anxious to be a good wage worker."[37] In some schools, indoctrination was very explicit. A Bluecoat (orphanage school) boy remembers having to call everyone "Sir" or "Madam" and reflects, "I didn't look back with any ill feelings, but I did have the idea that there's something odd that I'm doing it and that no one else seems to be doing it."[38] Such an emphasis on respectfulness (as opposed to the authentic working-class concept of "respectability") may not be surprising in such a setting, but the son of a highly paid shipwright and eventual foreman likewise remembers that "you were pretty well taught at school that people that were above your rank … that you always called them Sir or Madam … [I was taught] to lower my head lowly and reverently toward my betters – and you were told that these people were your betters."[39]

The elementary school, then, confined itself to basic literacy and numeracy, a class-biased view of history, an imperial view of geography, and a physical education syllabus slanted toward drill and designed to "make better soldiers, better servants and better workmen."[40] Attempts to teach anything else were liable to incur the wrath of either the board of education or the ratepayers. In 1908 an attempt in one school to teach the violin in the last twenty minutes of the day was quashed. Two years later, a scheme to teach French to older children was stopped in Burton-on-Trent. Generally the board was nervous of being attacked by those who deplored waste and extravagance in the educational system. It allowed dancing as part of the physical education syllabus only with the greatest reluctance, fearing a backlash from the economists.[41]

Besides an education characterized by standardization and rote learning, children also found the schools to be harshly disciplinary. Paul Thompson has labelled teachers as "the most persistently violent Edwardian adults," stating that "the number who showed signs of definite imbalance was considerable."[42] Stephen Humphries has gone further; in his study of childhood from the 1880s to World War II, he has located the schools at the centre of a continuing class battle over the control of ideology, with teachers as foot soldiers and the cane as the principal weapon.[43] Oral and autobiographical evidence goes far in supporting this view of school as battleground. "They was proper brutal to you, some teachers was," remarked a respondent, who on one occasion was knocked out of his seat by a blow directly to his ear.[44] Others provide evidence of the frequent corporal punishment that descended on children at the slightest provocation.[45] "Caning was the usual punishment for more than the mildest offences," says one, while another notes, "We used to say that they was four – basic lessons at school: reading, writing, arithmetic and stick."[46] A Barrow respondent remembers of his schooldays: "if you were late you got the cane. If you were late you had to stand at Holker Street in the passage and the headmaster would come round. There would always be about half a dozen lads who'd been late and you stood there and held out your hand and got the cane. If it was once you got one cane but if it was twice you got it more. It didn't pay you to be late often."[47] Since "discipline was meant to encourage subservience and to squash rebellion – very undesirable in children who would grow up to obey orders from their betters,"[48] it was not surprising that "the really vicious beatings were strictly on a class basis."[49] The willingness to resort to violence was given sanction as well by the contemporary notion that "children were not ... mentally deficient. The idea was that every child could do the work if he tried hard enough. And he was made to try by the threat of punishment."[50]

Children, however, were not entirely powerless in the face of this threat. The most common response of children who found schooling uncongenial was simply to stay away, and, as we have seen, this was very much a viable option in the late nineteenth and early twentieth centuries. It could even be accomplished with the permission of the school authorities; a London boy explains one technique. "I was a rare one for hopping the wag ... what I used to do to get away from school [was] I used to get a button ... and I used to press it in me throat just before I went into class see, and I used to go up to the head mistress and say – mother said could you tell me what this was? Oh, – ringworms, oh. I was away from school three or four months at a time."[51] Besides these normal subterfuges practised by children in all ages, the working-class child often had important allies – his parents. The *Board Teacher* was wont to complain of the number of assaults perpetrated on staff by the irate parents of beaten children.[52] One headmistress was forced to hire a male teacher, seeking "a protector as much as ... a new colleague" for the numerous occasions when "the rough Irish parents came barging in threatening murder." An anecdote from Preston illustrates well the fear of parents among many teachers. The boy had ripped his trousers on a nail protruding from his school bench and explained the mishap when he arrived home. "My grandmother was there, and she immediately got a hammer and went across the street to the school to do something about it. When a young teacher saw a woman with a purposeful look on her face and a hammer in her hand, she fled to the headmistress shouting, 'There's a mad woman here with a hammer!'" Fortunately, the headmistress knew the grandmother well, and "the offending nail was knocked down."[53]

Children were also liable to take mass action in response to intolerable conditions. "Resentment at the cruelty of certain teachers led to their being mobbed by the boys after school hours. More than once I took part in waylaying a teacher, booing and hissing and shouting names at him on his way home."[54]

Another tactic was the school strike. "The immediate result was the removal of the teacher in question, and a better disposition on the part of the remainder of the teachers," remembers one budding activist.[55] For another the immediate result was a caning for him and his companions.[56] Children could also petition the headmaster for the removal of a teacher who was inordinately fond of corporal punishment, and this alternative was successful on at least one occasion.[57] Faced with a teacher with a penchant for the cane, boys about to leave school in any case had little to lose by retaliating in whatever way they could.

Evidence such as this, as well as the fuller data collected by Humphries, should not, however, lead to a picture of the classrooms as arenas of a class war, or of teachers as wholehearted minions of the ruling élite. The teachers were themselves drawn largely from the class that they educated and knew, perhaps, better than anyone the rigid self-discipline and hard work that was necessary if even the limited social mobility they represented was to be wrung out of the existing system. The teachers as a body were also often opposed to the system under which they worked. They were early opponents of the Revised Code, criticizing the constant interference of Whitehall and arguing for a broader conception of education.[58] They were generally enthusiastic supporters of the higher grade schools, recognizing much more clearly than the central government the special needs of working-class children who wanted to continue their education.[59] Teachers were also very conscious of their low status in the eyes of those who controlled educational policy. The officials of the education department, usually university trained and upper or upper middle class in origin, "treated elementary education and elementary teachers with contempt,"[60] while in 1886 the *Board Teacher* complained that the Cross Commission, appointed to look into elementary education, had no teachers on it and had yet to call a single teacher as a witness.[61] Teachers as well as pupils were expected to know their place in the educational system. Their attempts to gain a professional status and wider discretionary powers were thus often consistent with the program of progressive educationalists, who sought to broaden the conception of working-class education, making it more responsive to the needs of this class. Many teachers proved to be reluctant drill sergeants and, given a chance, would probably have reacted positively to the creation of a more liberalized and humane school regime.

Schoolchildren who came into contact with such teachers have a different set of memories from those analyzed by Humphries, and there is little reason to doubt that instances of kindness and understanding were as numerous as those of brutality. A London respondent states that many teachers bought undernourished children breakfast from their own pockets,[62] a practice confirmed by an ex-teacher, who remembers that "teaching was looked upon as a type of social work in the East End, far more than it is now. It wasn't the money you got, it was helping children."[63] Teachers who bent the curricular rules are also remembered with affection,[64] while some children even recognized the necessity of the cane in overcrowded and unruly classrooms.[65] Faced with indifference or hostility on the part of many parents, disdain from Whitehall and rebelliousness on the part of their charges, teachers in the elementary schools of the period had a very uneviable position. If we deplore the often excessive use of corporal punishment by this group, we must take into account in mitigation not only contemporary standards of behaviour (for example, the disciplinary regime of the public schools) and prevailing notions of social work, which emphasized the formation of individual virtues, by force if necessary, but also the circumscribed and frustrating nature of their occupation.

Overriding all the other disincentives of the school system itself was that of the social environment beyond the school gates, and the effect this had on children's view of education. Quite simply, they were often at a loss to perceive the utility of education in respect to their future lives, or its ability to help them decisively to alter their chances in life. In this sense, the social indoctrination practised by authorities was a two-edged sword; because it could promise little to "good" students, it got little in return. Although self-help and hard work were preached, social mobility was never held out as a realistic prospect, the emphasis instead being put on the production of obedient workers. Few were the children who responded positively to such a bleak doctrine. Workhouse children were often educated separately and given special industrial training apropriate to their station. Class barriers were almost visible to such as these.[66] But this feeling of limited horizons and limited choices was pervasive throughout the working class and was by no means confined to its lower or more unfortunate sections. The children of the skilled rarely connected education with advancement to a higher social level. The son of a well-paid mule spinner in Manchester says of his education, "I didn't feel I was getting anywhere, because ... I thought it was only a matter of the teachers getting their time over 'til you was twelve years of age." For such a boy, life's prospects were predetermined: half time at twelve years of age, followed by the various stages of piecing and the long wait – sometimes into the thirties – for the chance to become a spinner.[67] A Wolstanton respondent, who followed his father down the mine at sixteen, says of the chances of social mobility, "No, I never thought it would be possible, no, I didn't, no. I didn't see how I could do it."[68] The utility of education was hard to see when you were "destined for the mill when you finished school, you know. That was your object in life more or less."[69]

Those students who enjoyed learning and who took their lessons seriously often found that it was indeed only a matter of "the teachers getting their time over." This was particularly the case with the Standard VII or Ex-VII scholars. Usually these students were so few in number that they were bunched in with one or more other standards and given very little in the way of new work.[70] One boy, bright enough to have completed all seven standards by twelve, simply ran messages until he was thirteen and could leave.[71] Another ran errands, monitored, and even did the headmaster's gardening.[72] Such treatment of the cream of the elementary school crop was hardly designed to encourage a respect for the potentialities of education among working-class children as a group. By contrast, in those towns where a good selection of secondary facilities existed, it was noted that an appreciable percentage of children stayed on past the minimum leaving age. It was in communities where Ex-VII scholars kicked their heels that mass defections took place.[73]

Isolated examples may be found of cases where good conduct and intelligence opened a few doors. In a Nottinghamshire school, the headmaster would get the brighter boys into the local colliery offices as junior clerks.[74] In Liverpool, one company director on his own initiative decided to examine and hire elementary schoolboys for clerical positions rather than automatically take boys from the secondary schools. In this way, a shipwright's son was able to move into the lower middle class (where he probably made considerably less than his skilled father).[75] On the whole, although schools may have aimed at producing good workmen and conscientious clerks, they had very little to do with employers and, until the very end of the period, had no organized job counselling system. As an early observer stated, "It seems to me as if the State now opened the doors of the School and shot the children down into an abyss."[76] As we shall see in the following chapters, the entry into most trades was contingent more on geneology and connections than on any high standard of educational attainment, while boys who found themselves in unskilled positions did so overwhemingly by their own efforts and through their own contacts. Boys thus had little reason to be regular attenders, to pass through all the standards, or to be model students in their classroom conduct, because neither the rewards nor the penalties for one's educational efforts were very large. School was seen by many boys as a disagreeable period that had to be gone through before they could begin to work, not as a process that could radically change their prospects in life.

For these reasons, schooling for the majority of working-class children ended in the elementary school, usually as soon as could be arranged. In many parts of England, school exemption certificates, often requiring a "Labour Examination" could be obtained at age twelve or thirteen, and many children (or their parents) took advantage of these clauses to end their education.[77] A London respondent makes a revealing comment on this practice and its implications. "If you passed through [the Labour Examination] you was allowed to leave early, go out to work you see, so it was like the opposite system to what is now, now you sit to stop in."[78] In other words, in the eyes of many boys, such a reward as existed for educational attainment was that it allowed them to escape as early as possible from further education, and begin their real life as a worker and wage earner. If necessary, forged certificates were not hard to produce and were widely resorted to.[79] At the end of the Edwardian period, 32.5 per cent of children left school either between twelve and thirteen or on their thirteenth birthday, while 79 per cent of those who remained left in the following year. Only 14.5 per cent of children continued elementary education beyond their fourteenth birthday, even to the extent of finishing the term or year.[80] The practice, in fact, was to leave on the day or week in which the birthday occurred. As a Keighley respondent says, "You started same day as you were twelve, never mind within a day or two."[81] Rowntree tells a story of a boy who left in the very hour that he had been born, refusing to stay a moment longer.[82]

Given the type of education offered in the elementary schools, the disciplinary atmosphere to be found there, and the attenuated relationship between educational attainment and future prospects, it is perhaps surprising that a good many children wanted to go on. For children in many areas throughout these decades, such a desire could be satisfied only in the grammar schools, with their attendant difficulties regarding finance, curricula, and clientele. From the mid-1870s, many areas, however, particularly in the north, began to press for some form of additional education beyond that sanctioned by the code. Thus the higher grade schools began to spring up, the first established in Sheffield in 1876–80. They had "a strongly scientific and somewhat technical character," with the aim of preparing students for manual work of the higher kind.[83] These schools were, unlike secondary schools proper, "an organic and natural outgrowth of the elementary school system."[84] Their curricula were specifically designed to dovetail with the teaching given in the elementary system, and they provided the kind of training that made sense to working-class boys with working-class lives ahead of them, concentrating chiefly on physical sciences, drawing, and applied mathematics. The Cross Commission found them to be "meeting the actual wants of more people than are the secondary schools, more especially because [they] are cheaper,"[85] while the Royal Commission on Secondary Education argued that these schools filled a legitimate need and should not be suppressed.[86] This was especially the case with working-class children; in 1897, 32.7 per cent of the males at higher grade schools were the sons of skilled artisans, and 7.3 per cent were the sons of labourers, while in the secondary schools only 8.1 per cent were from the skilled working class and a miniscule 1 per cent came from labouring families.[87]

The higher grade schools, however, had their critics. Particularly vocal was the Science and Art Department at South Kensington, which early on forbade any child on an elementary school roll from receiving its grants. By the 1890s, the Science and Art Department was taking the view that the higher grade schools were technically elementary schools administered by the school boards, and this prohibition was extended to them, blocking a source of funding vital to the full and proper teaching of science.[88] The effect was "to cut off the Public Elementary School from the government grants for Science and Art instruction, to deprive the 'industrial classes' of the Science and Art grants provided in the first instance for their benefit, and to divert such grants towards the Secondary and Grammar Schools."[89] Other critics were the managers and headmasters of the "true" secondary schools, who argued that the higher grade schools, subsidized by the ratepayers, competed directly and undersold the secondary schools. The proponents of the higher grade schools denied this, replying that, "for one boy who may be withdrawn from the grammar school, there are ten in the modern secondary school who would have no instruction at all were it not for the new educational development."[90] More important to the fate of higher grade schools than the wrath of grammar school masters was the fact that they were, strictly speaking, illegal, as the Cockerton Judgement of 1900 made plain. Dismayed by this decision, numerous schools boards and trades councils pressed for legislation to correct this, but received little sympathy.[91] The secondary schools set up or co-opted by the 1902 education act soon became fee paying (over £3 per annum) liberal arts schools with a limited number of scholarships, and as such were not designed to continue or supplement the education of appreciable numbers of working-class children.[92] To the newly erected financial obstacles for working-class students wishing to go on was added a large educational hurdle, since the "primary education [for a secondary school student] differs in character and method from the elementary instruction which the Public Elementary School affords."[93]

Even in the pre-Cockerton, subsidized days, the path to further education was strewn with obstacles. For those boys bright enough to sit for scholarships, a knowledge of Latin or other esoteric subjects was often required; the result was that "they are at sea in the classes of the new school. Much of their time is wasted in getting into the new groove."[94] In any case, in a poor area such as Lambeth, only one-third of the scholarship winners had parents wealthy enough to let them accept.[25] After the 1902 education act, the lack of choice in and inappropriateness of secondary education that had characterized many areas became general, as the curricula of all secondary schools, including the co-opted higher grade schools, increasingly began to reflect the grammar school model.

Beyond these institutional obstacles, further ones lay for the individual working-class boy and his parents. Given the structure of the working-class family economy, it is obvious that the individual desire and ability of the child would often not be the determining factors in any decision of a boy to avail himself secondary education. To the parents, additional schooling may not have meant a very large positive outlay, but it did mean the loss of the boy's income at what was often a critical period in the family's history. For one boy, a family crisis dashed all hopes of going on. "Well, yes, it would have been my father's [wish], he did contemplate my going to the high school, but as he died, well, it never materialized ..."[96] More usually, simple financial need forced boys to reduce their expectations. "The root of the trouble was when you got out, was the finance – to keep you at the other school, you see," remembers the son of a Darlington railway guard.[97] These constraints operated as well among the skilled; the eldest son of a carpenter in the Stoke area spent three years at a secondary school, with the eventual aim of becoming a teacher. A prolonged spell of slack employment for his father ended these dreams, and, "owing to the labour position again, Father said I had to get out to work."[98] A stonemason's son in Barrow spent several years at the local higher grade school, where fees were charged; even though his father earned 36 shillings per week, the boy knew that "it was a bit of a strain" to keep him. At age fourteen he therefore left to go into engineering.[99] The fourth of seven children of a Nottingham carpenter who left full-time education at thirteen notes that "in those days ... it were the economics, you see, ... that played a large part – especially where there's a large family."[100] The child of a Rhondda pit-winder simply remembers that, along with his brother, "I passed higher grade. I had to go to the pits." His elder brother, already in the secondary school system, gave up at the same time, as the family needed the two boys' income in a period of labour unrest.[101] The case of a Nottingham boy illustrates both the choices facing a bright student in the elementary school and the usual option exercized. He passed the grammar school examination, "but father couldn't afford it so I went and passed the other one then" – the Labour Examination, which allowed him to leave school at thirteen and move, like his father, into the hosiery trade.[102]

With the advent of the reformed secondary school system after 1902, substantial outlays were added to the loss of income, unless the boy won a scholarship or a free place. Even then there were considerable deterrents. "Me father couldn't afford to pay for the books, you see, and then when we come to uniform and that, well ..."[103] Many schools required in addition a written undertaking by parents that the student would remain in the program the full four years. This was especially insisted upon for scholarship boys, whose parents could least likely sign such a bond or look with equanimity upon the threatened £2 to £5 fine if the boy was withdrawn.[104] It is evident that, faced with these hurdles, it would take a very tenacious boy and understanding parents to see the course through.

Students who braved all these financial and educational obstacles still had to contend with cultural and social ones. Scholarship boys, or "Boardy blags" (=blackguards?), were persecuted or simply ostracised.[105] One woman remembers that "quite a few of the girls who were fairly comfortable, had good positions and got lovely clothes and that kind of thing ... they'd sort of pull aside, they wouldn't pass you on the stairs if they could help it."[106] Many were the students who "fled from this daily mortification."[107] Others stuck it out, "but they had to slave and crush part of their lives, to machine themselves so that they became brain alone. They ground away at their lessons, and for all their boyhood and youth and perhaps all their lives, they were in the ingenious torture chambers of the examination halls. They were brilliant, of course, but some when they grew up tended to be obsequious to the ruling class and ruthless to the rest, if they were not tired out."[108] Such were the joys of social mobility. Late Victorian writers were proud that "there is being prepared, there now seems within measurable distance of completion, the ladder that will enable any English boy and many English girls to accomplish the ascent from the gutter to the highest teaching of the University."[109] This process, however, involved a formidable series of curricular, financial, and cultural hurdles, including one whereby the boy "is to be separated from the class in which he was born and his brains recruited for the governing minority."[110] Perhaps, looking back, a man who had accomplished the climb would envy his former schoolmate, who "always came top in arithmetic and [who] was leaving to become a van boy."[111] The latter represented the usual, and in the circumstances perfectly reasonable, response to the question of secondary education among working-class children of the period.[112]

A young worker who had gone no further than the elementary school still had an opportunity to extend his education through the agency of the continuation or evening school. Such schools first received government aid in 1851, while the elementary school boards after 1870 were allowed to use their taxing powers to provide elementary education in the evenings for students up to the age of sixteen. In 1856 the Science and Art Department began its program of grants for part-time technical education, intended for the higher grades of manual and clerical workers. From small, haphazard, and uncoordinated beginnings, the evening school movement grew, aided by a progressive relaxation of the required syllabus and a greater generosity in grants. In particular, as the effects of the national educational system began to be felt, there was less need of remedial work and greater opportunity to develop courses that assumed and built upon a basic acquaintance with numbers and letters. In effect, the same process was at work in the evening schools as in the elementary system; the more progressive boards set up higher grade evening schools and used both the elementary school rates and the Science and Art Department grants to pay for them. This wider scope, especially after a more liberal and regulatory code was established in 1890, is reflected in enrollment figures; the numbers admitted to such schools rose from 115,582 in 1892–93 to 509,251 in 1899–1900.[113]

The Cockerton Judgement, however, proved to be as much a nemesis of the evening schools as it was for their day-time counterparts, declaring that evening schools teaching beyond the three Rs could not be supported from the elementary school rates. Such work was properly the sole concern of the technical education boards of the county and the county borough councils set up after 1888, supported by the Science and Art Department and by a limited (one penny in the pound) rating power. After the 1902 act, the two systems of elementary and technical contining education were fused, and all publicly supported evening schools essentially came under the aegis and control of the technical education boards, whose experience in continuation schools had always been associated with South Kensington's higher syllabus.[114] This syllabus presumed a better primary education than the elementary school normally provided, and the Science and Art Department, as one of the protagonists in the Cockerton Judgement, was even more determined after 1900 to see that its grants were not "abused" by night schools teaching elementary courses.

Nevertheless, by the Edwardian period, the evening school system had developed into one that attempted to respond to diverse needs. There still existed courses that had as their aim the teaching of elementary subjects. Higher grade continuation schools catered largely to the lower middle class and concentrated on commercial subjects. Polytechnics and schools of art catered mainly to apprentices in the higher technical industries, while commercial schools (often developing from the higher grade evening schools) specialized in languages, commercial geography, and accounting. Finally, university extension classes represented the highest form of part-time education.[115] In addition, a very few large firms, usually in engineering, ran or cooperated in the running of continuation schools for their apprentices.[116] Some boys' brigades and clubs also organized their own classes, but these usually failed (see chapter 7).[117]

The evening school movement as constituted by the 1900s thus catered mainly to the clerical and, to a lesser extent, the higher artisan classes. Of 4,775 class entries in Birkenhead in 1903–4, only 870 were in elementary continuation classes. Of the remainder, only 744 were for courses in industrial or technical subjects. The majority of students in the evening schools were there for instruction in

Table 1
Continuation Class Enrollments, 1902–7
(Number of students admitted at any one time in the year)

Age at entry	1902–3	1906–7	Per cent change
12–15	147,191	132,898	− 9.7
15–21	348,353	362,627	+ 4.1
over 21	162,050	240,987	+48.7
TOTAL	657,595	736,516	+12.0

Source: Sadler, ed., Continuation Schools, 111; Greenwood, Juveline Labour Exchanges and After-Care, 20–1.

languages and commercial subjects and for science instruction well beyond that achieved in the public elementary school.[118] The evening school movement was essentially by this date a lower middle class phenomenon.

Turning to national enrollment figures, we find that despite the hopes raised for evening schools as remedial agencies and as replacements for a withering apprenticeship system, they had reached a saturation point for teenagers fairly quickly. Table 1 shows the figures for government-aided schools for 1902–7.

It is clear that it was the older groups that were being increasingly drawn into the night schools, perhaps when the economic consequences of being an unskilled labourer or half-trained artisan were driven home. The changes for the younger groups are meagre by comparison; they actually show a decrease in the youngest bracket, for which the principle of "continuation" was designed. It would seem that the younger evening-school clientele 1902–3 was swollen by the type of students who would later go on to the day secondary schools. We must, however, be wary of these figures, because serious students attending two schools would be counted twice and about one-third of the pupils to be counted would fail "to complete the absurdly small minimum of 14 hours attendance during the session" that would qualify the school for the grant.[119] These dropouts were most likely to be the youngest, who "come, most of them, because forced to do so by parents, or because they think they could have a good time, and they leave if order and work are enforced."[120] The evening schools indeed experienced a rapid turnover of students. A thriving school would have 800 names on its registers by November and 500 by Easter. But most of the 500 would have enrolled in January, and very few of the original 800 would have survived the course. Even fewer would ever complete an organized three-year course.[121] In Birkenhead in March 1904 the effective roll was 74.4 per cent of the number who had registered for classes in the previous fall, but the attendance at the same date was only 48.9 per cent.[122]

In 1909 a government committee estimated that of the youths between the ages of fourteen and seventeen in England and Wales, 86.8 per cent were not attending any type of day school. Of this percentage, only 14.6 per cent were attending an evening school. In other words, 74.1 per cent of the young teenagers of the nation were not under instruction.[123] It is not hard to guess who these youths were. As early as 1887, an observer stated that evening schools were "attended by the children of the *élite* of the working class and by the children of the lower middle class," and that it was "an impossibility almost to get a boy who has left school to think of coming to an evening school. There is a bad odour associated with the name of the night school; and there are other reasons which lead a boy and girl positively to object to going any more to school."[124] Since that date, the evening schools had increased their slant toward commercial and higher technical training. The inroads upon the mass of unskilled or "blind alley" boy labourers had, all admitted, been negligible.[125]

Too many factors worked against the evening schools. Having escaped the primary school, the young teenager was now very loath to return to a classroom. The hours that boys now worked also prevented them from attending. "Well you just fancy boys working 'til eight o'clock at the night; [by] the time they came home they didn't want to go to evening classes."[126] Van boys and errand boys, the group most needing remedial or lower technical training, worked very long and irregular hours, and effectively barred themselves by their jobs from attending. Factory boys, while working shorter hours, still put in 55 hours a week and might be called upon to work overtime at hours conflicting with their schedules. If they were un-indentured boy labourers, the likelihood of their being let off early was remote. Those boys who tried to attend classes were often too tired to continue or found the conflicting demands on their time insurmountable. One boy, after a few years on the docks, wanted to get away from it; "I went for engineering and drawing with a view to try to get a job but there was a lot of overtime at the dock and I couldn't continue the course because of the overtime. It kept being broken."[127] Above all, the night school system seems to have been defeated in advance by the elementary school. "School days are not remembered with pleasure by the working lad, and his whole nature rebels at the thought of going back to the premises and often to the teachers of his much restricted youth."[128] For most boys, schooling meant childhood, dependence, and discipline, and, unless there were strong vocational reasons for attending, they would have none of it. The defects of the educational system, the behaviour of teachers, the attitudes of parents, and the economic pressure to earn were combined with a natural desire on the boy's part to put this symbol of restriction behind him.

Nonetheless, the night schools were attended by a section of working-class boys; about one-sixth of the oral history respondents investigated had been attenders at one time or another. With few exceptions, such boys were either apprentices (usually in engineering) or embryo clerks. They used their night school classes in industrial art, mathematics, engineering, or bookkeeping to supplement their apprentice training,[129] to put themselves on the path to a foreman's position,[130] or to obtain or keep a place as a clerk.[131] Night school for these boys was very much a vocational option exercised to gain a more secure and higher paid place within their own class, rather than to open new doors of opportunity so they could escape completely from their childhood origins. This applies even to the clerks; of the four trainee clerks who attended night school, three were employees of the Co-op, which insisted on attendance for its junior staff. Indeed, one of these respondents explicitly states that a limited move out of manual work was really possible only through the agency of working-class institutions themselves, such as the Co-op and the Workers' Educational Association (WEA).[132]

Thus, the experience of the child in the elementary school and a realistic view of life prospects coloured the youth's reaction to the evening school movement. Beyond a minority of boys, evening schools attracted only where tangible rewards were clear, such as a journeyman's ticket, higher wages, or continued employment in a firm. Given this, the continuation schools' attempt to fulfill a remedial function among the mass of boy workers was virtually a complete failure.

The national educational system erected or overseen by the state in the nineteenth century, especially after 1870, is one of the more impressive examples of Victorian social engineering. Its avowed aims were to educate the "new masters" of England, to supply an obedient and literate workforce, and to strenghten the bonds of social cohesion. As one historian of education states, "It could be said that the function of education emerging from the measures adopted at mid-century was not so much that of ensuring the *reproduction* of society with a divided social structure as the actual reinforcement and more precise refinement of an hierarchical society in which each stratum knew, was educated for, and accepted, its place."[133] In other words, the Victorian and Edwardian school system not only reflected class differences, but "deliberately planned to perpetuate them."[134] As such, the system has often been presented as a classic case of ideological hegemony and social control in action.[135] It could also, in this view, adjust itself when necessary; the threat represented by the "broad highway" of the earlier higher grades schools and the democratic leanings of the large urban school boards was dealt with by firmer Whitehall control and the narrowing of the highway to a "scholarship ladder," thus ensuring that the few successful students who scaled it would take on the norms and values of the ruling élite.

The administrative history of English state education provides much compelling evidence for such theories. Yet social control as a concept has some problems as an analytical tool. For one thing, we must beware of interpretations that concentrate on the central figures and ignore both the social context and the responses of those who are to be controlled. Theories that see "educators as *only* and *merely* policemen without boots," while useful perhaps as starting points for inquiry, are too crudely reductionist to capture the complexity of the processes of work.[136] Even at the higher levels, such theories tend to ignore the real differences among the policy makers, managers, and implementers of the system. Although it became more so over time, as centralized Whitehall control became tighter, the educational system was far from monolithic; the presence of go-ahead school boards and local education authorities, using their statutory powers to the limit (or beyond it), and of progressive teachers with a genuine interest in their charges ensured that education more suited to the taste and needs of working-class children was always possible.

Beyond this, hegemony and control as concepts imply a relationship – a dialogue – between those who wish to impose their values and those who are the targets of such attempts. To assess the real success of the system, one must therefore "disentangle intent from practice, and practice from effect."[137] Stephen Humpries, recognizing this, has attempted to set the pupils' own reactions to the system at the centre of his history. Yet his interpretation goes perhaps too far the other way. Social control is seen as a given aim, to which all educators at all levels subscribe, and the schools are thus pictured purely and simply as class battlegrounds, where bourgeois and working-class values fought for dominance, leading to the formation of an embryo class consciousness among students in reaction to the attempt to impose upon them an alien ideology.[138] Under such an interpretive schema, the schools in fact worked against themselves; in the absence of any effective carrots, they fell back on a liberal application of stick, and in doing so discredited the very ethos they were attempting to propagate. Given this premise, every act of rebellion, every subterfuge practised, and even passive indifference, may be interpreted as a subconsciously political act. There is plenty of evidence in oral history material, however, that teachers were often liked and admired, that some children at least wanted to continue their education, and that many were gripped by a desire to learn.

These desires were usually frustrated by the deficiencies and obstacles of the educational system itself. It is certainly clear that the elementary schools could not, and did not, act as "social elevators" for working-class children and that social mobility via the secondary system would also be extremely difficult.[139] Finally, it is clear that children themselves, and their parents, were all too aware of this state of affairs and expected little from the years in the classroom even when they did their best to profit from them. If the school system then was structured, consciously or unconsciously, to mould its charges by an appropriate scale of rewards and punishments, it did a remarkably poor job of accomplishing its aim. What it did, instead, was to gather the children of all sections of the working class together, to impose an increasingly uniform experience upon them, and to make it obvious that their education was to be different in aim and kind from the rest of society. Moreover, the limited opportunities that it offered were available to all working-class children, thus helping to break down the older barriers between skilled and unskilled.[140] In short, education usually provided social mobility within the limits of the working class, helping to reinforce and consolidate this section of society and to set it apart from other sections.

In this sense alone, the educational system may be said to have achieved its aim of reproducing a hierarchical class society, but in a curiously self-defeating way. If social control was the ultimate goal of the school system, the agonized studies of the Edwardian "boy problem," the statistics on school attendance and school leaving, the failure of the evening schools to touch the mass of working-class youths, and, perhaps most revealing, the sharpening social and political divisions of the period would leave one with the impression that this goal was far from successfully reached. Nonetheless, education may well have been exaggerated or misunderstood as a means of social control. It lacked two of the vital ingredients of such a structure: a set of real sanctions and a set of tangible rewards. What is most obvious from oral history evidence is how little the school seems to have meant to the majority of children. Conduct at school and educational achievement had little effect on the choice of jobs or apprenticeships available, and since schools did very little until the very end of the period in their role of fitting children into the workforce, their influcence on the behaviour and attitudes of children, for good or ill, was problematical at best. Such sanctions as existed could operate only within the school walls and took the unimaginative form of physical punishment; to extend these into future life would have required a far closer relationship between education and work than existed at the time. In fact, employers were becoming less rather than more selective of their youthful employ-ees, as unskilled and "blind alley" boy labour increasingly became the norm. Economic pressures from the family and the all too ob-vious barriers to higher education cut off this potential reward to any but the most headstrong and intelligent. If the school system failed to produce a docile and obedient working class in the years from 1870 to 1914, this probably had more to do with its ultimate insignificance to the average boy than with a conscious reaction to its overt class bias.

In short, for the average working-class child or youth, education meant little because it could promise little. His most probable future was to work in a world in which educational attainments counted for virtually nothing and in which tangible and immediate rewards were offered to those who elected to leave school behind. As a formative influence, the school could not compete with the omni-present realities of working-class life in the home, the street and the workplace. Social control, or ideological indoctrination by the middle class, paradoxically had little overt success because of the pervasive economic control exercised by the same class and because of the responses to this environment created by the working-class family. For these reasons, it would be wrong to conclude that education for the working class increasingly "came to occupy the centre of the stage, replacing religion and work as the dominant life experi-ence."[141] For some this was undoubtedly true, but for the majority the inference is clear; they voted with their feet as soon as possible and headed into the inevitable, yet seemingly free and exciting, world of work.

CHAPTER THREE

The Youth Labour Market

The working-class adolescent of late Victorian and Edwardian England was, for at least one-third of his time, an actual worker, employed in a multitude of functions among the nation's industries and services. With one exception, however, the phenomenon of boy work has not been the subject of any sustained historical analysis in recent years.[1] This is a surprising gap, since a perusal of the literature of social issues of the period would show that it was a major topic of debate. Trade unionists cited the growing use of boys for non-vocational labour as a major source of journeyman unemployment, while middle-class observers of the youth scene bemoaned the decline of apprenticeship, the progressive loss of control over the youth's life that this involved, and the dangerous amounts of money to be found in the boy labourer's pocket. It was generally feared that industrial developments were tending to create a mass of unskilled or low-skilled adult workers with little craft pride or industrial discipline from a growing army of boy labourers unbound by any system of trade teaching and unmotivated by any incentive to develop job skills. These fears disguise the true nature of the processes at work, but they do reveal an awareness among contemporary observers of the dynamic element involved in teenage labour, and the effects that changes in the boy labour force might have upon the adult workforce of a future period.

Beyond this, changes in the boy labour market have a direct bearing on the process of skill transmission among the working class in these years. The issue of skill is an important one, and is central to a vigorous and continuing debate about the extent of structural change in the working class in the period from 1870 to 1914. The question of structural change, in turn, has important ramifications for the interpretation of the rise of "New Unionism" and class politics. The older view that these years witnessed the creation of a more homogeneous and less stratified working class has been challenged by scholars who posit, instead, a continuation of the fragmented, hierarchical, and occupationally distinct nature of the Victorian workforce into the pre-war period.[2] In such a debate, changes that can be noted in the youth labour force may help shed light on wider structural changes within the workforce. I will argue that there was, indeed, a gradual but widespread extension of skill among the working class and a relative decline of the position of the artisan elites of the earlier period. This process took place through changes in both apprenticeship and boy labour, which had as their overall effect a greater access to skill among unindentured boy labourers and a gradual devaluation of the technical expertise acquired through apprenticeship. These trends explain in part the emergence of a large body of semi-skilled workers, a group that grew out of the new kinds of boy labour becoming predominent and around which a less stratified working class could crystallize.

The late Victorian and Edwardian period saw great changes in the nature of the juvenile labour force, primarily due to developments in education and changes in the industrial structure of the country. Perhaps the greatest single factor in the production of the boy labour "problem" was the impact of the successive education acts, beginning in 1870, which swept all but a handful of children into the elementary schools within a few decades. Among a class in which the obligation and necessity of working was imposed on virtually all members of a family, children in the pre-1870 era often competed with juveniles for available jobs, with predictable consequences on wages. Child labour certainly did not disappear in the subsequent years, especially in rural areas, but the various education and factory acts made full-time child labour in most industrial areas uncertain in its supply and exposed its users to legal hazards and social opprobrium. Essentially, child labour was pushed out into the fringes of the working world after 1870 and reduced to a multitude of part-time and half-time positions, which were themselves increasingly regulated. By 1900, with the exception of the textile industry's half-timers, the sight of children in factory, mill, or workshop was rare. This development left employers seeking cheap full-time labour with fewer alternatives – namely, women and teenage girls and boys, at a time when their industrial strategy consisted primarily in the increased exploitation of their workforce rather than in expensive and potentially inflammatory schemes of mechanization.[3] It was to a considerable extent the operation of the education acts and the factory acts that allowed youths to augment their status and their bargaining power in the years after 1870.

If the education acts concentrated available younger labourers into the teenage range, they did not by themselves create the specific demand for non-vocational boy labour which, in the eyes of both trade unionists and social observers, was increasing in these years. This demand for boy labour per se, and for a superfluity of apprentices to supply journeyman ranks, was the result of a number of developments within the structure of British industry. Among these changes were the trend toward larger firms, the spread of piece rates, the rationalization, breakdown, and, to a lesser extent, mechanization of industrial processes, and the growth of certain trades, pre-eminently transport, which relied heavily on an army of boys. The first two trends made the teaching of a trade in the old way more difficult; the other trends made the value and necessity of old-style apprenticeship questionable.

The system of apprenticeship that had its origins in the medieval craft guilds had industrial, vocational, and disciplinary characteristics. In its ideal form, a master of a trade contracted to teach the apprentice the techniques of the particular skill and to see to his moral and physical welfare, in return for a premium and the obedience and labour of the youth. In this way, the craft was perpetuated, a skill was procured, and the youth's behaviour was supervised. Whatever the gap between ideal and reality in earlier ages (and this was probably large), the enshrinement of economic liberalism and the coming of industrialization saw a widespread abandonment of this method of trade teaching. By the late nineteenth century, a new type of apprenticeship had evolved among those trades that had resisted casualization through the establishment of the New Model unions. By the 1860s, the skilled unions had captured the apprenticeship system and begun to use it effectively as a means of protecting their scarcity and their incomes. These skilled or highly paid workers were primarily to be found among many of the new occupations arising from the Industrial Revolution.[4]

In this system, the apprentice almost invariably lived out, and his leisure hours were accordingly unsupervised by the master. Nor was the master often the teacher; shops had become too large for this, and in many cases the master had become the capitalist, with no claim to a knowledge of the trade's techniques.[5] Instead, instruction was turned over to the journeyman, who had no contractual obligation to teach and often had positive incentives to teach poorly – incentives that increased in the late Victorian period, as employers sought to maximize productivity in an era of falling profits. If the journeyman was on piece rates, as he often was, the motivation to teach was lessened and the boy was often reduced to repeating a single process so that output could be increased.[6] In addition, since every apprentice represented a future threat to the position of the journeyman, his welcome in the workshop was by no means always warm. One engineering apprentice recalled that, "the chief preoccupation of the man over me was to prevent me from learning how to do his work – the poor devil was driven like the rest of us by the fear of hunger – and he hardly spoke to me all day."[7] Despite some employer's use of cash payments to journeymen to teach,[8] artisans by the nature of things had less incentive to teach well than formerly. Under the new conditions of industry prevailing in the late nineteenth century, complained one trade unionist, the employer had "a constant tendency to substitute boy labour for adult labour wherever there was a possibility of doing so,"[9] and many artisans saw the increased numbers of apprentices taken on as a prelude to their own ultimate supersession.

By the latter half of the nineteenth century, then, apprenticeship as an institution had changed radically. The boy lived out, the disciplinary character of the system had lapsed, the setting had often changed from owner-craftsman workshop to large factory, and the vocational aspect had become increasingly haphazard and problematical. Other trends in many industries were working to do away with apprenticeship altogether. These were the progressive rationalization and mechanization of processes. The ultimate effect of these trends was to break down the process involved in the manufacture of goods, reducing the need for all-round skill and allowing the introduction of semi-skilled or unskilled adult, boy, and female labour. These processes, of course, already had a long history. In the era of the Great Depression and the Second Industrial Revolution, however, they often began to affect industries in which the mid-Victorian labour aristocracy was strongly entrenched.

By the late Victorian period, the boot and shoe industry was perhaps the best known example of an industry that increasingly relied on boy and other cheap labour. Even in the early part of the century, subdivision of the trade had been pronounced, but with the advent of closing and rivetting machines in the 1850s the skill required in these processes was reduced, so that rarely was anything needed beyond an ability to supply power by hand or foot and a basic agility.[10] Clicking – or the cutting of the leather segments – remained skilled, but the introduction of machinery in the other sections led first to a speed-up of the clickers and finally to the widespread use of boy labourers, who were set to cutting the simpler patterns and leathers. The apprenticeship system began to erode, "the indenture period dwindling over the years from seven years to five, from five to two, and finally disappearing altogether, swamped by subdivision of function and boy labour."[11] With the introduction of clicking machines in the 1880s, the de-skilling of the trade was almost complete. Within a generation, the industry had gone from one relying largely on skilled outworkers to one where semi-skilled and unskilled factory production predominated. Along the way, it had seen the influx of Jewish immigrants, industrial school and workhouse "apprentices," and large numbers of boys. A witness to the Royal Commission on Labour in the 1890s termed boy labour "the greatest evil we have in the trade" and asserted that 35 per cent of the clicking workforce was composed of juveniles,[12] while actual instances of sons replacing fathers had occurred.[13] The number of men aged twenty to sixty-five in the industry actually dropped, from 171,358 in 1871 to 134,560 in 1911,[14] giving credence to the trade unionists' fears of de-skilling and loss of employment in the wake of mechanization.

Although the boot and shoe industry illustrated in an extreme form the results of mechanization, other industries were also affected. When one of the first composing machines was installed in a Bradford printing shop in 1868, it was manned, prophetically, by four youths – one composing and three distributing type.[15] The two major printers' unions were successful, however, in opposing a wholesale introduction of the machines until the 1890s, when, making the best of the situation, they came to an agreement with the employers on numbers of apprentices per machine and on new piece rates.[16] By this period, males under the age of twenty made up 37.6 per cent of the workforce in large works, 49.1 per cent in small works, and 22 per cent in newspapers, compared with 32.8 per cent for the whole industry in 1871.[17]

Within the skilled trades, unions frequently attempted to limit the number of boys taken on as apprentices, often embodying this desire in contractual arrangements with employers. Nonetheless, the latter used whatever loopholes were available to cut their wage bills and attack apprentice limitations. It was a common practice for employers to use older apprentices exclusively for any overtime that might be worked, while the journeymen were sent home.[18] In a trade dispute on Tyneside, one-quarter of the engineers' places were taken by apprentice blacklegs, these jobs being permanently lost when the strike ended.[19] During slack times as well, employers had a tendency to keep boys on and let the men go. As one employer disingenuously explained, "We do not think it is fair to the lads. They have no one to protect them, so we look after them."[20] Among foundry workers, "the [threat] which loomed largest in the moulder's mind was that of 'too many boys.'"[21] To the skilled worker, an inundation of apprentices was a prelude to the overstocking of the trade, the simplification of processes, and the gradual dilution of the industry with all forms of unskilled labour. A plethora of apprentices represented in a concrete form all the major threats to the journeyman's position, and around the figure of the apprentice his fears often crystallized.

A host of smaller industries were also affected by the introduction of machinery. In the silverware stamping trade, it led to the increased use of juvenile labour.[22] Mechanization of the ropemaking industry, noted Charles Booth, "has brought in a large number of boys; men from twenty-five to forty-five are missing; but the old men linger on."[23] The same development could be seen in brush making and in the manufacture of tin cans.[24] In brick making, new machinery had entirely de-skilled the trade and had caused a rise in the ratio of boys to men from 2:3 to 1:1.[25] A representative of the cabinetmakers noted that "where a large amount of machinery is used there is no doubt, in many cases, boys can do men's work" and stated that in many shops there were now more boys than men.[26] In glass-bottle making a typical new shop might have twenty-five hands in five "groups," composed of fourteen lads and boys, and eleven men. The new situation was cited as a major cause of journeymen unemployment.[27]

The breakdown of industrial processes and their rationalization also led to the increased employment of youth rather than adult labour. In these cases, articles formerly made by a journeyman were now often produced in parts by boys and assembled by adults. Cabinet making suffered as much or more from this trend as it did from mechanization, as did brush making and tinsmithing.[28] Engineers' accessories, light leather goods manufacture, and brass finishing were other industries in which subdivision resulted in a large number, or even a majority, of boys being employed.[29] In mattress making and upholstery piece shops, the men frequently complained of the number of boys employed. The same was true of the London stove-making trade.[30] In Sheffield, subcontracting and the subdivision of processes led to de-skilling and the virtual disappearance of true apprentices in sections of the cutlery trade.[31] In the docks, a simple rationalization enabled employers to increase the use of boys. Before, in the relay system, the men would take turns, one using the barrow while the other did the heavy lifting. By the 1890s, however, boys were wheeling the barrow while men ruined themselves with constant lifting.[32] The substitution of boy for adult labour extended into the dock office, according to one witness.[33] In another case, the simple introduction of pre-sawn (and hence lighter) pit props allowed the replacement of men by boys in the docks of northern England.[34]

Throughout the nineteenth century, but especially in the latter half, there had also developed industries that relied heavily on youths and females for their labour power.[35] In particular, consumer goods that had been manufactured at home or on a small scale were now increasingly made by large concerns that could benefit from the economies of scale. Biscuit making was one example of this industry,[36] as were the jam and chocolate industries and those of candle, soap, and glue.[37] In addition, such industries as lead and zinc goods, dye, ink, and paint manufacture, paper and stationery, and fireworks, cartridges, and matches all relied heavily on juvenile and female labour.[38] The transfer of these industries from home-based and incidental manufacture to factory production considerably widened the field for youthful employment.

Perhaps the greatest magnets for boy labour were the transport and distributive trades in all their variety. Transport as a whole was increasing in importance throughout this period, as the growing maturity of the British economy resulted in a need for the more orderly and rapid conveyance of goods and information. Transport grew both absolutely and relatively, engaging 5.1 per cent of occupied persons in 1871 and 8.0 per cent in 1911.[39] Moreover, as the economy developed a need for professionals, clerical workers, and others of the administrative classes, its appetite for messengers and errand runners likewise increased. At the same time, shops, through advertising and through developments in public transport, widened the catchment area of their clientele, necessitating a growth in the number of delivery boys. Altogether, the conveyance of goods and messages occupied 42,274 males under twenty in 1861; this figure had risen almost three and a half times by 1911, to 143, 146, by which time over to 70 per cent of the workforce in these occupations was under the age of twenty.[40] Nor do these numbers include the many shop, office, and factory boys who were in reality messengers and errand runners.

These types of jobs were so ubiquitous that for many boys they were the first, and natural, employments entered into once school was left behind. In Liverpool in 1909, 37.7 per cent of boys leaving school became errand boys, van boys, or messengers.[41] Even in Norwich, neither an entrepôt nor a port city, 31 per cent of fourteen year olds were engaged in errand or van-boy employment in the same period.[42] In the early Edwardian years, messenger work alone absorbed 8.5 per cent of employed boys under fifteen in Birmingham, 9.1 per cent in Leicester, and 11.1 per cent in Salford.[43] Altogether, such jobs provided a virtually guaranteed employment for young teenagers fresh from the schoolroom.

The trend noted and deplored in other industries was, moreover, also at work in the field of transportation. Former van boys, complained one cabbie, were now often licensed at sixteen or seventeen, undercutting and competing with the adults who traditionally had made up the workforce.[44] A carman stated that youths were also taking over meat delivery from men in the metropolis and being paid 1s.6d. instead of the normal 2s.6. for the night runs from station to market. It was also asserted that large London firms were buying out smaller ones, after which "the old hands in the firm get discharged and boys are taken on in their place."[45] Thus the growth of the distributive trades provided not only a growing market for recognized boy labour positions, but also a widening of the types of jobs available within it.

By the latter half of the nineteenth century, the new types of boy labour had come to the fore. As the Webbs noted, "It is no longer a case of ... an undue multiplication of apprentices, leading in time to an unnecessary increase in the number of competent workmen seeking employment"; rather, "the employers are endeavouring, by an alteration of the manufacturing process, to dispense with skilled labour, or, indeed, with adult labour altogether."[46] Even in such highly skilled crafts as gold and silversmithing, apprenticeship was dying out.[47] In the new kind of industrial organization, "the lads are not taught a trade or how to take an interest in the trade, but only a process or part of a process. They are encouraged to become proficient in one of a few operations, not to gain a general knowledge of a trade or its interests."[48] Henceforth, the efficient conduct of economic life would become "dependent on a great aptitude for learning by most workers of all types than on any formal steps which business firms took to ensure a labour supply satisfactory in quality as well as quantity."[49] Put simply, in many of the industries of the nation, the skilled/unskilled dichotomy, underpinned in part by the apprenticeship regulations of the skilled, was giving way to a workforce composed largely of a growing group of semi-skilled workers. In the process, apprenticeship was developing the characteristics of exploitative boy labour. Speaking of engineering apprentices, an observer noted, "the lad who is going to be a fitter goes straight to the fitting shop and learns nothing else; a lad who is going to be a turner goes to the machine shop and does not learn fitting ... They are not taught; they are made to work."[50] A favoured few might be put through the whole trade to become foreman or machine setters;[51] however, "some employers state that the 'engineer' of the future will be a specialised machine-minder at 22s. to 28s."[52]

The tendency to turn apprentices into a cheap supply of machine minders, or practitioners of a single subdivided process, was combined with the growth of trades and industries relying heavily on non-vocational boy labour to significantly open up the availability of employment to youths. Their bargaining power and wages rose accordingly. The "slave markets" for boy and girl labour held in mid-Victorian London disappeared in the 1870's as the younger children were sent to school and the elder ones were no longer forced to put themselves up for auction.[53] Along with the auctions went the shoe-black brigade, numbering up to 2,000 boys, which the Ragged School Union had set up in 1851. By the turn of the century, all such boys had found better jobs, leaving this precarious employment to older men, epileptics, and cripples.[54] By 1900 a former glut of office boys had turned into a drought, as boys moved away from these positions because of low wages, an uncertain future, and a new social stigma against the clerical ethos.[55] At the same time the Shipping Federation felt impelled to devise a new and more attractive apprenticeship system, with higher wages, no premium, and a gratuity at eighteen, in order to increase the number of British seamen.[56] A decade later, a proposed clause in the Mines Bill that was intended to prohibit underground work under the age of fourteen, brought a large deputation from Lancashire mine-owners to London; there was a shortage of juvenile labour in northwest Lancashire, and, if textile factories were allowed to snap up the boys at thirteen, the mines would find it difficult to recruit, despite the high wages and the shorter day they offered to boys.[57] By the eve of World War I, a juvenile employment agency in Cambridge was filling only one-quarter of its vacancies in errand boy positions, noting two years later that "some employers, in despair of errand boys, have had to resort to the services of old men."[58]

Writers throughout this period were unequivocal about the availability of employment for youths. "In a great city ... the demand for boy labour is virtually unlimited," said one, while another asserted that "there is no problem of employment in connection with boys and youth; the demand of employers for this type of labour appears insatiable."[59] In London, noted Booth, there was an "immense ... demand for boy labour."[60] Although no truly reliable statistics on unemployment exist from this period, I will cite some figures from local studies in order to corroborate these statements. In Birmingham in 1901, 94.5 per cent of all boys aged fifteen to twenty were employed; for Rochdale the figure was 96.6 per cent, while for Oldham it was 96.7 per cent.[61] In Northampton in 1913, 94.5 per cent of boys aged fourteen to eighteen were working, while in Warrington in the same year 96.5 per cent of this group were employed.[62] When we

Table 2
Youths as the Actual and Projected Proportion of the Male Workforce
in Selected Industries, 1871–1911

Industry	1871	1911	1911 (projected)
Railways	14.3	9.6	9.7
Road transport	10.0	11.1	6.8
Messengers	62.2	71.3	42.4
Printing	32.8	21.5	22.4
Engineering	18.7	17.0	12.8
Building	13.5	7.5	9.2
Shipbuilding	12.9	14.1	8.8
Woolen and worsted	30.6	28.1	20.9
Cotton	35.7	30.1	24.4
Coal mining	27.7	19.9	18.9
Glass and pottery	28.2	23.2	19.2
Iron and steel	21.6	11.5	14.7
Boot and shoe	13.2	15.9	9.0

Source: 1871 Census, p. xii, p. xliii, pp. xxxviii–xliii; 1911 Census, p. 1–24.

consider that these figures refer to boys of all classes and conditions, it is evident that the working-class component of these groups was virtually all employed.

The growing demand for boy labour, moreover, was counterpoised by a reduction in its supply, due to two causes: the diminution in the proportion of the ten to twenty age group in the general population and, more important in its effects, the growing proportion of this age group that was still at school and thus unavailable for full-time employment. Altogether, these factors reduced the proportion of the total male population in England and Wales that was *available* for employment who were aged ten to twenty from 22.3 per cent in 1871 to 15.2 per cent in 1911.[63] Thus, although many industries show a drop in the proportion of boys employed over this period, this reduction is rarely as large as the reduction of the number of boys available for work. Table 2 illustrates the persistence of youth in the labour market, by listing the actual percentages of youths in various industries and the projected percentage given the overall change in the labour force.

In many of the nation's most important industries, therefore, youths under age twenty played a role equal to or greater than their overall participation in the labour market. This was true not only of the so-called "dead-end" positions such as messenger work, but also of such skilled or heavily unionized industries as engineering, shipbuilding, coal mining, and printing.

Along with high demand for their labour went relatively high wages. Boy labour was still cheap in comparison with adult unskilled labour, and many jobs, as we have seen, could be performed, and were increasingly designed to be performed, by just such a type of labour. This constant demand led to a general rise in wages for all types of boy workers. In engineering, noted one writer, "the wages of learners have undoubtedly increased, and not only are they higher to start with, but they progress more rapidly from year to year."[64] In the 1880s, an apprentice began at 5s. per week, with annual 1s. increments. On the eve of World War I, boys in the trade started at 8s. per week, with 2s. or 2.6d. annual increases.[65] For office boys, 8s. in 1900 was "almost as common a figure ... as five was not long ago," and, throughout the industries of London, "many large employers of boys have had to recast their whole scale of wages."[66] From 1886 to 1906, the proportion of boys earning over 15s. per week in the textile trades, engineering, metal working, and shipbuilding doubled.[67] A more important point for social critics of the period, however, is that, for an adolescent worker, the weekly pay packet was an ever increasing one, giving him within a few short years two or three times as much money as he had possessed when he had begun to work. Demand for his labour ensured that his wages would be relatively high and often growing. It also resulted in a marked quality of mobility or, better, transiency, among boy labourers. Because of the demand for boy labour, dismissal from work meant very little to the youth beyond a few days' holiday and a short scout for another position. The employer could not take up a disciplinary stance where the school left off and, for various reasons, the home was also reluctant to provide it.[8] Boys, said one author, obtained and threw over work lightly and upon the smallest excuse, while another stated that they "often do not lose by doing so."[69] Speaking of the factory boy, a writer complained, "Let his foreman speak to him harshly, let him be asked to do one tittle more than he considers the fair amount, and more often than not ... he will throw up his employment and join the ranks of the unemployed."[70]

A report from Glasgow suggested that most boy labourers and learners (as opposed to bound apprentices) passed through at least six jobs between fourteen and twenty-one; more often the figure was twelve jobs, while figures of twenty to thirty were not unheard of.[71] Although certainly the reason for leaving a job in some cases was injured amour propre, the most immediate reasons were to obtain more money or access to further industrial skills (see chapter 4). This ability to give up one job and find another quickly, often at higher pay, astonished most investigators. The fluidity of the boy labourer in the industrial landscape caused one observer to comment that "no one who has not actually seen it can easily realize how lightly boys move from job to job."[72] The apparently carefree quality of a youth's movement within the labour market contrasted strongly with that of the adult worker, for whom dismissal often signified disaster.

The relatively strong position of the boy labourer was a result of his ability to perform the easy but essential tasks necessary to industrial life – simple machine minding, errand running, sweeping up, helping on a van – at a lower cost than that of adult labour. When the youth reached manhood, however, and demanded a substantial increase in wages, his value to the employer was not so apparent, unless he had contrived to learn the rudiments of a skill in the preceding years. The nature of many youth employments was also such as to preclude a large intake of the employed youths into the adult ranks. Few van boys could obtain work as drivers, while in many of the factories and shops using juvenile and female labour the adult male component was small. This was true of textiles, clothing, shoemaking, and the distributive and messenger services, as well as of the myriad London industries such as furniture making, canning, rope making and bottle manufacture. Even the virtually all-male industries such as shipbuilding, engineering, and building had a disproportionate number of boys employed as errand runners or odd jobbers who were not expected (at least by employers) to continue on in the trade. Many of these boys were even dignified by the "apprentice" appellation, yet found themselves at twenty or so without employment or saleable skill.[73]

The end of adolescence, then, was often a period of uncertainty and dislocation for the youth. Unable or unwilling to continue in a boy labourer's job, he was cast adrift into a much more competitive adult labour market. A period of prolonged unemployment might follow, until the young man found himself some precarious niche in the ranks of the unskilled or semi-skilled industrial workers. The growing insecurity of these years may have affected such trends as marriage patterns as well; the proportion of unmarried males age twenty to twenty-five rose from 767 per 1,000 in 1871 to 857 per 1,000 in 1911.[74] Many never found their niche, and one author's comment about the metropolis was equally applicable elsewhere. "Crime and the recruiting sergeant draw upon much the same class in South London."[75] A large proportion of applicants to the Distress Committee in Norwich were young men, cast out of low-skilled

Table 3
Nature of Youth Employment of Applicants for Relief, Liverpool 1908

Occupation	Percentage
Apprenticed to a trade	5.30
Errand boys and shop boys	28.34
Farm, garden, stable, and van boys	9.84
Yard, works and factory boys not learning a trade	42.00
Sailors	5.45
Street traders	4.20
Miscellaneous	4.37

Source: Tawney, "Economics of Boys Labour," 534.

industrial work and employment as errand boys.[76] The percentage of unemployed to employed at different ages in London in 1901 eloquently illustrates this coming of age: seventeen, 2.5 per cent; eighteen, 10 per cent; nineteen, 14 per cent; twenty, 21 per cent; twenty-two, 26 per cent.[77] It was at the latter ages that the harsh economic and social penalties of being an unskilled or low-skilled worker became apparent, since there was a strong correlation between "blind alley" boy labour jobs and subsequent unemployment. Table 3 shows the descriptions given by applicants for relief in Liverpool of their occupation when aged fourteen to seventeen.

Nearly 85 per cent of these applicants had spent their adolescence in the highly paid but uncertain boy labour positions, acting as errand boys, van boys, general labourers or street traders. By their early manhood, the relatively strong position of boy labourers had turned into the relatively weak one of young adult workers, as the supply/demand equation for unskilled and semi-skilled labour reversed itself. This "manufacture of inefficiency," the creation "of a future crop of unemployed adult labour,"[78] was a trend deplored both by middle-class commentators increasingly anxious about national efficiency and by trade unionists worried about the effect of mechanization and rationalization on their status and income.

Middle-class observers of youth were convinced that the breakdown of apprenticeship and its replacement by the various types of exploitative boy labour were potent factors in the creation of a lawless and asocial youth. The attitude of these writers toward the family was generally one of fearful contempt; to this was added apprehension as to the effects that high wages, lack of industrial discipline, and job transience would have on the teenage worker. According to these writers, the family provided little moral guidance, especially once a boy was working, while his work environment not only failed to supply the requisite discipline, but also inculcated harmful traits.

Singled out for the disapproval of these observers was the position of van or errand boy. "The work itself is full of incidence and adventure, more attractive to a fidgety boy of fourteen than the office or warehouse." The job provided higher wages than that of learning positions, as well as freedom and excitement, "but in three years' time comes unemployment and poverty."[79] "The boy is exposed in a marked degree to the temptations of the streets. His work demands little intelligence or sustained effort, and is apt to breed lazy and careless habits."[80] "He seems to care for nothing but amusement; the theatre, the music-hall, or the football field are his main interests ..."[81] Worse than this was to follow. "After several years of blind-alley work, a youth of eighteen is generally unfitted for learning skilled work. He cannot apply himself to the task or will not submit to the discipline and control necessary for learning a trade. He will not take a boy's job, and cannot get an man's job; and a few weeks spent in looking for a job is often enough to make him degenerate into a casual worker or loafer."[82] Nor was it true that a few years' work as an errand or van boy was a common prelude to an entry into a trade among the mass of youth, as a recent work has suggested.[83] A contemporary study emphatically stated that "the theory that boys can become errand boys for a year or two, and then enter skilled trades, cannot be maintained. Very few boys can pick up a skill after a year or two of merely errand boy work ... The vast majority become workers in low-skilled trades or general and casual labourers."[84] The same was true of van boys, to an even greater extent.[85] Table 4, a chart of occupations at different ages in Norwich illustrates this truth.

It seems clear from this chart that errand boys, along with boy labourers in low skilled industrial work, became general and casual labourers or soldiers, rather than artisans, whose ranks remained steady throughout. It is likely that those "errand boys" who became artisans were earmarked for apprenticeship already and that they spent several years learning tools and observing processes as odd jobbers before formally entering their time. For the vast majority of errand boys, no such future could be predicted. That some craftsmen had once been errand boys does not mean that errand boys often became craftsmen.

While errand or van-boy positions were generally considered to be the worst, it was recognized that many of the other industrial positions that boys found also had a "blind alley" character. Low-skilled factory work in many of the industries mentioned in this

Table 4
Occupational Distribution of Youths at Age Fourteen and Twenty, Norwich 1909

Occupation	Percentage at age 14	Percentage at age 20
Skilled work	4	4
Clerks	4	2
Low-skilled factory, excl. boot trade	25	8
Boot factories	19	21
Car men and van boys	1	5
General and casual labour, incl. unemployed	14	52
Errand boys	30	0
Army	1	6

Source: Hawkins, *Norwich*, p. 20. The numbers have been rounded.

chapter are examples of these. Such "'Improver Blind Alleys' ... leave a youth on the threshold of manhood without trade or occupation."[86] Adult unemployment was often the result, since the boy had become used to casual work and was in many cases too over-specialized to slot himself in somewhere else when the industrial rite of passage was reached.[87] This phenomenon was prevalent throughout the urbanized areas of the nation – as true for London soap making and furniture manufacture as it was for northern engineering, shipbuilding, and the cotton trade, where the cotton spinners "go so far as to insist on there being always ten times as many [boys] as would suffice to recruit the trade."[88]

To middle-class observers, then, the dangers of the late Victorian and Edwardian youth labour market were clear. Loose family ties and early independence from both parental control and the questionable discipline of the school gave the youth an ominous illusion of freedom. The workplace failed to take up the slack, as it had in the (probably mythical) past and, indeed, actively promoted fecklessness with an easy labour market and a dangerous prodigality in wages. Freedom and affluence would be followed in many cases by unemployment and casual labour. In their eyes, the growth of this "residuum" in the heart of the nation's cities was doubly disturbing, as it would be composed of a better educated group than formerly – one, moreover, that had been reared for half a decade in affluence and industrial indiscipline. The future to these writers looked far from bright, especially when they cast their eyes across the Channel to Germany, with its emphasis on technical knowledge, its lively youth movements, and its compulsory continuation schooling.

These men and women varied in their proposed solutions. Some continued to hark back to the days of old-style apprenticeship, stating that no other way of training for a craft was recognized or available and pressing "the urgency of diminishing the supply of unskilled and clerical labour by diverting young boys to the more skilled industries."[89] Another, not surprisingly a cleric, held that the solution was partly to be found in a moral regeneration on the part of employers. Apprenticeship had decayed principally because of the renunciation by industry of any regard for posterity or the common weal. Exploitation for the present had replaced training for the future. A recognition by employers of their responsibilities would go far toward rectifying the situation.[90] Others were more practical, realizing that old-style apprenticeship was disappearing in all but a few industries and areas. "The question, therefore, is not as to how the old forms of apprenticeship can be grafted on the new organization of industry, but how the spirit of the old system, its control, discipline, and training, may be infused into modern conditions."[91]

These writers therefore suggested the creation of an interlocking series of educational and advisory agencies to help the youth establish himself as a trained member of the workforce. Juvenile advisory committees were proposed, made up of representatives from the educational, health, and industrial branches of government. These would get touch with parents of children about to leave school and impress upon them the need for their children to avoid "blind alley" work and to continue their education.[92] "The boy and his parents [must be] fully persuaded that along this line lie welfare and happiness."[93] Juvenile labour exchanges would then take on the responsibility of fitting each boy in his place.[94] Voluntary agencies, such as boys' clubs, were also seen to fulfill a vital purpose in guiding the boy into a worthwhile trade and in urging upon him the need to receive additional education. In London, the Mansion House Advisory Committee of Associations for Boys existed to coordinate these efforts among 30,000 boys' brigade and boys' club members.[95]

To these social workers, the collapse of the old training system would be best replaced by a more flexible and more open system under the aegis of the state. With the statistical and information resources of the state at their disposal, such agencies could better respond to emerging demands for types of labour, could gain a national industrial picture, and, in coordination with continuation schools and boys' clubs, could divert youths into more profitable training and more hopeful positions.

Although it is certain that some boys profited from the growth of these agencies, which were given official sanction and support under an act of 1910,[96] their overall success is debatable. Essentially, they were trying to apply a statist approach to an economic problem that was very much a product of a free market. They could place boys only in positions that industry wanted and saw fit to advertise and could fill positions only with boys who took advantage of their offer. Since genuine apprentice or learning jobs were snapped up quickly by boys, industry placed orders for boys for the positions it had trouble filling – namely, van, errand, or other "blind-alley" jobs. Since younger boys had little difficulty finding employment, the juvenile exchanges were used primarily by older teenagers who were too late to begin a trade and whose place in low-skilled positions had been usurped by another generation of school leavers.

Of the vacancies posted in 1910–11 in the juvenile labour exchanges in the country, by far the largest "trade" was "conveyance of men, goods, and messages" – in other words, van and errand boys – with 42.74 per cent of all openings and 43.79 per cent of all placed boys in these jobs.[97] The exchange was acting, in effect, as another avenue open to employers through which to locate boys for low-skilled work. As for the boys themselves, the experience of an exchange set up in a Manchester boys' club is illustrative; the average age of applicants was eighteen and a half.[98] Younger boys needed no help in finding van boy positions, while the type of employer who could lead a youth to steady and skilled adult work had little need to advertise. For these reasons, the juvenile exchanges operated in much the same fashion as their adult counterparts, which they were never intended to do. They functioned as lubricants in a too-static labour market; they could not shape that market to their liking.

A similar result was experienced by the trade boards set up after 1909 to set minimum wages and standards for all workers in low-paid industries such as chain-making, tailoring, paper box manufacturing, and lace. The boards' attempts to set minimum wages for adults were frustrated, since they soon found that workers were being dismissed when they became old enough to claim such remuneration. To counteract this practice, the boards often set a high rate for adolescent workers, which had as its effect the attraction of many youths into these low-skilled but highly paid "blind alley" industries. The boards then tried to deal with this problem by instituting an increasingly onerous "learner certificate" program in order to limit the numbers of juvenile workers and to ensure that youths in these trades received some training. This program quickly became an administrative nightmare, which took up more and more of the boards' time and energy, particularly as no real training was needed in many of these industries. By 1914 the Board of Trade wanted out of the whole scheme, recognizing that it could not impose training requirements on industries in which the modes of production made them superfluous.[99]

The fears of trade unionists and other workers were more immediate than those of the middle-class investigators. In the late Victorian period, indeed, as the Royal Commission on Labour put it, "the apprenticeship question remains, in many cases, one of the leading points at issue between employers and employed. A frequent object of trade unions is to secure that no one shall enter a trade without serving a five years' apprenticeship between the ages of sixteen to twenty-one, and that there shall not be more than one apprentice to every three or four journeymen. It is on this last question of proportion that disputes on this subject commonly turn."[100] Trade unionists saw the changes in industry as direct threats to their bargaining power and status, which would lead in time not only to a general de-skilling among adults, but also to a situation in which they might be forced to compete with their adolescent sons. They recognized, however, that their fight in this regard would be difficult. "No Trade Union has been really able to enforce a limitation of apprentices if new employers are always starting up in fresh centres; if the craft is frequently being changed by the introduction of new processes or machinery; if alternative classes of workers can be brought in to execute some portion of the operation. These are precisely the conditions which are typical of most of the industries of the present century."[101] Moreover, by the turn of the century, "a positive majority of Trade Unionists now belong to occupations in which no shadow of apprenticeship has ever existed."[102] Although it could with truth be said that "whatever remains of [apprenticeship] is chiefly owing to [Trade Union] action,"[103] unionists realized that "the apprenticeship system, in spite of all the practical arguments in its favour, is not likely to be deliberately revived by a modern democracy."[104]

How then to go about arresting or reducing the use of boy labour in the industrial world? The solutions proposed and the strategies adopted were numerous. From the beginning, technical education was seen as a possible answer.[105] A full system of "practical training by competent trade teachers" would ensure the survival of industrial skills, while getting around the major objections to apprenticeship: its haphazard method of teaching, its undemocratic selection of boys, and its tendency to create a monopoly of skilled workmen.[106] Such proposals, however, foundered on the rock of industrial reality. Technical education, until the latter part of the Edwardian period, was limited almost exclusively to actual or aspiring foremen, draughtsmen, and managers,[107] and it was becoming increasingly superfluous to youths who most likely would find themselves possessed of knowledge and skills that they could not use in the modern factory or workshop.

Trade unionists therefore attacked the boy labour problem in different ways. The president of the National Union of Boot and Shoe Operatives, in his capacity as member of the Leicester School Board, went after truancy and campaigned for the abolition of homework and the tougher application of the factory acts. His strategy was to cut out child labour, and hence homework, and to completely unionize the resulting all-factory industry. With additional bargaining power, he felt that juvenile and low-wage labour eventually could be dealt with. His cause was aided by the radicalization of the clickers – the "aristocrats" of the trade – who were angered by the introduction of boys. Previously contemptuous of the Operative's Union, they were organized and affiliated to the larger union by the early 1890s.[108] Results on the boy labour question followed soon after; at a conference of union and employers in 1892, a one boy to three men rule was worked out, with a procedure for appeal in certain cases. This was the best that the union could do, however, and it was only with difficulty that it got this rule extended for three years when it expired in 1896.[109]

The experience and strategy of the boot and shoe workers became a common one for many unions, and opened the door to the formation of general or industrial unions combining all workers in an industry. Recognizing that the apprenticeship system and exclusive craft unions were no longer a viable method of restricting competition, they sought to strengthen or to universalize their union's position in the industry and to obtain collective agreements that would simply seek to restrict the number of boys, whether apprentices, learners, or boy labourers. Some craft unions, however, were initially loath to abandon the exclusivity on which their power was based, until experience brought home to them its reduced viability. The boiler makers, for instance, issued their own apprenticeship cards and refused to recognize journeymen without them. This tactic, which might have succeeded a few decades earlier, failed, since it effectively promoted the growth of a blackleg workforce, and the union fell back on the instrument of the collective agreement to limit numbers of apprentices. In 1893 a pact was signed setting the apprentice/journeyman ratio at 2:7 in shipyards.[110] By 1901 the union had found it difficult to keep the employers to this, however, and had to settle for a promise by employers that they would not overstock with boys. In 1906, with a better economic climate, the union fought back and, by threatening to strike, was able to achieve some reduction in apprentice numbers.[111]

In the printing industry, likewise, a series of agreements was worked out in the provinces and in London between the unions and the companies on the use of apprentices on composing machines.[112] In the iron foundries, disputes in the first decade of the twentieth century often hinged upon the number of boys in the industry.[113]

Other types of unions tried different tactics to reduce the threat of boy labourers. In cotton spinning, a big piecer could usually spin, but often found it difficult to gain a secure place as a spinner. The Spinners' Union, previously craft exclusive, therefore forcibly organized the piecers and paid them if a strike was called in order to discourage scabbing. Although the spinners were willing to help the piecers fight employers, they would not support them in any attempt to better their position vis à vis the spinners themselves.[114] The Amalgamated Society of Engineers also tried to organize apprentices and improvers, sometimes being forced to recognize boy blacklegs in order to prevent a repetition of these occurrences.[115]

The Dockers' Union, typically for a general union of semi-skilled workers,[116] pressed for statutory legislation in the fight against boy labour. Asserting that he had "known these boys sleeping at the winches although the lives of the men below were dependent upon them," one Dockers' Union member recommended the prohibition of youths under eighteen on lifting machinery. Others echoed his call for state regulation in other parts of the docks.[117]

The decay of apprenticeship and the widespread introduction of boy labour were factors that helped prompt the formation of general and industrial unions and the organization of lower grades of workers by the craft unions. With de-skilling taking place through changes in apprenticeship, the amalgamation of all occupational groups in an industry became both possible and increasingly necessary, and a prominent item on the unions' agendas by the Edwardian period was often the question of boy labour. This development is illustrated clearly by the history of the boot and shoe workers. In addition, since apprenticeship was no longer a viable method of restricting competition and upholding industrial status, unions were increasingly forced to think about social, educational, and political, instead of purely industrial, methods of attack in their attempts to safeguard or ameliorate their members' position.

The years from 1870 to 1914, then, witnessed various developments in British industry that made the old system of apprenticeship increasingly outmoded and superfluous. In the industries on which England had based her economic superiority, such as cotton, engineering, and shipbuilding, rationalization and the more intensive exploitation of labour led in these years to a declining need for all-round journeymen and an increased need for semi-skilled workers. In a host of other industries, most producing for the home market, the trend was the same. In printing, furniture making, clothing, and food processing, to give a few examples, the introduction of machinery and the subdivision of processes led to a simplification of work in which a solid knowledge of the whole trade was unnecessary. The invention of the automatic lathe, of the composing machine, and of boot and shoe machinery were signposts along a road paved with a multitude of changes tending toward the more "efficient" and "rational" use of manpower.

It is true that this period also saw the rise of new industries that depended upon a higher grade of technical expertise. The chemical, electrical, and, toward the end of the era, automotive industries were examples of trades that called into being, and relied upon, a whole new body of skilled workers. Yet, in these industries, the old style of trade teaching was inappropriate, and recruits into the higher manual branches of these industries needed a theoretical base of knowledge that could come only from a thorough technical education, which most working-class boys were unlikely to possess. In any case, Britain was very slow compared with her trade rivals in building these new industries. Instead, the nation in these years tended to retreat ever more into its established industries, with modernization confined to the use of cheaper labour, rationalization, and the practising of economies of scale rather than the development of new products and technologies.[118] In such a situation, apprenticeship was bound to decay, and a new type of highly skilled workforce, trained by new institutions in new methods, was unlikely to emerge in large numbers.

On balance, then, while retaining an awareness of continuing diversity and stratification in the workforce, one should return to the earlier view, in which, in this period, "the working class became more homogeneous – a phenomenon which is generally accepted to have occurred, but which is rarely satisfactorily explained."[119] The increase in exploitative types of boy labour was both a symptom of this trend and a factor in the creation of a new working class. With each succeeding generation of boys passing into adulthood, the differences among apprentices, learners, and boy labourers lessened imperceptibly, and the basis upon which artisans maintained their economic superiority over unskilled labourers became less tenable. The youths of the late Victorian and Edwardian years were the first generation of this new workforce and new working class and formed the seedbed from which it grew. As such, studies of the rise of the new unions, of the growing homogeneity of the working class, and of state intervention should include an examination of working-class youth, the youth labour market, and generational change in this period.

The results of these trends for boys themselves were a less restrictive labour market, higher wages, and, generally, less industrial discipline, as industry developed a need for immediate labour rather than a future source of well trained craftsmen. It also eventually meant, however, a much more uncertain industrial career for the boy. Henceforth, advancement in industry and the winning of a steady position would be much more the result of the boys's own efforts to gain a saleable skill.

CHAPTER FOUR

The Experience of Boy Labour

For a male member of the working class in the late Victorian and Edwardian era, there was rarely any neat chronological division between school and work. Long before the adolescent school-leaver began full-time employment, he was likely to have been in some way a member of the workforce. Throughout his childhood, the working-class boy had usually acted upon any opportunity to earn that had presented itself, these efforts ranging from occasional errand running to permanent and time-consuming employments out of school hours. Investigators in this period were often shocked at the proportion of schoolchildren who were part-time earners. In 1910, 23 per cent of Liverpool elementary schoolboys aged eleven to fourteen were working, while in Nottingham the figure was 25 per cent.[1] One author estimated that in London roughly one-half of working-class children worked before or after school.[2] A committee investigating in 1901–2 thought that perhaps 300,000 children worked while still at school, equalling about 8 per cent of the total population below the age of fourteen.[3] These were, however, figures from single points in time. The oral evidence suggests by contrast that virtually every working-class boy had an after-school or before-school job at some time during his pre-teen years. These employments could be temporary or permanent; a matter of a few hours or the equivalent of a full week's work.

The working schoolchildren who came under the notice of legislators and authorities usually fell into one of two groups: half-timers and street traders, each with its own special characteristics. Half-timers were largely defined by geography, being mainly confined, with the exception of rural areas, to the textile areas of Lancashire and Yorkshire, while street traders were recruited largely from the poorer children in urban areas throughout England.

Beyond these special groups, however, was a large and shifting mass of working schoolchildren, employed in a host of jobs and experiencing a range of different conditions.

Partial exemption from school in order to work half-time was possible in some areas until the end of the First World War, although many local authorities (notably London) had used enabling powers to prohibit the practice at an earlier date. The major exceptions were rural areas and the cloth towns of the north, where half-time work continued to be common until the end of the Edwardian period. Children who availed themselves of the half-time provisions had first to pass an educational exam and undergo a medical check-up. The latter was rather perfunctory, while the former was an open farce. "I never knew a single case of a child failing this examination," remembers one woman,[4] while the future activist Harry Pollitt, himself a half-timer, stated that "the mill-owners who controlled the educational bodies took precious good care that the biggest dunce in the school could pass it."[5] Unless a child was obviously physically unwell, there was little to prevent him being sent half-time to the mill as early as ten years old in 1870, eleven in 1883, or twelve in 1899.[6] Half-timers worked in the mills either mornings or afternoons on alternate weeks, the early shift going from 6 A.M. to 12:30 P.M., the later from 1:30 P.M. to 6 P.M.[7] The consensus seems to be that morning work was the worst, especially in the winter. "It was a rum job getting up at half past five to run and start at six o'clock,"[8] and half-timers were notorious for falling asleep in afternoon class.[9] The governments of the day took the view that the half-time system in general was beneficial rather than harmful, being educative, remunerative, and character-building. More plausibly, civil servants also noted that the prohibition of half-time might simply swell "the numbers of children employed in the irregular or unskilled occupations which can be followed out of school hours."[10] There was, in fact, much to this latter argument; in areas where half-time factory work was common, parents often used the provisions to get children working half-time in other employments. Where half-time was prohibited, children instead usually worked part time (often for long hours) after a full school day.[11] Nonetheless, the defects of the half-time system were increasingly noted by social workers in this period, and calls for its abolition became more strident. Half-time employment usually precluded the accomplishment of any serious educational work in the school portion of the week, since the children were often too tired to concentrate. In addition, half-time work was probably physically harmful; half-timers had a rate of physical disability five times that of their full-time schoolfellows.[12] The working conditions for half-timers were also rather reminiscent of the early industrial age. Half-timers were sometimes forced to sweep the looms while they were running – "it was illegal, but it was done"[13] – and seem to have often been the victims of casual violence by overlookers and adult workers when they were not quick, nimble, or subservient enough.[14] For these dubious "educative" benefits, a half-timer earned an average of 3s.6d. in Lancashire and 3s.8d. in the West Riding in 1908.[15]

Although the numbers swept into this system generally fell over the years, there were important fluctuations in the trend. While, for instance, the number of half-timers fell from 110,654 in 1897 to 47,360 in 1906, the figure nearly doubled again to 84,298 the following year.[16] Employers were not averse, obviously, to employing these young children if the exigencies of trade demanded it. It would take prohibitory legislation to finally extinguish the practice. Having its origin in the first attempts to regulate the lives of child labourers and to ensure that some provision for their education was made, the half-time system is an example of a reform that becomes in time an abuse. Once compulsory elementary education had been introduced, the usefulness of the half-time system was apparent only to those who directly profited from it, yet the fact that these included adult spinners and weavers as well as employers delayed its abolition for half a century.

Street traders as a group also came under a good deal of investigation and were subject to various attempts at regulation in the Edwardian period. The street arab of Dickens' time was, by the Edwardian era, seen as a sociological problem rather than, as in the United States, a sentimental or exotic character practising the bourgeois virtues of independence and initiative. Newspaper and match boys had a tendency, said one report, to spend their earnings immediately on sweets and cigarettes, music halls and gambling,[17] while another report noted that "such street employment also seriously interferes with the education of many children of young age, and frequently leads to begging, street gambling, sleeping out and felony ... the majority of children sent to Certified Industrial Schools have been engaged in street work ..."[18]

Many of the street traders came from homes where incomes were less than 20s. weekly, yet it was claimed that few of the pennies earned on the street made their way back to the family exchequer. In many cases, this was because there was no family; 30 per cent of Liverpool street traders in 1900 came from homes in which one or both parents had absconded, were dead, or were in gaol.[19] It was held that "street trading has a disastrous effect on the character of every child who has the misfortune to get there," and many traders were thought to end up as "race course touts, ... travelling thieves, and loafers."[20] In Birmingham in 1901, of 550 boys under sixteen who were engaged in street selling, 419 had been prosecuted for various offences in the previous six months.[21] An interdepartmental committee investigating the problem in 1901 produced recommendations that were put into effect in the Employment of Children Act 1903. Aimed mainly at street trading, the law prohibited children under eleven from any selling and those under fourteen from selling before 6 A.M. or after 9 P.M. These hours could be moved inwards by local authorities, who were also given enabling powers to establish a licencing system. In fact, since 1889 municipalities had had precisely these powers under Section 3 of the Cruelty to Children Act, yet only four towns had made use of them.[22] While the 1903 act set minimum standards throughout the country, an investigation by the Home Office seven years later revealed that the act was a dead letter in most of England's larger cities. By-laws had rarely been passed and were not enforced where they had been.[23] As one former street seller notes of the supposedly licenced and regulated Liverpool, "a boy could stop there 'til eleven o'clock or twelve o'clock at night. Make no difference."[24] Buying twenty-six half-penny papers for 8½d., selling them for 1s.1d. plus tips, and often employing younger boys, the street seller was not an easily regulated animal.[25] The fluid nature of his 'work and his ability to lay low whenever enforcement was fitfully attempted ensured his continued presence while profits were to be made.

Although one author thought large sums were to be made in the job,[26] the reality was more prosaic. Most boys earned between 3s. and 8s. for a very lengthy week.[27] Most ended up, not as racecourse touts or thieves, but as van boys or as boy labourers in textile or other factories. The pay in such occupations was just as good as or better than in street trading and more assured, and the hours were usually shorter.[28] Working schoolboys who sold papers in the mornings and evenings usually did so from the pressures of economic necessity and from the desire to furnish themselves with small luxuries that their parents were unable to provide. Trading rarely became a career once better prospects were in view; for most boys, this coincided with their departure from the elementary school.

Beyond these regulated "special cases" was, in fact, a large schoolchild labour market. Among the most common schoolboy jobs was that of helping on a milkround, since it could be performed before or after school hours. Most deliverers worked one to two hours per day for 1s. or 1s.6d. per week,[29] but cases of up to seven hours a day have been reported.[30] Another common employment was that of lather boy in a barber shop; this was considered to be a harmful employment, since foul language was common. In addition, barber shops rather than pubs were principal sites of adult gambling because of dangers to the latter's licence.[31] Acting as a delivery or shop boy was another prevalent schoolboy job, one that perhaps resulted in the longest hours worked: twenty-five hours a week for one Thompson respondent, forty hours for another, and forty-two hours for a Lancaster boy.[32]

Many other schoolboy jobs could be listed, such as cleaning fish, working in a bakery, selling cakes on weekends, cleaning cutlery door to door, and so on. They illustrate the multitudinous ways by which a boy could earn some money and highlight the ingenuity with which pennies were often pursued. An example, albeit an extreme one, is the case of William Luby, born in 1883 in Manchester into a drunken and destitute Irish family. His first job was leading a blind man about for 6d. a week. During this period he also sold matches, later graduating to newspapers. When needed, he would spend whole nights helping a local sweet boiler, once going off with this man for weeks to sell sweets in the north. At the age of twelve and a half, being tired of school, he used his brother's papers to prove he was fourteen and embarked on full-time employment.[33] Such a career illustrates the ways in which a bona fide street arab could keep himself alive in the nation's cities, by assiduously following up earning opportunities.

Part-time jobs can be seen as providing an "apprenticeship" of sorts to working-class life. They taught boys where and how to obtain employment and reinforced the message that, as members of the working class, they must never pass up any opportunity to gain income. Boys were also in many cases introduced to the culture of the workplace. Half-timers especially were often used partly as errand or tea boys and were thus made familiar with the various departments and the hierarchy within the mill.

There is little evidence of any resentment among schoolboy workers about the need to earn, except among the early-rising and often tired half-timers, and in these cases the resentment is usually directed against the necessity to stay in school. This is not to say, however, that this lack of bitterness can be wholly explained by a widespread devotion to an ethic holding that "work had an intrinsic *moral* value."[34] Boys generally went out to work because of the economic imperative to earn, because delivering parcels around a city was as entertaining as staying at home, because going to school half time was preferable to full-time attendance, and because children were unable to conceive, given their probable future, of any reason why they should not work when able to do so. Part-time work, and more important, earning, were seen less as moral duties than as pragmatic necessities to be enjoyed if possible and endured if not. As such, schoolboy work prepared children well for the full-time employments that awaited them.

By the age of fourteen, a minimum of 80 per cent of working-class boys had left the schoolroom behind, most of them forever, and had entered the full-time labour market. This market was, however, a boy labour market, distinct from that of men. For a period of roughly five to seven years, whether as an apprentice, learner, or boy labourer, the youth had a boy's duties and a boy's wage. When this period came to an end, the consequences for the youth, for good or ill, were considerable.

Although, as noted in the previous chapter, apprenticeship was declining in many industries in this period, it was by no means completely extinct. Generally, in cases where the size of industrial concerns was small or the techniques used were traditional, apprenticeship often still lingered. In such a city as Norwich, the giving of premiums and the practice of indenturing were still common in 1910, especially in the printing, carpentry, plumbing, and masonry trades.[35] The Webbs noted that "it is in especially ... such homes of the small-master system as Sheffield and Birmingham; and in such old-fashioned handicrafts as glass-blowing and hat-making, that the archaic apprenticeship regulations linger."[36] Nonetheless, when added up, these industries still represented only a small fraction of the English industrial population. Of 1,490,000 trade unionists at the turn of the century, the Webbs estimated that only 90,000 belonged to unions in which apprenticeship regulations were actually enforced.[37] Beyond the non-apprenticed unionists, of course, were the millions of non-unionized workers in industries in which apprenticeship had never existed or had long disappeared.

Despite their relative scarcity, then, bound apprenticeships were still a possible option even at the end of the Edwardian period. It was an option, though, that many boys found difficult to exercise. Where premiums were still demanded, their cost put them out of the reach of most working-class lads, unless a charity stepped in to help. For most London boys, a further obstacle loomed; in engineering shops, cooperages, foundries, and locomotive works, sites of still flourishing trades, most of the apprentices were relatives of the skilled workers employed there.[38] Elsewhere, the same pattern prevailed. A Salford fitting apprentice won his position through the intervention of an uncle, while a Barrow lad became an engineer's pattern maker because his father was a friend of the foreman.[39] In an extreme case, 80 per cent of the Thames lighterman apprentices were bound to their own fathers.[40] As one respondent remembers, "Parents made a desperate effort in those days to get their sons into ... an apprenticeship, and that was one of the main things ... therefore [in] each generation [that] came up there were these crafts-man families."[41] An engineer's son did not necessarily become an engineer, although he usually entered some craft comparable in status.[42] But "if the father is not himself in a position to get the boy into a good trade, he does not know in many cases how to manage it."[43] "In those days they were very strict about how many appren-tices there were in a shop where there were so many men ... [It needed] a lot of wire-pulling to get in."[44] The chance to learn a trade was closely connected to the position of the boy's father and had little to do with the boy's own aptitude or educational attainments, so in the competition for access to valuable skills, it was almost always the labourer's son who lost out. Oral history material does furnish evidence of the sons of the unskilled obtaining apprentice-ships, but these examples are the exceptions proving the rule that connections of one kind or another were what mattered. A Keighley youth who became a foreman in a mill may have been only the son of a low-paid coachman, but the coach belonged to the Cloughs, the proprietors of the mill in which he became apprenticed.[45] A Barrow youth obtained his position as a co-op apprentice because his neigh-bour was on the co-op committee, and the family, although poor, was known to be respectable and steady.[46]

The obstacles to a recognized trade were compounded by such forces as the overstocking of apprentices, the breakdown of pro-cesses, and mechanization, which tended to reduce the value of a journeyman's ticket over the years in the minds of youths. An ex-ample of one danger in apprenticeship in the new age could be seen, said one author, in "a small trade which consists of a particular form of glass-cutting." Chemical processes were replacing hand ones, and "the boys, with several years of their apprenticeship still to run, are tied down to a trade that will soon be as extinct as a dodo."[47] Many boys from poorer families, cognizant of lower apprentice wages, simply could not afford to make such an uncertain investment. For these reasons, the apprenticeship option was becoming in this pe-riod both more difficult to exercise and less attractive to the boys themselves, even when disqualifying circumstances such as poverty or the father's position did not rule it out in the first place.

Many boys who became apprentices did so after a few years of other work; for example, in trades such as plumbing, smithing, boilermaking, and bricklaying, the dangers or physical strain of the work involved made these trades unsuitable for young teenagers. Some trades such as printing, however, often insisted on a full seven-year apprenticeship, which, since indentures were void at law at age twenty-one, meant that only those fourteen years old or younger were taken on.[48] In other trades, the length of indentures was flexible: seven years for a fourteen year old, five years for a sixteen year old, and so on.[49] Up until the time that a boy entered a trade, his occupations might be quite varied. Among northern engineers, it was common to begin as a half-timer, then become a full-timer in a textile mill before entering a fitting or turning shop.[50] A London boy worked as a page, a shop boy, and a messenger before beginning an apprenticeship as a wood machinist, while a Staffordshire lad, predictably, spent three years in the potteries before switching to the carpentry trade.[51]

By the late Victorian period, the formal training characteristics of apprenticeship had been considerably reduced. Apprentices were therefore much more likely than formerly to take advantage of night schools, although such classes were rarely insisted upon by employers.[52] Indeed, bound apprentices were often forced to act unilaterally in order to obtain a wide knowledge of their trade, undertaking continuation education at their own initiative and expense.[53] Within the shop itself, the youth also had to fight to learn. An apprentice automobile mechanic noted that the journeymen in the garage "weren't so keen to learn a young boy as ... they are today. But you was alright if you poked your nose in ... you know, and had a good look round and see what he was doing. You sort of learnt yourself."[54] Employers, as well, would often leave a boy to repeat a simple process, so that an apprentice eager to learn had to insist on his right to be moved around.[55] Along with a general rise in wages in this era went a decline in the readiness of employers to train fully their future workmen. The production of a competent all-round journeyman was hence much more than formerly the result of the boy's own efforts. Conversely, in firms that paid abnormally low apprenticeship rates, teaching was more likely to be an organized part of workshop activity. At Waring and Gillow's in Lancaster, for example, the paltry 9s.6d. weekly made by a sixth year, twenty year old apprentice was consonant with the large amount of training that was carried on there, the very high level of craftsmanship displayed in the firm's furniture, and the quality of material used.[56]

Apprentices had a more onerous workshop existence than did boy labourers, and they often recognized and resented the fact. "The craftsman ... had to go to the technical school two or three nights a week and work for little wages. And they were kind of jealous of the information and knowledge that they got," says one fitter.[57] Another notes, "When you're serving your time you got a poor wage. But them as is going to be labourers got fabulous money some way or another, nearly three times your wages. But when you came to a craftsman you got the big difference." The same lad, weary perhaps of night schools and low wages, really wanted to be a teamster, "sightseeing and getting paid ... I thought all along for years that the employers were making money out of me."[58] This wistful longing was by no means unique; another budding engineer records, "I envied the van drivers and the draymen perched in their high seats, seeing things happening all day."[59] It was recognized that adult labourers made less than journeymen, but as another remembers, they were not also constantly queried about the pace of work or whether the work done paid the firm sufficiently.[60] With greater prospects came greater responsibilities and a higher standard of diligence, as many apprentices ruefully learned. Apprentices were also more likely to be disciplined by foremen or journeymen, or were at least less able to react to such treatment than the boy labourer, who could walk out without leaving too much of a vocational investment behind. As an apprentice, it was expected that you would "behave yourselves and ... do as you were told";[61] the result of failure was likely to be "a good hiding" or a "back hander" from the superior.[62] Discipline was tight even as the youth approached manhood. A trainee iron moulder was once told to hurry up by his superior, "and I called him a lazy devil ... And I had to run out of the foundry 'cos [if] he'd have got hold of me he'd have given me a good hiding." When the lad's father found out, he told the boy, "'Now when he ever asks you to do anything never answer him back.' And I were nearly eighteen year old then."[63] Nor were apprentices encouraged to enter the conversations of their betters. "Lads sit with lads, men sit with men, you understand. Now you never got into a conversation with them, you were a lad and had to stop a lad. Now when you come twenty-one and you come out of your time, you went sitting with men. You left the lads you see, you were a man then, but you didn't speak when you went sitting with men – not 'til you were a matter of about twenty-two or twenty-three, 'til you started voicing your opinion to 'em."[64] Although in these respects an apprentice's lot was perhaps harsher than that of a boy labourer, numerous compensations existed beyond the obvious one of a more secure and affluent future. The oral and biographical material shows that many workshops had a varied and rich day-today life and that apprentices and learners practised (or had practised upon them) many customs stretching back in some instances into the pre-industrial era. In addition, the process of learning a craft and of working with machinery and tools had an intrinsic attraction to many boys. "I loved wandering through the works, fascinated by the steel-pressing, galvanising, brass founding, acetylene-working, and blacksmithing being carried on, and also by the men's talk," remembers one.[65] An apprentice smelter concluded by observing the men that "there was the satisfaction of creation in every pot of good steel. That made up for a lot,"[66] while Will Crooks, the future M.P., remembered a man in his cooperage who circled around and admired every barrel that he had made.[67] By such observations, apprentices could glean a little of what it still meant to be a craftsman in terms of the dignity and pride of labour.

An apprentice also had an interesting social education to undergo. "There are traditions, customs, and usages interwoven with, and indeed in a great measure constituting, the inner and social life of workshops," wrote Thomas Wright. An apprentice who failed to learn this side of workshop life would, no matter how competent a workman he became, "find the workshop world a harsh, unsympathetic, and unjust world."[68] For an apprentice, the first test in the syllabus was usually the willingness to take a joke. A boy might be asked to fetch "a half-round square, or some other non-existent and impossible tool" or be sent out to buy "belt-oil" and, given this by a knowing shopman, be instructed to pour it on the pulley belts, causing them to slip and the boy to be spattered.[69] In a Salford fitter's shop, first-year apprentices were forced to put on a variety show at Christmas, "and if they thought you was lousy, whether you were lousy or good you'd get all blacking bags out of the foundry ... and they'd wet and they'd throw 'em at you."[70] In Preston, apprentices traditionally took a half-holiday on Shrove Tuesday, "but custom said that they had to escape, and the older men tried to catch them leaving at twelve o'clock. If they were caught they probably got their faces blackened before they were allowed to leave."[71] New apprentices were also expected to "keep nix," or to watch for the appearance of authority, and were rated by the workmen on the ingenuity they displayed in smuggling drink into the shop.[72] Such pranks and tasks were designed to judge the apprentice's worthiness as a potential fellow craftsman and unionist, his willingness to work, and his overall disposition. A boy who displayed petulance, sycophancy, or some such other trait would likely experience a miserable and unprofitable period of indentures.

Among apprentices themselves, various sanctions existed to protect individuals from each other and from adults. A persistently late or lazy apprentice would, for instance, be ambushed by the other lads and thrown into a water trough.[73] In a railway works, if "one of the boys proves to be a bully and a terror and plays ducks and drakes with the rights and privileges of others, the boys will not be satisfied until the tyrant is humbled and punished."[74] Nor were adults immune to such practices as "small-ganging," a concerted attack by the youths upon "some particularly obnoxious man." Adults had "a well-grounded dread of it, which is a great protection to the boys."[75]

As well as the clear demarcation between themselves and the journeymen, there were gradations among the apprentices according to age and experience. Younger boys on Saturdays "used to have to clean all the moulding shop up," relates one Bolton ironworker, "collect all the spades and oil 'em and you worked an hour longer." However, "as you left from being a shop lad you went a little higher, then you went a little higher 'til you were top lad ... You'd turned twenty [by] then you see. So at Sat'days, instead of you doing any work, ... you sat on boss's step and you told t'other lads [to] collect all spades but you got your hour overtime just the same ..."[76] Soon after this, a young man would leave the ring of apprentices at dinner time to go to sit with the men and would, within a year or so, be "putting in his word" and expecting it to be listened to.[77] The formation of a journeyman in social as well as industrial terms would be complete.

The occasion of an apprentice coming out of his time was usually one of celebration. When a cooper's apprentice had finished, for instance, he was put into a hot barrel until his clothes were singed, then he was taken out and tossed in the air. The new journeyman then had to buy bread, cheese, and beer for the whole shop.[78] In a Lancaster mill, a similar custom can be found. "Once a boy got to twenty-one he had to treat all his intimate workmates, those he associated with, generally a cigar round and the apprentices got a bob. Every apprentice got a bob off the one that was going out."[79] It was at this time, as well, that the young man became a full-fledged member of his trade union, though he had often been admitted on a provisional basis earlier.

The end of apprenticeship was also, however, often a time of dislocation, since the immediate aftermath for the new journeyman was the necessity to go "on the tramp." This was because many young men still had to struggle with their own firm to prove their bona fides and to obtain full journeyman wages.[80] "If the rate was two pounds you got ten bob less than the rate and you had to advocate to get your rate within twelve months. Every three months you had to go cap in hand for an increment."[81] Most young journeymen refused to put up with this and left. "I worked for about a week to see what the gaffer were paying and I got thirty bob. I packed it in on a Saturday and got the same night's boat over to Belfast and got two pound seven and six." Harry Pollitt, faced with two years of "improver's" pay, left to join another firm, while, in another company, apprentices were given three month's notice at twenty-one and "out you went ... you've got to go and get experience elsewhere ... that was what they call the good old days."[82]

Bound apprentices in this period continued to undergo many of the same experiences as their predecessors of the mid-nineteenth century "labour aristocracy." As apprentices, they were introduced to the customs and usages of the workshop and were expected to conform to the disciplines of a hierarchy based on skill and experience. They were also made aware of craft pride, which was an essential element of artisan culture. Yet in many ways their position as budding tradesmen was changing and was beginning to approach that of other types of boy work. Their status as apprentices was no longer an automatic guarantee that they would gain access to an arcane and valuable skill or that they could look forward to a relatively secure and highly paid working life. Henceforth, a secure position would be gained as much in the technical school classroom as in the workshop, while within the workshop itself knowledge in many cases had to be wrung out of employers. Boys who failed to take these steps to ensure their future, while contractually on a par with those who did, would likely end up closer to semi-skilled operatives than to true artisans. The production of a craftsman in this period was beginning to be much more than formerly an act of self-creation.

Of those boys who eventually found themselves a skilled trade, only a certain percentage were actually bound apprentices with signed indentures. The majority were "learners," "improvers," or unbound apprentices. Some skilled and highly paid trades, such as mule spinning, had no apprenticeship regulations, while in many others the practice, as we have seen, was dying out. The learner was in fact, the standard industrial trainee of the future, and probably many self-styled apprentices were in actuality members of this group. It was distinguished in large part by the unregulated, non-contractual, and informal methods of its trade training and by the large degree of initiative it presupposed on the part of the boy.

An investigator in the Edwardian era compiled a list of the main types of learning. Besides formal apprenticeship, he identified five major learning methods. "Verbal apprenticeship" referred to cases where a contract was lacking but a tacit agreement existed that the boy would stay the full term and learn. "Employment during good behaviour" was the term given to a job wherein the boy was given the chance to learn but no promise of being kept on either as a youth or an adult. Another method was "working and learning," in which a boy was more or less on his own; by working hard and gaining promotion, he could advance to more complex processes. In sawmills, shipyards, and glassworks, a boy could learn by "following up"; a boy doing this acted as the helper of a skilled man and observed his techniques. Finally, in the less skilled and more mechanized trades, such as boot and shoe manufacture, a boy could "pick up" a facility in a trade by moving from simple machines to more complicated ones, becoming efficient on each in turn.[83] Although these terms and distinctions are useful and highlight the main methods used by boys to gain a skill, it is probable that the majority of youths used an amalgam of two or more of these means in their adolescent industrial careers.

Learning, as opposed to bound apprenticeship, had certain advantages from both the employers' and the boys' point of view. For employers it meant a more flexible youth workforce, unencumbered by contractual arrangements or by the obligation to teach. Youths could be used simply as labour, with a few boys picked out and taught needed skills in response to a shorter term demand. Given an economic system beyond their control, the learner method also made more sense to the boy. The pay was higher than that of an apprentice, since the labour to learning ratio was higher. There was less chance of being stuck in a soon to be extinct craft, since learners were not legally tied to an employer. Above all, the future, given the overall economic constraints, was in the individual youth's hands. By pushing foremen and masters, by requesting changes in tasks, and by attending night school, an adolescent could carve himself out a niche as a highly skilled worker despite a lack of credentials and in spite of a chequered employment history.

Many firms practised forms of tacit or verbal apprenticeship in these years. In this, a boy would be taken on in a menial capacity but would be given the opportunity to better himself and to rise in stages through the workforce. These stages were sometimes marked by examinations. Thus, a Darlington boy passed from engine cleaner to fireman to driver on the railway, with examinations and medicals at each step.[84] The Port of London Authority gave its messengers examinations in order to determine which were potential clerical and supervisory material.[85] In both these cases, the employers merely provided an opportunity to advance, making neither arrangements for the boys to learn a syllabus nor any promises that the boy would be able to continue in the firm's employ as an adult.

Much more common were the other methods of learning, in which the boy rose by demonstrated efficiency rather than by success in formal examinations. In the textile industry, mule spinners had no recognized apprenticeship, but rather won their position by a combination of learning and luck. "You had to wait on someone dying or leaving before you was moved up. It was a very slow process, there was people ... I recollect, that was in their thirties before they began spinning."[86] As each spinner supervised (and paid) a little piecer, a big piecer, and a minder, there were three youths and young men training for one adult job.[87]

In the collieries, boys would also have a more or less set career path, from lamp boy to door boy to pony driver to coal filler to collier.[88] On this route, sheer size and strength were probably as important to advancement as familiarity with the workings of a mine were. Similarly, in tinworking, the very high wages paid to adult workers reflected more the workers' stamina and strength than their skill, which was, nevertheless, not inconsiderable. A boy learning this trade could proceed only as fast as his muscles, as well as his expertise, would allow.[89] An example of "following up" can be found in the case of a Nottingham factory worker. Starting as a shop lad in Raleigh's bicycle works, the boy fetched tea, ran errands, and swept up. From there he was set to putting spokes in the wheels, along with other girls and boys below the age of fifteen. After this age, the boys would be set to "rough true" the wheel by tightening the spokes. Finally, after a few years, the better boys would be kept on as wheel truers, who would supervise and finish the work of the adolescents.[90] In this scheme, an exploitive factory system relying heavily on juvenile labour did not prevent a relatively skilled trade from being learnt by a few boys through observation and practice. Those whose dexterity was greatest and whose behaviour had been acceptable would presumably be considered for adult positions. A similar career was followed by a cane furniture maker, who simply learnt this intricate craft on the job.[91]

Another common method of learning was by moving from shop to shop. As we have seen, many investigators associated this habit with adolescent fecklessness and indiscipline. Others were more perspicacious, seeing the motive behind the many moves. George

Askwith, after noting that employers often complained of boys leaving just as they became useful, explained. "Of course they are. It is the attempt of the lad, by himself or through the advice or need of his parents, to better himself and to go where he thinks there are higher wages, better conditions, or more chances of advancement."[92] Another observer gave as an example of this method the career of a typical boy worker in the London furniture shops. "A 'little boy' of fourteen comes into the shop at 6s. a week to run errands. He does not do the work or possess any tools, but from watching the men at work he gets to know how it is done. His wages rise to about 9s., the most he is worth as an errand boy, and when he asks for 10s., he is refused and leaves. He gets another job for about 10s. a week, saying he can do some simple thing, and on being sacked or leaving that place, he gets another [job] to do a harder piece of work at a higher wage. This he may not yet have done, but having seen others do it, he contrives to carry it out sufficiently well to keep the place. Thus he gradually makes his way, until he can earn full money."[93] In the building trades in London, as well, there was "a widespread opinion ... in favour of 'picking up' a knowledge of the trade – of going first as a boy and then as an improper, and of moving from shop to shop in order to secure the advantages of various experiences."[94]

By this system, employers paid for actual skills, while boys could progress at a rate consonant with their quickness and their temerity. Youths often preferred the migratory method of learning a trade, sometimes supplemented by night school, to the lower wages and more onerous discipline of apprenticeship.[95] Moreover, a boy did not have to wait for some arbitrary date to be reached before considering himself a journeyman. As a Barrow youth explained, "When you felt you could take charge and you knew all there was to know, you then applied as a baker and confectioner and you just went. If you couldn't do the work, you got the sack and that was it, it was up to yourself." By the same token, a boy could set limits to the tasks that he was willing to perform. The trainee baker, after about a year and a half in one shop, moved to another to gain access to more skills. "All right, I was an improver, I already had the rudiments of m'trade so I went to another shop as an improver. I got a raise in wages. As an improver, you didn't expect to be the one called upon to grease the tins and mop the floor and wipe the table." Soon after starting at the new site, however, he was asked to fill in one day for the missing errand boy. "I said, 'I'm not an errand boy now, I've done all my errand boy jobs. I've worked hard in my life and I'm not doing any more errand boy work.'" The result of this display of honour was the sack, but another job was quickly found.[96]

Clearly, in these methods of trade training, a type of dialectic was at work. Boys made progress as the result of a constant struggle with superiors over wages and access to more complex processes. Progress itself was measured empirically, by demonstrated ability rather than by time put in. In this dialectic, a boy might exercise his own will, measure his chances, and choose his options relatively freely. Thus, for instance, faced with the alternatives of becoming clerks, with a smaller wage but more security, or labourers, with the reverse, many boys intentionally failed the Port of London Authority examinations.[97] To claim that such boys were masters of their fate would be to discount the powerful economic and social forces arrayed against them; clearly, however, teenage learners were able to act as responsible agents in the labour marketplace and to influence their own destiny. Most investigators of the time tended to ignore the resilience of youths themselves when faced with a perceived threat of de-skilling in the workforce.

Learners no less than formal apprentices were subject to the social codes and traditions of the shop and were often the victims of initiation rites. Perhaps the most famous of these customs was practised in the textile mills. As Harry Pollitt explains, "The usual tricks played on a learner were played on me, but the weavers, being a cut above the cardroom operatives (as they thought), played only polite, ladylike tricks on me. It was left to the buxom girls and women in the cardroom to break me in by taking my trousers down and daubing my unmentionable parts with oil and packing me up with cotton waste."[98] In a less drastic way, other boys were introduced to sex when they began to work, either through the talk of older men or their peers. As an Oxford native notes, "Them old men'd learn you better than any book or anything else. They took you in their confidence you see ..."[98] A former telegraph boy and trainee postman from London remembers, "See you mix with a lot of lads of your own age ... – between thirteen and eighteen – and ... from getting amongst them you learnt things that you'd never heard of before. I mean I was quite innocent – absolutely innocent of anything ... – when I started work."[100] Learners, being rather freer from disciplinary restraints than apprentices, were more given to horse play, "singing and shouting at the top of their voices and slopping water over each other." Occasionally such boys would be sent home for a few days, "but they do not care about that ... they do not feel to be bound down hand and foot by the employment, and even if they should be discharged altogether they will not have lost very much."[101] Nonetheless, in many trades the learner, like the apprentice, was made aware of the privilege inherent in the position and the pride that men took in their job. Spinners, in particular, considered themselves to be true labour aristocrats, going to work in bowler hats and tailcoats, and jealously guarding their supervisory status over the piecers.[102] The miners' self-esteem was also well attested, and boys who went down the pit had a conscious feeling that they were joining a select band of men distinguished by their courage and stamina.[103] Tinworkers likewise felt pride in their ability to stand the heat, the hard work, and the pain of frequent cuts and burns.[104]

From the beginning of the Great Depression onward, employers attacked what they saw as the unnecessarily restrictive practices of the craft unions. Wherever possible, they fought for a more flexible and fluid workforce and attempted to divest themselves of the constraints imposed by a true apprenticeship system. Boys entering the workforce under these conditions found their path to a skilled position to be considerably less assured than in the past. Nonetheless, youths were able in many cases to gain a valuable skill precisely because of this new flexibility. The more extensive use of boys posed a threat to craft status, but, conversely, allowed boys to move freely from shop to shop and to fight, often successfully, for access to positions where a skill could be gained. The growing presence of these types of learners made the old artisan-labourer dichotomy increasingly untenable, and employers, by their use of a less formally trained type of labour, promoted the increasing presence of a group of workers around which a more homogeneous working class could form. This class was itself the product of innumerable individuals attempting to gain a secure position in a rapidly changing economic environment.

Below the apprentices and those learning a trade, estimated as about one-fifth of the youth population,[105] was the army of so-called "dead end" or "blind alley" boy labourers, situated in van-boy, errand-boy, or unskilled factory positions. These boys usually had a much more chequered industrial career than the others, with the exception of the consciously peripatetic learners, and there is very little evidence of continued education. It is often difficult to determine the subsequent histories of their careers, since in many of the oral history interviews no information beyond 1918 is given, and, in any case, World War 1 provided a distorting factor in many of these boys' industrial lives. Nonetheless, it would seem that despite their position as the least favoured type of boy worker, most of the "dead end" youths had begun to establish a permanent position for themselves by the time they were eighteen or so.

As with apprentices, many of the youths found their jobs through relatives, though on a less exalted level. Although sacked once already for playing cards on the job, a Hanley boy obtained another position in the same colliery where his stepfather worked.[106] Another boy got a van-boy's job in the same firm that employed his father, while another became an engine oiler on the railway where his father worked as a guard.[107] In one case, a boy disregarded a vicar's attempt to put him into the printing trade, preferring his brother's scheme to get him a job as a van boy with a railway; the father's £1 per week wage as a docker probably counted for much in the decision to forgo the low-paying apprentice position.[108] Most young teenagers probably welcomed the opportunity to work with relatives, but would have had little difficulty finding themselves similar positions without such help. One boy searching for employment was "not long in finding it. Two shops in Victoria St, Manchester, next door to one another, were advertising for errand boys, one at 6s. per week, the other at 5s.. Needless to say we applied for the six shillings ..."[109]

Where did jobs like these lead? According to the observers of youth, the most likely destinations were casual labour, loafing, the army or crime. Although the sample is small and the information incomplete, the oral evidence rarely bears this out. While only a few boys ended in secure and steady clerical jobs, and very few as artisans, most boys who began as messengers or van boys found relatively steady low or semi-skilled positions. Thus, a London respondent from a poor family, successively a milk boy, delivery boy, and stable lad, found himself a position as a helper in the local butcher's shop in late adolescence and learned the rudiments of a trade.[110] A Liverpool native, who spent seven years in an orphanage, began as a messenger, yet found steady work as an engine cleaner at age eighteen and retired as a driver.[111] An errand boy, clothing club collector, and newsboy obtained a labourer's job in a biscuit factory when sixteen years old, and eventually rose to foreman, while a boiler firer and gardener from Durham became a low-paid but secure railway shunter.[112] Finally, a fish shop lad became a goods porter on the railway at seventeen and ended his career as an inspector.[113] There is little doubt that many boys did fall into casual employment, but such was not the inevitable fate of van boys, errand boys, or other "blind-alley" boy labourers, especially those who worked for large concerns such as railways. Moreover, given the common educational opportunities offered to the entire working class, it is probable that boys from poorer labouring families were as likely to end up as clerical workers as were their contemporaries from the families of skilled workers. Thus, the son of an ex-soldier and labourer began as a messenger and errand boy in an office and then became a clerk, fulfilling his mother's ambition that he work in a white collar. [114] The son of a poorly paid railway labourer in Barrow was given a chance to work for the co-op because of neighbourhood connections and eventually qualified as a grocer. [115] The son of a part-time prostitute whiled away much of his childhood in reading, and then rose from an office boy position to that of a nationally known sports and music critic. [116] The oral history material also includes examples of the sons of late Victorian labour aristocrats moving into the lower middle class; a Liverpool youth, whose father was cargo checker on the docks, went from office boy work into the grocery trade, eventually becoming a qualified grocer – a decision he regretted all his life because of the poor pay. [117] The son of a highly skilled dipper and fireman in the Potteries began as a warehouse lad and rose from this position to that of a railway depot clerk by the turn of the century. Again, the idea that this represented true social mobility may be doubted, since, two decades before, his father owned three houses and could afford annual holidays in Blackpool for the whole family. [118] Many in the working class may well have been contemptuous of "twopence ha'penny toffs ... all dressed up and no food in the house,"[119] but for labourers' sons this was probably as realistic an ambition as that of aspiring to become an artisan. Thus, while boys from tradesman families were certainly more likely to gain entry into a skilled trade, boys from poorer families were perhaps as likely to rise into another social strata.

Unfortunately, the reaction against clerical work that became noticeable in the Edwardian period rested upon a well grounded recognition of its decreasing status and rewards. One respondent's brother provided an object lesson in the pitfalls of social mobility – one that was probably not lost on many who surveyed the increased "opportunities" created by the universal educational system. "He was a white collar, and he lived with us and what we say the poor class, and I've seen him have little paper collars on, and at one time he wore spats; ... he'd cut boots down, make a pair of shoes of 'em just to keep up appearances. He was a clerk in the City you know. And he tried to be different to us in his way but of course he still had to come down to our level [as] regards his food and one thing and another. He's a nice enough chap, but he was a white collar worker. And I suppose he didn't ought to have been really; he couldn't keep up to it you know."[120]

Van boys and boy labourers also underwent an apprenticeship of sorts. "The art is to bear the daily burden of tiredness and boredom equably, to know the limit of one's strength and to husband it." Getting to know the rhythm of the pick, shovel, or hammer was an essential part of this education.[121] Van boys were required to inure themselves to long hours, since they "used to start at six o'clock in the morning and finish work when you'd done at night – not before. Seven, eight, nine, ten, eleven, twelve o'clock at night. Start again at six o'clock next morning."[122] Such boys also knew that their future was far from secure. A London railway, for instance, gave each van boy a medical examination at eighteen in order to determine which youths would stay on. Hard workers were always passed, while those that the company had no use for were invariably failed.[123]

Despite these drawbacks and hazards, boy labourers had certain advantages over their apprentice peers. Their jobs, particularly that of van boy, were rarely boring, were comparatively free and easy, and often took place in the open air in the bustling streets of a large city.[124] Their initial wages were quite high, and they could often set a low limit on the amount of discipline to which they were willing to submit. For boys who had often spent their childhood in a penurious and gloomy environment, such factors may well have provided a sufficient return for future insecurity, which all the facts of their existence, in any case, had shown they could do little to avoid.

Observers of boy labour were fearful that the course of economic development was inexorably leading to a general de-skilling of the workforce and the creation of a future generation of rootless and casual workers. With hindsight, it can be seen that what was occurring was a process that would begin to break down status barriers within the working class and would promote instead a greater homogeneity. This process was given a large impetus by, but was certainly not created by, the First World War. Its roots, in fact, go as far back as the last three decades of the nineteenth century.[125] As was their wont, middle-class writers of the time were apt to extrapolate purely economic factors and so arrive at their dire predictions; they tended to ignore the reaction of workers themselves. Part of this reaction was the formation of viable industrial and general unions that could fight for higher wages and security and thus soften the impact of de-skilling and casualization. Another facet was the reaction of individuals, who, finding themselves in a changing environment, used the resources of technical education and their greater ability to move freely in the industrial landscape in order to gain as secure a position as possible in a capitalist society. In this changing environment, and despite the continuing strength of craft barriers, individual boys could develop valuable skills from a seemingly directionless and casual industrial career. Those who painted the picture of the "blind alley" boy or the peripatetic learner in such dark colours were positing a lack of intelligence and resourcefulness on the part of youths that an examination of oral and autobiographical evidence belies.

Whatever the long-term prospects, little doubt exists that the years from fourteen to twenty were a high point in the life of a male member of the working class. After the discipline and boredom of the elementary school and the often financially difficult and controlled atmosphere at home, the boy of thirteen or fourteen could strike out into the world of work, where employment was easy to find and where wages meant a modicum of independence and affluence. In the culture of the working class, reaching the school-leaving age was a rite of passage initiating a half-decade period of little responsibility and considerable freedom, tied inevitably to the economic basis of working-class life. If the poverty cycle constructed by Rowntree graphically depicts the long-term economic insecurity of much of working-class life, it also outlines the main phases of the lived experience of the individual worker. Of these phases, the one representing adolescence, when both the boy worker and his family dragged themselves above the poverty line, was one of the most optimistic and heartening, whatever the future might hold.

For the majority of boys, freedom from school was accompanied by freedom within the home. Discipline with regard to conduct and hours of coming and going was progressively relaxed, until the older teenager assumed the position and perquisites of a favourite lodger – one willing to lend a hand when needed, and bound by ties of intimacy and love, but one ultimately unfettered by family control. After the often penurious years of childhood, the youth also had substantial money in his pocket for the first time. Whether this was pocket money doled out by parents in the early years of adolescence or larger sums retained by the older boy after paying for his "lodging," it often amounted to a matter of several shillings a week, to be spent as the youth saw fit.

It may be argued that when the boy left the classroom, he exchanged the discipline of the school for that of the workplace. There is undoubtedly much to this; whether in a factory, shop, or office or on a van, the working boy was in a menial position in relation to adult workers, and in the factory or shop the working class as a whole was subject to the discipline of work procedures arising from the methods of production. In addition, hours of work were often very long: in 1906, fifty-five and a half hours on average per week in textiles, fifty-two and a half hours in clothing, and fifty-nine hours on railways.[126] Van boys often worked seventy to eighty hours a week.[127]

Yet even in work the boy achieved some measure of freedom, arising from the nature of the job market and the nature of much of boy work. As we have seen, job transience among youths was high, and the majority of youths had an option not possessed to the same degree when they became adults – that of quitting an uncomfortable position and seeking a new one with a good chance of finding one quickly. The nature of much boy work also encouraged the feeling, if not the reality, of freedom and independence. In a shop or factory, errand running, taking messages, and the like formed some part of the boy's tasks, promoting an atmosphere of diversity and novelty in the boy's working experience, while in many positions the learning of new processes and the working of new machinery and tools formed a larger or smaller component of the daily round.

Work, then, for most boys was not the inescapable mechanical drudgery it would soon become, but often a refreshing and exciting experience after the world of the classroom. Moreover, it provided the means whereby the boy could purchase a measure of independence from the potentially restrictive family. School and its ethos dropped behind the horizon of childhood for the majority of boys, and sizeable sums were found for the first time in these boys' pockets. It was against this backdrop of new-found independence from family and school, relative wealth, and job transience that the working class youth sought his entertainment and amusement.

CHAPTER FIVE

Youths on the Street

From his earliest years, the working-class boy had found the street, with its endless tapestry of inconsequential occurrences, to be his main source of entertainment and diversion. "'When we were kids anything pass which was at all unusual attracted our attention – fire engines, which we chased; funerals, which we lined up to watch pass."[1] It was in the lively street rather than in the dreary home that the young child was usually to be found out of school hours, indulging in games such as "whip and top, leapfrog, football, guinea, [and] lurky", which often had histories stretching back into the remote agricultural past,[2] or getting up to mischief. "Our pranks used to be the old parcel under the lamp post tied with a bit of black thread. Persons coming to pick it up and it would be pulled away from them. Going down yards and tying a bit of cotton to the window with a little pebble on it to make somebody come out. Tying two doors together and knocking."[3] It was here that the child would often just sit and watch the eternal theatre in progress. On weekends, buskers and organ grinders would journey from pub to pub and street to street, playing their instruments for coppers; "yes, barrel organs ... And then Saturday evening you'd see 'em dancing round it, yes. Yes, it was part of the entertainment."[4] In Tottenham, outdoor songbird contests, whippet racing, even cock fights were common.[5] In the north, "there used to be the German band used to come round. Then there was the chaps with the monkey that would go up on the roof. Then there was the hospital parade."[6] In addition, Russians with dancing bears and Italian organists vied for the attention of the promenaders, while at all times muffin men and hot potato sellers announced their wares.[7] After the excesses of Saturday, Sunday would be given over to more ethereal and abstract matters; Sally Ann preachers and bands spoke and sang of repentance at street corners, while socialist orators promised a more immediate millenium.[8]

On special occasions, the streets became even livelier. Elections in particular are remembered as being "much more exciting things than they are now."[9]

They took elections seriously. You see ... you'd no means of communication; there was no TV or radio or anything so the candidate, no matter who he might be, had to get his message over to the people and the ward he was standing for. They used to take a hall or a school and we kids ... used to collect at the committee rooms and they'd have photographs and they'd give you some to take round the houses and summon them to a meeting. By golly, they attended the meetings and the candidate would address them and we as kiddies used to have a political party you belonged to. You got a picture of the candidate and you put it on a stick and go round the streets shouting, "Vote, vote for Mr. Smith," and there was a rival crowd coming round the corner and there would be a bit of a fight. That was our election rule in those days.[10]

Children, in fact, were largely introduced to politics in the streets, each election coming complete with parades, scuffles, and yelling and with the area and its inhabitants decked out with the parties' rosettes. "It was good entertainment for the children. They used to roll up their peaked hats and tie them on a string to be used as a weapon in fights."[11] In the north, besides elections, children could look forward to the Whitsun processions, when the friendly societies and the trade unions all marched with banners and bands. Children would often collect pennies from onlookers on this day.[12]

For children, then, the street was both a source of, and an arena for, their amusement, and their play activities would only rarely take them beyond their immediate neighbourhood. Their special celebrations, such as singing door to door on May Day or collecting pennies for Guy Fawkes Day in November, were likewise street oriented. A travelling fair might lure them a distance of a few miles, or outside agencies such as parish or school might take them to the countryside, but otherwise their immediate environment represented their world. Even on country visits, protested observers, the destination often had all the urban vulgarities – slot machines, shooting galleries, and ice cream shops.[13] As one author noted, "The children ... care nothing for the country. They like going because children like going anywhere ... but let no one think that they pine for the fields. The street is their real delight and favourite playground."[14] The parochiality of the young can perhaps best be illustrated by the experience of one boy, who became in later life a renowned critic of both classical music and cricket. Until the age of twenty-one, he had spent his life "within a three and a half mile radius of bricks and mortar."[15]

With the coming of adolescence and the youth's entry into the labour force, his horizons broadened considerably. As often as not he took a tram to work, and in his leisure hours he became much more likely to travel out of the area of his home. But the street continued to be a strong magnet to him in his free hours. No longer, however, was he prone to play games; the working boy set the seal on his new status by beginning the practice of street lounging and, in doing so, effectively became part of the panorama. "Every evening crowds of [young people] come back from their work and loaf about the streets; they join in with whatever is forward, and are an embarrassment if there are no places of amusement for them to go to."[16] As another author put it, "Working class lads, no matter what their occupation may be, from fourteen to sixteen years of age, spend their leisure time largely in standing at particular street corners, making themselves more or less of a nuisance to the householders in their immediate neighbourhood."[17]

Coming home from work, the boy would have a "sluice," or a wash, then change into his good coat and don a bright tie and a clean collar. After taking his tea, he would stroll out to join his mates at about 7 P.M. "Nearly every street had its own little gang of corner boys," and each "click" or group had its own meeting place – usually a street corner, railway arch, or pillar box.[18] Although some groups were formed from boys at the same works, geographical proximity and personal affinity were normally the main determinants of friendship.[19] This is understandable, since the trade union ties and friendships arising from long acquaintance at work, which operated among adults, were not applicable to most youths, whose tendency to change jobs precluded such affinities from easily forming.

Parents who tried to control their son's choice of friends on the basis of "respectability" often had little luck unless their street was unusually socially homogeneous. Except in mining villages, neighbourhoods usually contained a mix of workers in different trades, possessing different levels of skill, as well as a local élite composed of shopkeepers and publicans. A typical court in London at the turn of the century, for instance, was inhabited by milkmen, gardeners, navvies, chimney sweeps, blacksmiths, and carpenters.[20] The streets of even a supposedly single-industry town such as Preston contained quite diverse inhabitants; a crane driver's son lived in a street of millworkers, railway employees and dockers, while the son of a stable hand grew up among mill and rail workers, engineers and foundry workers.[21] Even in childhood, parental authority in the matter of friends extended only so far, as the desire among many adults to "keep oneself to oneself," though sometimes attempted, was difficult to enforce among young offspring in the street. With the coming of adolescence, these dictates ceased to have any real meaning outside the home.[22]

Within the street group, conversation would be, said one author, "a desultory rechaufé of the evening paper and an athletic weekly."[23] Football would be the main topic of interest, with occasional erudite references to boxers, weight lifters, cricketers, and dog fanciers. Though this often may have been the case, boys also discussed more serious things on a regular basis. "Jobs in factory, pit, mill, dock, and wharf were mulled over and their skills explained ... Youths compared wages, hours, considered labour prospects, were advised on whom to ask for when seeking a job and what to say. All this was bread and butter talk vital at times to the listener, talk that had an economic scope and variety to be heard nowhere else."[24] Another working-class boy cautioned that "politics, too, got a good share of our attention. it is a big mistake to think that the corner boys spend all their time conspiring to attack old gentlemen and steal purses. There are many intelligent young workers in these crowds, and I have heard very fine political discussions, albeit amateurish and crude."[25] The street corner group thus performed functions and served as the forum for many other things besides idle chatter. Youth investigators were wont to castigate and fear these gatherings as being outside adult control and devoid of intellectual content. They were unable or unwilling to see that the "click" performed vital services to the participants, acting as informal labour bureaus and continuation schools, as well as providing the normal desiderata of good fellowship and diversion.

A habit reportedly on the increase in this period was smoking. Boys as young as eleven or twelve were now puffing away on street corners, one committee heard, while industry spokesmen estimated that 15 million of the 100 million cigarettes sold in the United Kingdom each day were bought by youths under sixteen. Various leagues were set up in the Edwardian years to combat the evil, which was blamed on unscrupulous sweet shop owners and on the attractions of cigarette cards, contests, and coupons.[26] The local sweet shop operated in fact as an alternative meeting place for the "click." There could be bought a packet of five smokes for 1d. or, for the affluent, the smoother ten for 3d. variety. Also to be had were "a host of fizzy coloured drinks, reinforced by a number of hot mixtures made from essence of raspberry, pineapple, ginger, or peppermint."[27]

For most boys, on most nights, the evening round would be taken up in these ways. The boy would join his group, where jokes, gossip, news about job openings, and other topics of general interest would be exchanged and bandied about. A trip to the local cafe or confectioner's would often afford a change of scene. Such "larking about" was perhaps the major leisure activity of working-class youth in this period. It was inexpensive and pleasant in itself and, often in an abbreviated form, would be the starting point for other activities. Acting as a conduit of information about the world at large, as an arena for the shaping of adolescent opinion, and as a convivial club, the importance of the street "click" as a cultural institution can hardly be overestimated.

The street also functioned as the forum for another leisure activity, that of gambling. For some, the practice had started early. One Edwardian stated that "nearly all day Sunday was gambling or getting up to some mischief, since I was eight years old," while a Barrow respondent remembered that "you could go and pitch and toss down the lower end of Hindpool and find a gambling school there any weekend."[28] These street casinos, where pitch and toss or halfpenny "banker" were played, often used young children as lookouts, thus introducing them to the habit.[29] For others, this introduction took place later. "You got about fifteen or sixteen, you took a pattern of t'elders what used to go on, where the gambling was – the pitch and toss and the card playing. The police was more concerned about catching you for doing that than any crime 'cos he knew there was very little villainy. And there was more youth summonsed for playing cards and playing pitch and toss than ... [for] committing any crime."[30] Other sites of gambling were barber-shops, tobacconists, and newsvendors.[31] It was, however, usually at work that boys were introduced to betting, sweepstakes often being organized for the major races by workers doubling as bookies' runners.[32] It was in the latter half of the nineteenth century, aided by a legal decision in 1874 allowing off-course wagers, the expansion of telegraphs and rail services, and the development of a large circulation sporting press, that betting penetrated to a large extent into the working class.[33] Nonetheless, street gambling had a long history among this stratum of society, and it was on the street that the youth usually developed a taste for the wager. By the Edwardian period, the habit was endemic among boys; a youth club worker reported that she "hardly dare attack the betting systematically for fear of losing her protegés. She found one lad actually receiving telegrams from France during the racing season."[34] With respect to gambling, the street "click" provided both the school and the forum, functioning also as a clearing house for the latest tips and for other racing or betting information.

Girl-watching formed another of the major pastimes of the street corner "click," since orbiting around these groups would often be similar groups of females. On most nights contact between the two groups would be limited to stares and would result in nothing more than subsequent fevered speculation. Among younger children, this speculation had, very often, the comic and ill-informed quality about it common to that age group in any time or place. But as we have seen, the working world provided boys with the deeper and at least the anatomically truer picture. It was as an apprentice, boy labourer, or van boy that the youth, surrounded by older workers, began to piece together a picture of this previously forbidden and murky realm; among the grafitti in the works' washroom and through the jokes and postcards circulated in the shop, "in sketch, rhyme, and apothegm, man's sexual activities, normal and deviant, lay fully exposed."[35] As one writer warned, "At the place of this work, pictures of vice will be passed around, little pamphlets of foul suggestion will be lent to him ... These vile seductions come to the boy at a dangerous age. The restless cravings of impurity within are fomented by the open tolerance of vice, and many a lad who left school in all innocence has fallen into evil ways before he is twenty."[36] For most boys, the unveiling of this new world was probably most welcome; as one man remembers, ignorance was certainly not bliss. "We grew up without the least hint or training about sex ... The result for me at least was a groping of my way through adolescence that almost tortured me out of my mind."[37] In such a situation, and with the quandary of boys in this matter in mind, the lending of pamphlets by older men might well be considered an act of kindness and a precaution against trouble, instead of the temptings of the Serpent portrayed by worried bourgeois writers.

In the streets in the evenings, these boys tried, as all youths do, to put this new knowledge into operation. On some nights – usually Saturday and Sunday – they succeeded, and connections would be made on the local "Monkey Parade." The boys, dressed in their weekend best, would circle warily around the girls in an effort to pick up or "strag" them.[38] "Girls were called 'tarts,' not depreciatingly as today, but as something sweet; 'bits of fluff,' 'bits of skirt,' and 'flappers' ... Smart young fellows were "Knuts' or 'Bhoys'. They wore socks with 'clocks' i.e. an embroidered pattern ... One might call the attention of one's pals to an approaching girl by s.o.s. or 'Stuff on skyline.'"[39] The forward and unrestrained manner in which this was done amazed (and amused) youth observers, as the following fictional account illustrates. "Billy Chope, slouching in the opposite direction, lurched across the pavement as they met, and taking the nearer hand from his pocket, caught and twisted her arm, bumping her against the wall. 'Garn,' said Lizerunt, greatly pleased: 'le' go!' For she knew that this was love."[40] Another opening gambit, according to one writer, was to shout a current catch phrase from the music hall, such as "Whoa, Emma!", "Does Your Mother Know You're Out?", or "Have a Banana!"[41] After this opening sally, both the conversation and the evening could proceed in more normal channels.

The oral evidence appears to support the descriptions of middle-class observers. One respondent remembers the etiquette of the Monkey Run this way: "Sometimes you'd get half a dozen girls all together and half a dozen boys, and of course they usually tried to connect in some way or another. Drop a handkerchief or something of that sort or trip over ... perhaps you'd pull a girl's hair ... She might give you a mouthful, she might be quite polite."[42] Another Londoner remembers, "Perhaps a weekend you'd walk up what we called Mare Street, that was the main road, and you'd just walk up and down and have a chat with girls and that."[43] An autobiographer supplies more colour when describing the local high street, which functioned as the weekend Monkey Parade. "For a hundred yards by West Green Corner, the wide pavements were thronged with groups of lads and girls ... Scuffles, nudges and shrieks of laughter came from every group." On the writer's first visit, shepherded by his shop mate, two elegantly dressed girls came along "I was amazed when Bert suddenly leaned forward and gave one of them a loud smack on the shoulder. And I was quite unprepared for the squeal of delighted laughter which followed."[44] A pairing might result in nothing more than a one-night diversion, or it might lead, eventually, to marriage. Even a reasonably steady pair, however, rarely met on set "dates," but would come together on occasions (usually Saturday or Sunday evenings) and at a place (usually the local Parade) that both tacitly understood.[45] In this way, walking out with a girl had a rather casual and unfettered air about it. It was "a trial trip in companionship, and the trip [could] be abandoned by either party without loss of prestige or severance of acquaintanceship."[46] Nonetheless, for many older boys the local Monkey Parade was no mere pick-up spot, but the arena for courtship, and many working-class marriages had their origin here. As one respondent laconically summarized it, "Well I was out walking one day and I met her. Started talking and – started walking."[47] Others tell the same tale; although the local Monkey Run was originally used for "looking for blondes,"[48] future wives were often met there.[49]

Thus, for both casual contact between the sexes and for more serious relationships, the local high street, park, or common – usual venues for the "Monkey Run," "Mare Street" or "Tip Top Parade"[50] – provided the setting. The street-based nature of the marriage market worried many middle-class observers; it was argued that the attempts by many working-class adults to control their children's choice of spouse often failed because of a stronger reluctance to admit the existence of sexual desires in their offspring and because of a reticence about sex in the home in contrast with the workman's habit of joking about it in the shop.[51] The parents of a teenage girl would rarely welcome a young man into the house, finding his presence both an embarrassment and a threat to her period of familial dependence. Courtship necessarily became illicit in these circumstances, and when a young man eventually did come to tea, it usually meant business, even though the candidate was often a dark horse to the parents.[52] Nonetheless, there is some evidence in the oral material that suggests that parents may have had at least an indirect influence in their children's choice of mate, precisely because of this tradition of introducing only serious candidates. One respondent remembers of his teenage years, "If I said I'm going out with a girl, Mum, [she would say,] 'Oh bring her home, lets have a look at her,' you know, but I didn't take any home until I got hold of the right one – no. I'd go, 'Oooo, this one ain't no good for my mother' – you know, you can weigh it up when you get older."[53] Even if these considerations were the norm, however, such a control was an extremely limited one. Once a future spouse was introduced, it is apparent that the father and mother had to accept their son's choice.

The common age for marriage, in London at least, was in the early twenties. When the weekly wage rose to approximately £1 a week, the young man became anxious to set the seal on his independence and finally to escape from his family.[54] It may have been true that many marriages were necessary, as one author put it, "in order to save a child from shame, and to earn for it the hollow blessing of a legitimate name," but the same author was forced to admit that "the real cause of most river-side marriages is love."[55] Another author with a wide acquaintance with the working class stated that most happy unions resulted "from boy-and-girl attachments and very early marriages" rather than from matches deliberately entered upon later in life.[56] The method of courtship practised by the working class seems to confirm this belief.

The desultory and ad hoc sparring on the street and the more highly structured and ritualized weekend promenade were customs made by and for youth, being "a club of the streets in which the spirit of youth ran riot."[57] Parents and those in authority may have found these practices threatening, but they fulfilled extremely important functions, leading in the end to a choice of life partner for the boy or girl. In this remarkably free love and marriage market, where personal desires and affinities were what counted, we may see one example of how working-class youth used the street in order to construct a cultural institution that gained for them a large measure of independence and autonomy from their parents and the authorities.

Working boys in their leisure hours also pursued many other interests besides talking and girl-watching. Of these, sports, walking, collecting, and reading were the major ones. Although often taking place in other areas, the street provided for each a setting for meeting, organization, and exchange. Boys collected and played marbles in the street, although interest in this game tended to wane in the adolescent years. They also collected and exchanged cigarette cards, with the street "click" again functioning as the local bourse.[58] As Roberts notes, "Before 1914 it would have been hard indeed to have found a boy in the working class without at least a few dog-eared cards about his person, dreaming of making up, by swap and gambling games, that complete set of fifty."[59] What may have been the attitude of many boys is revealed by the following excerpt from a Thompson interview.

Did you keep any pets?
Only fleas.
Did you collect anything?
Anything I could lay my hands on, I think.[60]

It is not hard to imagine the teenager in the "click," ready to pull out cigarette cards, marbles, postcards, and various bits of commercial and industrial jetsam in order to swap for something dearer to his heart.

Impromptu games formed another large part of the youth's leisure time, "cos in those days, nearly every street that was any street at all had a football team."[61] This was as true of Barrow as it was of central London. "We used to have a little gang on the corner, no fighting, just ganging up against one another. No rough stuff, and we used to play games. If we could get an old ball, rag ball, we used to play football and we used to do running about and jumping. We had to make our own fun and we'd no cricket tackle, no bat, and we'd trouble getting the ball."[62] For some boys, this was their major activity. Instead of Sunday school, which he attended as a child, one boy's Sabbath would almost entirely be taken up by football with the other lads.[63] Another spent most of his free time with friends, walking or playing football or cricket on Primrose Hill.[64] Although for the most part these were pick-up games, boys sometimes became intimately involved in organized sport. One Thompson respondent became secretary of a boys' football club while still a youth, while another was, at twenty, a founding member of the Bolton Harriers.[65]

Walking was another pastime engaged in by some boys. A Barnsley youth, surrounded by the wooded estates of Earl Fitzwilliam, would spend most of his free time exploring them,[66] while a Preston lad walked on occasion to Blackpool and back with two friends, a distance of nearly forty miles.[67]

The working class, especially the younger section of it, was an increasingly literate group in the period of this study, a development that the market reflected. Although Raymond Williams warns that such publications as the *Daily Mail* and *Tit-Bits* were not truly "mass" journals, it is undeniable that the latter half of the nineteenth century saw a great penetration of reading material, led by the Sunday papers, into the working class.[68] This development was aided by a significant rise in literacy, which increased dramatically in the years after 1850. Though the true rate of literacy is difficult to assess accurately, and was unlikely to be as high as some statistical evidence would lead us to believe,[69] the working class by 1900 was certainly a great consumer of the printed word.[70]

It is obviously dangerous to generalize too much about the reading habits of a class, since the very diversity of reading material would seem to preclude the drawing of hard and fast conclusions. A rough poll conducted in the northern town of Middlesbrough during the Edwardian period shows this difficulty. Considerable reading was done in sixty out of the two hundred households investigated. The tastes ran from Plato, Shakespeare, and modern greats such as Dickens and Ruskin down to the racing page of the Sunday paper, with no apparent correlation between quality of material and income, occupation, or education.[71] The same diversity among individual families appears in the oral material. In a poor London family in which the father was dead and the mother was a low-paid shirt factory worker, Dickens, Scott, and both daily and weekly papers were read, while in a Preston family with a similar income the children were not allowed to read even the local paper.[72] Reading among the working class, as among any class, was a highly personal and selective activity.

On the street, however, a reasonably specific type of literature circulated, again through the agency of the street corner "click." Roberts describes how conversation within the group would often turn to "matters literary." Newspapers, periodicals, and more adult offerings filched from home, such as *Tit-Bits, Answers*, and *Police News*, would be produced and exchanged.[73] That these and the more bloodthirsty types of boys' literature should be circulated caused predictable consternation among the middle-class observers of youth. A typical reaction was that of a vicar, who wrote to the Home Office at the turn of the century complaining of the effects on boys of the *Illustrated Police News*. Not only did this periodical advertise salacious photographs, but it was "the instrument for the publication of advertisements which are calculated to cause ... immense mischief to the family life of our nation," namely, for abortifacients and prophylactics.[74] Moreover, despite a long fight against them, in the Edwardian period there still existed "those execrable publications, known to lads as 'penny bloods' – tales of reckless and impossible daring, of bloodshed, of successful thieving, and ridiculous adventure."[75] In Northampton in 1904, it was stated that "clubs for the purchase of 'penny dreadful' literature, glorifying the crimes of hooligans, are becoming quite common among factory boys," and this practice was noted elsewhere before World War I.[76] In the same city, the axe murder by a fifteen year old of his young sister was blamed on his addiction to these tales.[77] The period of this study nevertheless saw the gradual replacement of the "penny dreadful" by a more genteel variety of boys' paper, in which blood-letting, if it took place, was located in the jungles and mountain passes of the newly expanded empire rather than in the streets of the nation's slums. Another species of boys' story that appeared, and that was to have a great impact, was the school yarn. For many boys, such fare proved to be an irresistable attraction. After a long diet of the classics, V.S. Pritchett was introduced to *Gem* and *Magnet* by a friend. "One page and I was entranced. I gobbled these stories as if I was eating pie or stuffing. To hell with poor self-pitying fellows like Oliver Twist; here were the cheerful rich. I craved for Greyfriars, that absurd Public School, as I craved for pudding. There the boys wore tops hats and tail coats ... they had feasts in their studies; they sent a pie containing a boot to 'the bounder of the Remove'; they rioted; they never did a stroke of work ..."[78]

A further illustration of the grip these tales could exert on a youthful imagination is provided by the present writer's grandfather, who, "absolutely rivetted" by the series "At Sea with Goldsharks" in *Chums*, conceived an unalterable ambition to go to sea, eventually persuading his father to put him on a three-masted barque as an apprentice mate.[79] For many working-class boys, Greyfriars became their "true Alma Mater," while the Famous Five provided them with their "ideals and standards" – a hazy ethos of fair play, moral purity, and genial contempt for "cads" and foreigners.[80] The reading habits of boys, in fact, were often twofold; while within a literary home, Verne, Dickens, and Corelli might be read aloud, the youth would obtain boys' papers on the street,[81] going so far as to smuggle them home and hide them up a chimney when parents disapproved.[82]

The tales of such authors as G.A. Henty and Frank Richards (creator of Greyfriars) struck a nice balance between adventure and sermonizing. The moral was usually pointed out tangentially rather than directly, with the desired code of values put across by the cumulative effects of scene setting, action, and the behaviour of the characters. In these stories, the middle and upper classes were portrayed as inherently noble and highminded, while their values were characterized as selflessness, fair play, and courage. Beyond this, Britain's empire was represented as the just reward for a superior race, and its daily life gave promise, to the young inhabitants of mean streets, of fascinating mystery and hair-raising adventure. Wrapped in such a subtle and palatable coating, the new types of boys' papers were probably more influential in reconciling working-class boys to imperialism and the class structure than were more obvious and purposeful agencies such as school lessons, sermons, or boys' movements. It was, therefore, with a "curious shock" of enlightenment that a boy discovered "that he himself was a typical example of the 'low cads' so despised by all at Greyfriars."[83] Paradoxically for such effective apologetics of a class society, the beginnings of class consciousness for many boys may well have sprung from such a snub, rather than from the tangible and weighty evidence of everyday life.

Many of the pursuits described above were frowned upon by authorities and youth experts, not to mention the parents of the youths involved. Other street activities, however, drew the direct intervention of authorities – namely, fighting and crime. Unlike girl-watching or the perusal of "penny dreadfuls," which authorities could do little to control, these two activities increasingly drew into action a host of agencies and institutions designed to punish and reform the perpetrators. For fighting, at least, the result was a major reduction in the scope of these conflicts, and the virtual disappearance of a youth subculture dedicated to brawling.

Youths were not strangers to fighting. Domestic violence was not uncommon in areas such as London, where the casualization of the labour market put a strain on both the family economy and the tempers of its members. "Of course, them days, ... most of the poor people ... was inclined to be short tempered and squabbling ... Things wasn't as comfortable as they might have been ... probably – about Wednesday you'd have perhaps two or three shillings to get to the end of the week with, and you were worrying how to get the next dinner and that, so the least little thing would upset you, you know."[84] As children, they had also often witnessed one of the major attractions of the street scene, the traditional Saturday night brawl, each major altercation attracting a crowd of youngsters "keenly enjoying the scene."[85] A Preston resident remembers, "I've seen fights galore, and the police walking about in twos ... fighting in the streets, fights anywhere, drunken fights ..."[86] In the rougher areas, these bouts often spread, as different factions among the street's adults formed around the original combatants. Occasionally a whole street might forget its internal differences and take on a neighbouring area in a large and violent free for all.[87] In a poor London neighbourhood, Saturday was, according to one boy, "a proper lively night. And probably six or seven fights all going on together." On one memorable occasion, this boy "saw one terrible affair; it was a street fight ... one of these men out of my turning – he'd been insulted down there by somebody and when he came back ... well, he set about the chap, and then from the market place they come on one particular day and set about all the men in this turning where I lived, and it ... ended up as a proper battle with police ... on horses and everything, trying to disperse the crowds. It really was a battle, too, and I think it unnerved me a bit being a youngster because I witnessed it."[88] Nor was this phenomenon confined to the slums; even a more "respectable" working-class street would sometimes go berserk, erupting into a brawl in which old scores were settled and new ones created.[89]

Fighting, then, was an inescapable part of the working-class street scene, and children began their involvement at an early age. Territoriality provided the most common dividing line for the opposing sides, but any perceived difference would do as well; for schoolchildren in Liverpool and in Lancashire, fights based on religion were not unusual. One respondent remembers regular Saturday battles between Protestants and Catholics, while another states, "We used to go to Mount Carmel School [the local Catholic institution] only a couple hundred yards away and attack the kids ... it was a – a tradition."[90] Although, in this area, religious differences provided the most easily identifiable demarcation when some excitement was looked for, they do not seem to have led to lasting animosities; the last respondent himself eventually married a Roman Catholic.

As a boy grew order, other causes and pretexts came into operation, although geography continued to play a part, including "certain amounts of gang warfare from different parts. Yes. They would ... refer to us as the South Street gang as against the High Park Street or the North Hill or the Admiral Street gang ..."[91] These gangs were, there seems little doubt, essentially passive "clicks" engaged in the pursuits described earlier. However, their members occasionally had to fight to defend their particular territory or what they perceived to be their rights, a concept that now usually included the area's girls. The willingness of the area's adults to themselves indulge in this activity lent it an aura of necessity and duty. This attitude, moreover, transcended occupational and status boundaries. "If anybody hit me I had to hit 'em back. I hadn't to let anybody hit me, that was a strict order," remembers the son of a Salford ironworker.[92] The child of a more genteel family, whose father was a Bolton gas meter inspector, recalled that whether he was punished for fighting depended on "whether I won or lost the fight."[93] In a London family, the postman father may have been a strict sabbatarian who usually enforced a rigid discipline on his children, but his son relates, "I came home one day with a black eye. Father said, 'Been fighting? ... What about the other?' ... 'Well, he's got two black eyes ...' He chuckled, you know."[94]The duty to stand up for oneself and for one's friends or neighbourhood was proclaimed in many families that otherwise exhibited the virtues of working-class respectability. Not surprisingly, then, physical violence was a common occurrence among the youth street "clicks."

An incident or an encroachment by another group would set off one of these tribal melées. "There'd be different streets ... at war with one another ... Used to get a heap of stones ... We'd barricade across the street and start aiming stones at one another, you see ..."[95] Everyone know the "relative status" of the various districts, moreover, which added a further element to amour propre.[96] For a low-class district to violate the prerogatives of a more "respectable" area was an insult requiring satisfaction. Conversely, however, the slummier areas often had the more battle-hardened warriors. Roberts notes that "each slum had its own cachet and fighting reputation," a factor that might influence the decision to fight or not. Roberts' neighbourhood in Salford would quite cheerfully take on Adelphi or Hulme, but would think twice about going up against poorer districts such as Islington Square or Ancoats, which had touchier and more ferocious inhabitants.[97] Likewise, in a Glamorgan village, the local colliers' sons were accorded considerable respect. "We used to have a lot of boys from the Constant. And when they got together it was look out. They were toughs ... They'd clear the place."[98] The imperatives of honour thus often clashed with more sobering factors such as the fear of physical injury.

These fights were, for the majority of boys, occasional and perhaps unwelcome occurrences, but the boy who managed to avoid them entirely must have been rare; they were one of the inescapable facets of urban street life, and they formed one the sacred, if rare, duties of a group member. Although loath to do so, a London boy was forced to join in with the neighbourhood youths in order to ward off a threat by the New Canning Town lads. The latter's special weapons were stones or bricks wrapped in a cap and tied on a string, but posturing rather than actual fighting apparently formed the major part of the subsequent confrontation.[99] Duty done in this way confirmed a boy's membership in good standing with his "click."

For some boys, however, street fighting was more of a vocation than an irregular civic duty. Youths of this type formed gangs, such as the "40 Row Gang" and the "Bengal Tigers" of Manchester, the "Peaky Blinders" of Birmingham, and the "Bermondsey Street Yoboes" of London, which would rush into combat at the slightest provocation.[100] These "scuttlers," as the northern variety were generally known, wore "peaked cap, hair curled well over the forehead, white neckscarf, bell-bottomed trousers, and sharp-pointed clogs with heavy brass nails,"[101] while their "Molls" wore clogs, shawls, and vertically striped skirts.[102] They tended to congregate at a favourite tavern, or "blood tub," "which none durst enter save its habitués."[103] For the scuttler, "war was his amusement and his avocation, and he must make war upon his neighbours of the next street. His gang must show its prowess by thrashing all other gangs." Twenty to thirty strong, and armed with water bottles, clubs, and heavily buckled belts, gangs such as these could terrorize a neighbourhood.[104] Although usually confining their violence to their peers, attacks on bystanders, sometimes fatal, are recorded.[105] In London, complained a writer in a teachers' journal, "Our daughters cannot walk the street without insult; our property is unsafe; the language on all sides is low and disgusting,"[106] while in Salford the scuttlers occasionally turned their energies from gang warfare to the trashing and burning of Jewish shops.[107]

Another street activity that unsettled youth investigators was that of crime. Among children and youths, this nearly always took the form of petty larceny, with the occasional dash of vandalism. A

London boy, for instance, would participate in organized raids on fruit wagons. While some boys distracted the driver, others would "break a case of oranges open at the back, pinch a few oranges and dive down the side turning."[108] Another metropolitan boy would steal bananas, rum, and wine from the docks, while some of his family's vegetables came free from the market.[109] A Salford lad would rob the local corner shop, with another boy acting as a stall; he later enjoyed a proportion of the proceeds of his friends' practice of rolling drunks.[110] In areas where the countryside was close at hand, boys had other avenues for the liberation of goods. A Cardiff youth supplied, from the Marquess of Bute's estates, the grapes with which his parents made wine. Up to twice a week, they also dined on rabbit poached from the nobleman.[111] For children, money left for the milkman and goods on the street provided the chief targets. Later, the habitual thief would graduate to shoplifting proper, "tea leafing" (robbing tills), forcing gas meters, and stealing from factory warehouses and sheds.[112] His first conviction was likely to be for "being on enclosed premises."[113] According to some authors, crime arose in part from an insufficient awareness of the law. "A great number of thieving cases consist of stealing iron from the scrap heaps, timber from the docks, and coal from the staiths, and *these offences are often committed under a mistaken idea that the acts are not criminal.*"[114] It is unlikely, however, that a youth brought up in a society where property rights were so entrenched, and where the principle of *meum* and *tuum* was expounded so regularly at school, would not actually know that he was breaking the law. Nonetheless, youths obviously thought of these activities as legitimate, if not legal, and this conception was reinforced by their elders. The parents of the Cardiff poacher were regular chapel goers, and the dock thief was often aided by his mother, while in a Guildford family notable for its deferential social attitude, poached rabbit was a regular part of the menu.[115] Perhaps such boys were "determined to get their own back" from a society against which they felt a grievance,[116] but this interpretation, as well as more elaborate theories of the social basis of crime, tend to ignore the very real economic motivations behind petty theft. Most probably such boys were simply responding to an opportunity to acquire needed goods, in much the same way that they had not forgone any opportunity to earn a few pennies, and they appear to have felt either little guilt or satisfaction in doing so.

The recruitment pool for scuttlers and casual thieves usually consisted of the lower and more nomadic types of boy labour. Van boys and newspaper sellers formed the majority – boys who had often had a few good years before growing out of their jobs and becoming unemployed.[117] The most common site for the congregation of these youths was the local railway station. Here, a boy could earn a few shillings a week carrying bags and running errands, a form of employment known as "working the rattler."[118] A study in Birmingham found the most common ages of these boys to be from sixteen to nineteen, with a range of fourteen to twenty-one. They earned an average of 8s. per week, of which 3s.2d. was spent on food, 2s.4d. on lodging, and the 2s.6d. remainder on cigarettes and gambling.[119] Described as "a very bad class altogether,"[120] "composed chiefly of idle, dissolute, outcast youths,"[121] these boys usually ended up, according to their own testimony, as "hangers-on at race-meetings, bookies' touts ... tramps."[122] Others held horses in town, alternating between the casual ward and prison, while others joined the army. A very few became regular or semi-regular unskilled workers.[123]

Such boys were targets of a good deal of moral reproach from middle-class observers, yet the latter's own research shows that the boys on the rattler were often there as a result of misfortune and economic pressures rather than defects of character. One or both parents of 77 per cent of the Birmingham boys, were dead, drunkards, invalids, or criminals; had deserted the home; or were permanently out of work.[124] Moreover, most of the boys had been employed, often for long periods of time, but had lost their positions as a result of slack times, the desire for a rise in pay, or disputes with foremen or employers. These boys were, in fact, the real casualties of "blind-alley" work, becoming unemployable in later adolescence except as casual and unskilled labourers. They formed the bottom rung in a fiercely competitive adult labour market, and, given the economic pressures impinging upon even skilled workmen, it is hardly surprising that such boys ran afoul of the law on numerous occasions.

Because of their home environment, 56.3 per cent of the Birmingham boys lived in common lodging houses.[125] Besides being unconducive to the formation of a sound character, these abodes presented a further obstacle to steady employment; they demanded cash down every night, and a boy on the rattler who obtained employment would thus have nowhere to stay until his first week's wages came in.[126] The station lounger therefore soon found himself in a vicious circle, where the circumstances of his life required casual and immediately remunerated employment, and where every day witnessed a struggle to find the means to meet pressing expenses. For most boys, even the army was no solution, since the majority were in poor health.[127] In the labour market that was emerging in the late Victorian and Edwardian years, they were the ultimate losers, and they would, for the most part, work out their penance for their failure to gain a skill of some type in the workhouses and prisons of the nation.

Even more unsettling to authorities and investigators than the pursuits of the normal working boy were the threats and problems presented by the subcultures of scuttlers, thieves, and station loungers. These groups were scrutinized by a host of writers and investigators, who put forward numerous suggestions as to these youths' origins, their outlook, and the best ways of dealing with them.

The work of Stephen Humphries has provided a valuable analysis of the concepts and motives impelling these social reformers. He sees the development of interventionist institutions as "powerful attempts to inculcate conformist modes of behaviour ... through various bourgeois agencies of control, manipulation and exploitation."[128] Working from theories of mass culture and cultural deprivation, often with a spicing of social Darwinism, these reformers saw such youths as anomic, emotionally backward, and often hereditarily unintelligent. What was required was to take these boys out of their environment and, via strictly controlled institutions, reintegrate them into the larger society by inculcating habits of thrift, obedience, and hard work.[129] The period under review thus saw the emergence or expansion of institutions such as the industrial school, the reformatory and the Borstal, which, each for their separate categories of "problem" child or youth, attempted to carry out this modification of behaviour and attitude in carefully controlled settings.

It is not my purpose to explore the development of these institutions, but to examine the ways in which such new pressures impinged upon the working-class youth of the time. In general, the effect of these changes was to increase the likelihood of an arrest, charge, and incarceration of a juvenile following the apprehension of an offence. Throughout the period, changes in the law, developments in the powers of judges (especially those of summary justice), and changes in police's and individuals' willingness to prosecute all helped to sweep into the juvenile system many youths who might never have found themselves there before.[130] By the end of the Edwardian period, youth observers were urging the incarceration and training of juvenile vagrants, station boys caught gambling, and even lodging house boys for the mere fact of being street sellers.[131] As well, these writers did their best to promote the new institutions, sure that "as soon as the growing elasticity and reasonableness of the present system is realised, employers will with confidence" prosecute their dishonest youth. It was argued that it would be to the boys' ultimate advantage to be arrested and convicted.[132]

For these reasons, criminal statistics, especially those relating to youth, tell very little about the nature and extent of crime in the late Victorian and Edwardian period. Instead, as J.R. Gillis has pointed out, they reveal changes in the nature of society's response to an old challenge or reveal heightened apprehension about a problem, such as youthful criminality, that may well have been stable or declining.[133] Indeed, given the more buoyant nature of the youth labour market, the greater access to education for all levels of the working class, and the establishment of settled and stable working-class neighbourhoods with their own system of behavioural sanctions, it is quite probable that fewer boys were drawn to crime in this era than in the preceding period of rapid industrialization and urbanization.

Moreover, despite the statistical evidence of growth in a regularized, bureaucratic response to social deviance and an expansion of its boundaries, it is clear from oral evidence that these years were still ones in which the older methods of punishment predominated – in which policemen, in other words, were just as likely to administer immediate corporal punishment as they were to hand children over to the correctional machinery. Indeed, if schoolteachers were, in Paul Thompson's words, "the most persistently violent Edwardian adults,"[134] then policemen must have run a close second. For children especially, older forms of punishment were usually still applied. In London, policemen often put ball bearings or marbles in their gloves and struck unruly children with them. "Cor. You used to ... hear bells in your ears."[135] To young children, policemen were figures to be feared – "all big men, slow moving men. Anything from fourteen to sixteen stone, and as one disappeared another was coming over the horizon."[136] A Preston respondent notes that, "if we were playing a game and there was anything doubtful about it, that is, if we thought that we were liable to get reprimanded by the police, one lad would be put on to what they called 'keep nix.' He was a look out."[137] Despite the innocuous nature of much childhood street activity, youngsters usually took good care to stay out of the way of the police. Even when only playing football, "as soon as someone said 'Look out, policeman's coming,' you'd to clear because you were committing a nuisance in the street. I think it was done really to keep the kids down ... think it was done because of damage in the main. They'd run away and windows [would be] broken and such like."[138] Another remembers of the police, "We knew what time they come round. We used to hop it whether he was after us or not."[139] Hitting with sticks and rolled or folded capes by policemen was also prevalent, and any child merely loitering in the street was liable to impromptu chastisement of this kind.

Nevertheless, as the old century gave way to the new, the operation of truancy laws, increased regulation of street traders and the activities of such groups as the National Society for the Prevention of Cruelty to Children (NSPCC) made institutional rather than ad hoc responses to misbehaviour more likely, while the definition of misbehaviour was itself being widened. In this context, the search for a more "efficient" and supposedly more "humane" method of dealing with problem children should probably be seen, in part at least, as an attack on the methods of the local policeman on his beat, who came himself from the working class and whose habitual use of corporal punishment seems to have enjoyed a wide measure of acceptance by working-class parents.[140] Given the alternative – their children falling into the hands of the judicial system – this is understandable. A Barrow respondent remembers a friend getting a six-months sentence for stealing turnips,[141] while the experience of another unfortunate made a deep impression on a Lancaster boy, whose schoolfellow, aged eleven, was caught stealing. "I always remember that he got three strokes of the birch up at the Castle, and the thing that sticks in my mind is that that lad came back absolutely cowered. He had no spirit at all. He used to be a bit of a lively card before, but he came back to school and he was absolutely shattered. As far as I could make out, he lived in Lancaster quite a long time; I could always spot him. I got the impression that it ruined his life."[142]

One of the major targets of this institutional counterattack by the forces of authority was the scuttlers, who began, around the turn of the century, to disappear from the youth street scene. The various boys' clubs and boys' brigades often tried to claim credit for this achievement,[143] yet this is unconvincing as a cause, since the section of working-class youth most likely to turn to scuttling was the group least likely to join the clubs. Rather, the more drastic measures being proposed at the time, such as training ships and labour colonies, where "discipline would be stern in the extreme,"[144] give a better clue to the factors at work. Acting from this groundswell of popular opinion, the scuttlers were put down, "not without trouble, by vigorous action on the part of the police"; "scuttlers appeared in droves before the courts, often to receive savage sentences."[145] Because of these and other pressures, the late Victorian scuttler gave way to the Edwardian "Ike," a more solitary, less forceful, and more dandified example of teenage rebel.[146] Such boys were often snappy dressers. "I was always one for dress ... I always had two or three suits a year when I was young," says a Salford respondent,[147] while a Londoner remembers his first outfit: "... cigar brown, and I had a brown felt hat – kid gloves, silver top cane, brown shoes. And I felt the absolute – real – sort of – Burlington Bertie sort of thing."[148] But probably as important a cause of this transition was the changing leisure patterns of these years, founded on the contemporaneous changes in the youth labour market. The Edwardian era, a time of high demand for boy labour, put money into the pocket of almost every boy, while new forms of entertainment and amusement gave him the opportunity to spend it in more peaceful ways. For these reasons – police repression, more affluence, and a greater scope for entertainment – the violent scuttler tended to give way around the turn of the century to a wealthier, more dandified boy in a smaller "click" looking for amusement rather than trouble.

The disappearance of the fighting gang in the Edwardian era has led one scholar to conclude that no subcultures seem to have existed in this period.[149] Sociological studies go further, arguing that youth subcultures themselves are a unique phenomenon of the post-World II period, arising from such factors as a new affluence among teenagers, mass entertainment, the effects of World War II and advances in education, which created a generation of working-class youth who were recognizably distinct from their elders in outlook and behaviour. Youth subcultures are seen in one theory as attempts to "magically" recreate the old community, or else to fantasize and to symbolize lifestyle options that do not really exist for the youth.[150] In this model, the Skinheads and the Rockers of the 1960s and 1970s are seen as examples of the first trend – an attempt to recreate the elemental forces of working-class life by emphasizing brutality and naked force. The Mods, and to a lesser extent, the Teddy Boys, with their parodies of the upwardly mobile and the man about town, are examples of the second option.

Apart from the dislocations caused by World War II, however, it could be argued that all these ostensibly new features and forces were active in the late Victorian and Edwardian years, which produced an increasingly better educated, more leisure oriented, and more affluent youth population. In this context, the scuttler, with his extreme working-class image – clogs, heavy belt, brass buckle – could represent a response to late Victorian change at the tail end of the Great Depression, centring on the breakdown of the older working-class lifestyle based on street corner, pub, and locally owned industry and reacting against the greater intrusion of the state in the lives of the poor. The Edwardian era, a time of affluence, for boy workers at least, and of rapidly expanding cultural horizons, saw the appearance of the smartly dressed youth and, indeed, what might be termed the original Teddy Boy, whose Monkey Parade outfit of tight trousers, walking stick, and fancy waistcoat can be construed as a parody and emulation of the contemporary Mayfair society man.

Beyond this, an examination of the street life of working-class youth as a whole gives evidence of a subculture, different from both the adult working-class culture and that of the larger society. The five to six years of adolescence represented a definite stage in life for most working-class boys in the area of leisure as well as work, separate from the relatively constrained nature of their childhood and from the responsibilities and cares of adult, married life. Through their relatively large discretionary income and through such institutions as the Monkey Parade and the street "click," youths in general were able to gain for themselves a considerable measure of freedom from both parents and authority, and to symbolize their outlook and their hopes by a selective and conscious use of distinctive clothes and practices. This period certainly saw a narrowing of the limits of behaviour that society would tolerate, but it also witnessed a growth of alternative and more peaceful leisure options of which youths would in any case have taken advantage. Beyond this, the core and foundation of youths' leisure activities, such as the "click" and the Monkey Parade – "those clubs of the street in which the spirit of youth ran riot" – were unamenable to control by either police or parents.

The final resolution of the subculture question awaits further exploration of the evidence, particularly that pertaining to the interwar years, and a sharper model of how and why such phenomena arise. Certainly, however, one can speculate that the roots of England's varied and vibrant history of postwar subcultures lie further back than most observers realize. English working-class youth since World War II have shown an amazingly creative ability to adopt and adapt the cultural artifacts of the larger society for their own use. This chapter, it is hoped, has pointed toward a conclusion that this ability is not a newly found one.

The street and the locale, then, provided for working-class youth the primary arena for their leisure activities, and "larking about" in the "click" was one of their major pursuits. It was inexpensive, pleasant in itself, and served as the forum wherein gambling and the exchange and assimilation of literature, news, and gossip all took place. In an abbreviated form, it was often the starting point for other activities, such as walks, sports, or a visit to the music hall or cinema. Beyond this, street lounging had wider implications for the older youth with an eye to courtship or marriage. To generalize, the small gang or "click" provided both entertainment and the forum for the discussion of further entertainment. Whatever the historical importance to working-class youth of newly appearing mass commercial entertainments, the vital role of the "click" and the patterns of neighbourhood life from which it sprang must not be forgotten. These factors and facets of street life formed the fundamental building blocks of working-class youth culture and the basic context in which it operated.

CHAPTER SIX

Commercial Entertainment and Working-Class Youths

The years 1870 to 1914 would rank as one of fundamental importance in any study of popular pastimes and recreation. Although the earlier characterization of the period 1820 to 1850 as the "dark age" of popular recreational history is no longer tenable,[1] the subsequent six decades witnessed the full fruition of previous trends and saw the emergence of a recognizably modern working-class style of leisure. In these longer-term developments, one can see the effects of the change from a pre-industrial, integrated way of life to an urban industrial and specialized lifestyle, in which leisure tends to become a discrete activity and to become localized in specific institutions.[2] It also becomes commercialized. The late Victorian and Edwardian period saw the evolution of the small tavern or beer shop concert into the rococo and highly capitalized music hall, the codification and professionalization of sports, the emergence of the popular seaside holiday, and the coming of the cinema – in short, the birth of what has come to be seen as the classic forms of working-class leisure.

In this leisure revolution, youth played a major and possibly vital role, as one of the prime consumers of these new forms of entertainment and as *cognoscenti* of their stars and their history. Youths were to be found in the music hall, on the football terraces, and in the cinema, usually in disproportionate numbers, and their allegiance was reckoned crucial by many proprietors. The emergence of the new commercial forms of entertainment in the decades before World War I was based in part on the simultaneous development of a working-youth population with considerable discretionary income eager to patronize these establishments.

The emergence on a mass scale of popular commercialized entertainment in the late nineteenth century has aroused considerable interest on the part of social and cultural historians in recent years. The development of the music hall especially has been treated as an archetype of the new leisure genres. In the process, the theoretical and explanatory apparatus for dealing with popular leisure has been refined in a number of ways. In order to "make sense of the music hall,"[3] it has first been necessary to strip away various self-generated and self-congratulatory myths surrounding this institution – both to lay bare to profit-seeking, capitalist imperatives behind the mask of friendliness and innocent fun and to locate the material itself in a truer perspective, less as the authentic folk songs of an urban industrial proletariat and more as mass produced and market-oriented offerings of a fledgling popular song-writing industry. This scholarly demolition of the old myths about the music hall is often carried out with the aid of the full vocabulary of hegemony, subordination, and co-optation. It is argued that the increased income and freedom squeezed by workers from their middle-class employers in these years were then taken away again through an exploitative and manipulative medium of entertainment that simply reinforced the values of the dominant élite and reconciled workers to the prevailing system. Given the general failure, by the mid-nineteenth century, of the consciously "rational" recreational movement to "reform" working-class leisure, the capitalists, it is argued, made a strategic adjustment. They began to provide more appealing, yet no less pacifying, leisure offerings to the lower orders – offerings that, moreover, had the added attraction of bringing in a healthy profit. In such a reading, the bourgeoisie got the best of both worlds; dividends rolled in at the same time that hegemony was maintained, in the very institutions that had traditionally been seen as the last bastion of an authentic working-class culture.

Such a revisionist assault on the original, cozy version of the music hall was necessary, but there was a danger that it, in turn, would become a reductionist orthodoxy. As scholars are increasingly becoming aware, however, the reality of the music hall experience is undoubtedly more complex. Even more than in such fields as eduction and organized youth movements, the history of popular culture can never be easily divided into simple issues of dominance by one class and resistance by another, even if it is accepted that this is one of the major mechanisms at work.[4] Too little is yet known about the multifarious and exceedingly complicated relationships between proprietors, performers, songwriters, audience, and the wider public, about the connections between music hall attendance and subsequent attitudes and values, or about the nature of the music hall experience itself, to encapsulate these into a simplified class-based dichotomy. At present, it is perhaps more useful to limit oneself to general hypotheses or observations about the conflicting and contradictory topography of what is still largely uncharted cultural terrain. It can be assumed, for instance, that the working class, including its youth, were never simply passive consumers of the entertainment that was presented to them, or that the mere fact of attendance led to acceptance of the views or values being purveyed; nor is there much evidence that they were actively and consciously engaged in fighting off the blandishments of modern, mass forms of escapism. The music hall, simply put, sprang from, and continued to draw sustenance from, the working-class life experience, at the same time exploiting these experiences commercially; it is this basic and inherent tension that ensures that the nature of the music hall is too rich and various to be easily reduced to simple categories.

The music hall was the premier working-class leisure institution of the late Victorian and Edwardian period. Opulent, gaudily decorated and loud, such hall as the Alhambra and the Empire summon up a vision of *fin de siècle* consumption at its most conspicuous. It would be misleading, however, to associate all music halls at all times with the behemoths of Leicester Square. Over the period of this study, the halls underwent considerable and uneven development, until by the end of the era they presented a range running from small converted beer halls to the glittering palaces of the West End.

Traditionally, the north has laid claim to the first "true" music hall; this was the Star at Bolton, opened in 1832. Attached to a large inn, it was built expressly to provide entertainment in a relaxed and licensed setting. According to this history, the success of the Star prompted imitators throughout the north, and in 1849 the music hall formula came to London with the opening of the Canterbury – built, like the Star, onto a large inn.[5] What can be said, with less certainty but perhaps more accuracy, is that the 1850s seem to have been the decisive years, when a number of diverse strands, such as the older concert clubs or song-and-supper rooms, usually catering to the wealthier bohemian sections of society, and the working-class taverns, came together. Thus, the sociable and the theatrical melded in an institution that, although characterized from the first with a working-class imprint, provided a setting where the community as a whole could meet.[6] The next half century witnessed the emergence of the music hall as the most important site of popular leisure and entertainment. By the turn of the century, every major town had one or more of the halls; Middlesbrough, with a population of 100,000, had ten, while Birmingham had seven large halls with a seating capacity of 16,530. The number of halls in London has been variously estimated as between sixty and five hundred, the latter figure including the multitude of East End beer halls.[7]

Yet the turn-of-the-century halls were quite different from their counterparts of the mid-century. A number of trends in the late Victorian period ensured this. One of these was the attempt by moral crusaders to "sanitize" the music hall, purging it of vulgarity, drink, and illicit (and often commercial) sex. In 1878 the sale of liquor was banned in the main body of the hall; this forced the closure of over 200 of the original type of music hall, where patrons sat at tables and drank while watching the show.[8] In London, in 1889, promenades were forbidden in new music halls, since as they were thought to provide a meeting ground for prostitutes and their clients, and in 1890 the London County Council formed a committee of moral watchdogs to scrutinize performances and to examine the conduct of the women. With the power to revoke licences, this committee prompted the "voluntary" destruction of promenades in many older halls and ensured the quick disappearance of any act or scene it found objectionable.[9] Similarly, in 1896, Bradford and Leeds lost their promenades as a result of a campaign by Mrs. Ormiston Chant's "Prudes on the Prowl."[10]

Even without the efforts of the purity crusaders, however, the music halls were moving in a more respectable direction as a result of another major trend. By 1900 many of the larger halls were in the hands of several national syndicates representing significant amounts of invested capital. With the emergence of syndicates came the "star" system, as each group vied for the public's custom. These stars began to make large salaries and increasingly used agents to obtain them.[11] With a weekly wage bill of over £3,000 or more, lavish productions of over 200 dancers, and elaborate sets, the managers of the new larger halls began to play it safe when it came to risqué content.[12] Noting that "Society" was beginning to be attracted to the halls, a trade paper cautioned that "the proprietors and managers will do well to conduct their halls on such lines as will ensure this patronage being steady and constant," advising that innuendo and *double entendres* be stricken from the material and that 'h-less, grammarless" singers and comedians be replaced by artistes of a higher social standing.[13] Most of this was wishful thinking, except in the big plush West End halls. When Grundyism threatened in 1889, proprietors banded together to fight it, with the result that hundreds of music halls came to light, of which nine-tenths flourished in the poorer districts.[14] Undoubtedly, here, working-class audiences continued to enjoy working-class artistes performing in front of a simple all-purpose backdrop. Nonetheless, it is probable that even the smaller halls were cleaned up to some extent in the wake of the twin developments of the late nineteenth century moral crusade and the late nineteenth century process of cartelization. By the turn of the century, then, patrons of the music halls were unlikely to meet with blatant solicitation or to see widespread drunkenness. Yet the attitude of middle-class observers or moral crusaders toward the music halls still varied from mild dislike to violent condemnation. The Salvation Army continued to regard the halls as "Fortresses of Beelzebub,"[15] while a writer in the radical *Contemporary Review* said of the songs, "What is most striking is the utter poverty and monotony of their topics, the sordidness of their view of life, the baseness of their ideals, the insincerity of their enthusiasms ... Intellectually, morally, artistically, this whole body of work is simply squalid."[16] Most youth observers, though, admitted – however reluctantly – that although sexual innuendo was a major component of most songs and skits, and that "no concentrated effort of mind, no fixed attention for any length of time, is required,"[17] the fare provided in the halls was on the whole relatively harmless.

By the turn of the century, as well, the music hall programs everywhere tended to follow the same pattern, consisting of ten to twelve "turns" of about ten minutes each. Juggling and acrobatics, magical displays, comic and melodramatic skits, short instrumentals, and a variety of songs made up the usual bill. Over time, however, changes appeared in both form and content. The longer melodramatic plays, popular in earlier years, gave way to shorter sketches or skits, while songs expressing the theme of tragic love, common at mid-century, were replaced by the serio-comic ballad.[18] By the end of the century, the love portrayed in the music hall "is a passion *sui generis*. It is a mixture of the valentine, the cosaque cracker, the penny novelette and the *Family Herald*." Young lovers were shown in an optimistic light, but, "once they are married, the voices are dumb, and all that remains to dominate the old harmony is the peevish cry of a child. In fact, anything more terrific or deterrent than the music-hall view of matrimony it is impossible to conceive."[19] In these transitions, we can see part of the process by which a national, or indeed international, repertoire of song and drama was infused with a new type of popular realism.

The precise nature of this popular voice has been a subject of scrutiny since the 1970s, and attempts have been made by such scholars as L. Senelick and G. Stedman Jones to elicit from music hall songs some kind of picture of the working-class mood in this period. Although such attempts are valuable and often revealing, various problems arise when treating songs as vehicles of working-class expression. They were the products of lower middle class writers in the main, or of such "artist-sociologists" as Albert Chevalier.[20] Song writers were poorly paid and, in order to survive, had to apply the techniques of mass production – in this case, "the assembling of recognized formulae to meet the known needs of a given genre and produce effects both predictable and easily assimilated."[21] Moreover, the songs were a good deal more rehearsed than earlier ballads and broadsheets and therefore less topical. As the music hall attracted more sectors of society, it also necessarily sought a middle ground in the nature of its offerings, attempting to please all and offend none.[22] Above all else, it was in the "patter," a changing melange of jokes and topical allusions interposed between verses, that social content appeared most markedly, and it is the patter – which, though rehearsed, was constantly modified – that, much more than the songs themselves, has slipped through the net of time and been lost. When *The Music Hall* advised on the desirability of a double repertoire – one for the East End and one for the West End – this suggestion undoubtedly included the patter.[23] A full analysis of music hall songs would therefore have to include in its material whatever fragments of the patter has come down to us and would have to locate it in terms of audience and contemporary events.

A study of the songs can be nevertheless instructive, since it is legitimate to assume that those songs that have survived as classics "illuminated or truly reflected some aspect of working class life,"[24] while more immediately topical songs may have represented in a more generalized and opaque way working-class concerns of the time. This is not to say that the music hall was an exclusively working-class institution. The proprietors and the songwriters were bourgeois, and there were suburban halls that catered largely to the lower middle class, offering fare portraying lower middle class figures – clerks, shopkeepers, and artisans – with sympathy.[25] These qualifications, however, point to a significant facet of music hall entertainment as a whole; it was an art form that was intensely conscious of and reflective of its audience. Questions of class, status, and the various strata, trades, and occupations that made up the clientele were always major preoccupations of the music hall entertainment, and the proprietorship of the halls in a very real way had to give the people what they wanted. Given that the music hall audience was overwhelmingly working class, it is not surprising that the majority of music hall songs dealt in some way with the experiences of the various groups that make up the evening's crowd. In addition, what was true of the audience was true of the stars; the Great MacDermott was a bricklayer, and Champagne Charlie (George Leybourne) started his working life as a hammer man in a steel mill, while Jenny Hill was a cabby's daughter, Bessie Bellwood a Bermondsey rabbit skinner, and Harry Lauder a Lanarkshire pit boy.[26] In short, while recognizing the impossibility of regarding music hall song as an authentic and spontaneous product of the urban workers, it is doubtful that audiences would have responded positively to the songs or the stars unless elements within them struck a responsive chord, reflecting in some way the desires and opinions of this group. Moreover, as we will see, youths composed an important part of most music hall audiences, probably forming a majority of the gallery crowd on certain nights, and at all times representing a stratum of the clientele that proprietors and artistes would attempt to please. An examination of the entertainment is therefore worthwhile in order to gauge this group's artistic preferences and to determine what attitudes and ideas they were likely to pick up from the music hall offerings.

It seems clear that music hall songs "never truly advocated social change or improvement," yet it is an exaggeration to state that they instead exclusively proselytised "the causes of chauvinism and imperialism."[27] Music hall songs, in fact, show a decrease in shrillness and flag waving from the Crimean to the Boer War and through to World War 1. The heroes of these songs meanwhile changed from officers to "the recalcitrant warriors of the barrack-room or below decks," of which "Private Potts," in his constant guerrilla war against authority, is perhaps the best example.[28] Officers, meanwhile, had become monocled idiots such as "Captain Gingah," who was "undoubtedly courageous, and undoubtedly a nit-wit: bursting with energy and incompetence."[29] The obverse of the original music hall jingo song can also be found in Herbert Campbell's version.

> I don't want to fight, I'll be slaughtered if I do;
> I'll change my togs, I'll sell my kit, I'll pop my rifle too;
> I don't like the war, I ain't a "Briton true";
> And I'll let the Russians have Constantinople.[30]

The Saturday-night soldiers also came in for their share of ribbing.

> Since poor father joined the Territorials,
> Ours is a happy little home,
> He wakes us up in the middle of the night;
> And says we must all be prepared to fight!

He puts poor mother in the dustbin to stand on sentry guard;
And me and brother Bert, In his little flannel shirt,
He keeps drilling in the old back yard![31]

Although hardly malicious, such songs should be kept in mind when discussing the overtly tub-thumping paeans of the same era, which may well have been primarily for middle or lower middle class consumption.[32]

Songs about work also underwent a change in these years. Harry Clifton's "Work, Boys, Work and Be Contented" and Albert Vance's "Act on the Square, Boys, Act on the Square," which extolled honest (and non-unionized) labour, are products of the early music hall. By the turn of the century, it is much more difficult to find such songs. Instead, "the attitude ... to work is sceptical: at best it is deemed a regrettable necessity, at worst a tyrannical imposition."[33] In addition, one might note that the swell song of the 1860s and 1870s, immortalized by Champagne Charlie, lost its popularity, and that the typical swell of the Edwardian period was usually a bogus figure, the target of contempt or derision, skulking home to his suburban cottage after painting the town. This transformation of the swell style may have been partly the result of the music hall's marked propensity to parody its own products, but it was also perhaps a reflection of a real economic and social transition, from a period of exceptionally high wage increases for skilled workers in the Champagne Charlie era to the much less buoyant economy of the Great Depression.[34] There appeared a growing awareness that "class was a life sentence," and while this was usually approached in a spirit of comic realism and gentle parody, it was also realistic and may well have acted as an agent of class consolidation and a spur to class amelioration.[35]

Although Queen (or King) and Country remained relatively, though not absolutely, immune to the barbs of the comic singers, other groups were not as protected. It was noted that "you can always make pretty sure of a music-hall audience ... by attacking the vices of the aristocracy,"[36] while in melodrama the villain was almost invariably a gentlemanly figure in linen and starched collar.[37] If not portrayed as positive rascals, such figures were often woefully unaware of social realities, as when "Bertie Bright of Bond Street" sings,

How on earth do those chappies manage
Who haven't got a man to help them dress?
Fancy, studding shirts and putting bally boots on,

I'd be fairy done I must confess,
Fancy, having to fill your bath each morning,
And shave your beard when that is growing long,
And yet I'm told there are some men who have to,
It's really simply absolutely wrong![38]

or when a similar figure exclaims,

I hear that folks are starving, what a rotten thing to do,
With heaps of first-class Restaurants about,
I know a lot of places where for half a quid or so,
You can get a really ripping good blow-out ...[39]

Although this type of song is far from revolutionary, its effect on youths who often passed their childhood in cramped and penurious surroundings and who often enough went hungry could hardly be reconciling either. While poking fun at the upper class in a gentle way, they also more seriously pointed out the need for a greater social awareness on the part of the rich, and gave eloquent expression to the social chasm that separated the classes.

Teetotallers and the clergy provided other favourite targets for the songwriters, the first group for their notorious sanctimoniousness, the second group for their hypocritical conduct and rich living.[40] The lower middle class also came in for its share of ridicule, primarily for its pretentiousness. One song tells of "Cuthbert, Clarence and Claude" at Brighton, with their latest "stop the traffic" ties, socks that "will kill at half a mile," and monocles, while back in London,

Each at a dingy desk
Chewing the end of a quill
Earning their twenty-five bob a week
Sit *Henry, Thomas,* and *Bill.*[41]

Likewise, as "Wotcher 'Ria," and "'E Dunno where 'E are" illustrate, working people who try to be toffs earn the disgust of their fellows or a well deserved comeuppance. As "'Ria," a girl "what's doing wery well in the wegetable line" learns, it does not pay to go sit below with the quality in the music hall. After being thrown out for actions considered normal among the group in the gods, she observes,

Next time I'll go in the gallery with my friends, you bet a crown. You won't catch me going chucking my money away, trying to be a toff anymore.[42]

Nor is this attitude necessarily evidence of a servile acquiescence by the working class to their station in life. Rather, it reflected a conscious and indeed strident assertion by this class of the value of their own customs and point of view. In the "popular" halls, the songs often contained "some very broad compliment to what are called the 'working classes' as the base – the inevitable, priceless, base – of society's column."[43] Those stars such as Marie Lloyd, Gus Elen, and Bessie Bellwood, who continued to hold the affections of the working class, did so because despite their wealth they remained close to their roots, eating bloaters and bread and dripping, and refusing to be over-impressed by their "betters."[44] Though undeniably conservative in one sense, the music hall reveals, beneath its surface vulgarity and inanity, powerful springs of cohesiveness for the working class in this period, particularly on the cultural level. As one song simply yet eloquently said with the audience joining in,

> We all go the same way home,
> All the collection in the same direction,
> All go the same way home,
> So there's no need to part at all.
> We all go the same way home –
> Let's be gay and hearty, don't break up the party,
> We'll cling together like ivy on the old garden wall.[45]

One might add that they all came the same way as well. From its earliest days, the music hall was to a considerable extent the haunt of youth. Music hall disasters in 1865 in Dundee and 1868 in Manchester show only a small fraction of the casualties to have been over twenty years of age.[46] Three decades later, a similar incident in Aberdeen left twenty-eight dead or injured, only five of whom were more than twenty years old.[47] A visitor to the Medley in Hoxton in 1883 wrote that, of 4,000 patrons on a Saturday night, "it may be stated without fear of contradiction that of the whole number two thousand at least are not more than fifteen years old." Many of the rest were older teenagers or young mechanics.[48] Indeed, along with our increased awareness of the social distribution of the music hall crowd should come an awareness of its age distribution. As well, the fact that most music hall panics or fires began in the gallery would indicate both that this was the recognized territory of adolescents and that the behavioural standards to be found there were lower or more liberal than in the main body of the halls. When the street corner "click" decided to seek out further entertainment, or when a connection was made on the Monkey Parade, the music hall was often the evening's ultimate destination. Such places as the Medley in Hoxton served as a "free and easy" for "the rising young costermonger who resorts thither with a short pipe in his mouth, his 'young woman' on his arm, and in his pocket a drop of something in a bottle to keep them in good spirits for the enjoyment of the performance."[49] Despite its bias toward "Society," even *The Music Hall* admitted that "the management look to the gallery as being a sure sign of prosperity."[50] While desirous of attracting the wealthier sections of the populace and willing to tailor material so as not to offend the respectable, managers could not afford to alienate the bread and butter stratum of their clientele, on whom their solvency ultimately depended. Indeed, one of the reasons behind the campaigns to purify the music halls was the very obvious preponderance of adolescents within the crowd. It was particularly emphasized by the observers of youth that teenagers were too prone to spend their free time and money on the music hall. The seventy-one Birmingham boys investigated by Freeman all went at least once a week – usually Saturday – and some went more often. One visit per week was felt by these authors to be the limit of safety, more frequent trips implying impending depravity.[51] Street vendors, with the time and often the ready cash to make the matinées, were particularly likely to make a habit of going three or more times a week.[52]

Youths often began their visits to the music hall as children, in the company of parents or other adults; aunts and uncles especially seem to have taken children to shows as part of a regular treat.[53] One schoolboy who worked received, as part of his wages, a weekly trip to the Regent with his greengrocer employer.[54] More often, relatives would take boys at a regular time such as the Thursday or Saturday matinée or Friday night.[55] This was clearly a high point in the child's week; one Thompson respondent vividly remembers, "We'd go down to the local Hippodrome and stand on the queue, and as soon as the door opened there'd be most awful rush. I'd rush up umpteen flights of stairs to the very top of the building while father got the tickets and followed me. And then we'd dive down the seats, which were just cement steps with a wooden platform on. So as we'd get in the front, and then we'd see the show."[56]

After the school-leaving rite of passage, such family excursions became considerably rarer. The young worker now usually visited the halls on a Saturday, and he usually went with his friends. "We didn't want our mothers and fathers with us."[57] Without a parent, relative, or employer to treat him, a visit to the music hall could be expensive. A Glamorgan youth's weekly trip set him back nearly a shilling: 3d. for the horse bus, 3d. to 4d. for the gallery, 1d. for Woodbines, and 3d. for fish and chips. Walking back home, he would have 1d. left for the Sunday collection.[58] A respondent from Nottingham also provides an inventory of an evening at the music hall. "You'd a seat booked [for 6d.], a pint of beer for threepence, four ounces of sweets for a penny and a packet of cigarettes for tuppence, more or less ha'penny on the tram each way, and you got your night out for a shilling … – that was my regular Saturday."[59] Yet, it seems that few working-class youths begrudged the expenditure. For a few brief hours, the youth could enjoy himself fully, joking with his friends and celebrating with the audience and the stars the best that his world had to offer. Looking back, a Preston native tried to catch something of the enchantement that was an evening spent at the hall. "There was magic in the theatre. The anticipatory hum of conversation from the audience. The shrill cry of the programme boy, 'Programmes, chocolates.' The scraping from the violins; the gentle bursts from the brass as the orchestra tuned up. Even the drummer had a share in it. Then the conductor appeared, the turn number had gone up in the procenium frame, the red signal lamp flashed near the conductor's music stand, the hubbub died away. The show was about to begin."[60] Both this essentially romanticized memory and the highly detailed reconstructions of the expense of a music hall evening certainly illustrate part of its nature as a site of "measured and commoditised abundance,"[61] where popular art and leisure were turned into products of consumerist escapism and doled out in weekly lots of several hours apiece; however, a concentration on music hall entertainment merely as commodity unduly devalues and reduces the complex texture of the music hall experience for the individual youth.

Although an integral part of the original, self-propagated, and largely discredited myth of the music hall, the analysis of the music hall as a participatory as much as a passive form of entertainment, whether on the emotional or critical level, still has a great deal of truth to it. Theatre and music hall audiences would regularly weep at a heroine's predicament or shout imprecations at the villain, and the actors responded to these situations; they "address themselves directly to the audience, and take comparatively little notice of each other, while the audience accepts their attention as part of the entertainment."[62] Boys in the gallery would shout out the songs they wanted to hear, and many stars obliged, while such stars as Bessie Bellwood and Marie Lloyd owed part of their popularity to their ability to hold, and win, rhyming slang matches with the gallery.[63] Similarly, audiences who found material or an artiste uncongenial also directly made their opinion known. The early halls often had wire netting over the stage and orchestra to protect entertainers from the gallery boys. In London, "you used to take oranges with you because the orange peel came in handy if you didn't like the art-istes."[64] Costermongers had a habit of ridding themselves of excess merchandise in this way.[65] In the north, iron rivets long remained a favourite form of projectile.[66] Music hall audiences thus made their wishes and opinions known in an immediate way; in an art form without any large body of criticism, the audience itself and its re-actions provided the basis of measurement for the popularity and worthiness of a star and his or her repertoire. Bourgeois ownership was therefore always tempered by a certain amount of working-class control.

Moreover, the relationships within the hall were by no means confined to those between proprietor and clientele or performer and audience. An important subset of the relationships within the theatre was those between members of the audience itself. Among these members were the youths in the gallery. The music hall gallery was a lively scene, especially on a Saturday night, with hundreds of teenagers of both sexes shouting insults at each other and engaging in horseplay.[67] A Manchester youth remembers going in a gang and tormenting the ex-policeman who was the bouncer by shouting in the dark and tripping and pushing him from behind.[68] In Not-tingham, the local theatre was "the Grand on the Green. We used to call that the place for ten murders for threepence you know ... always a fight on Saturday night in the gallery when they were drunk."[69] For one boy, the gallery, with its youths "hitting one another on the head with bottles and what have you," was too rough a place, and when he began to earn good money he would sit below.[70] Such fastidiousness, along with his smart clothes, earned him the sobriquet of the "Duke of Kent."

We cannot reduce the music hall experience, then, to a single, undifferentiated state of leisure consumption common to all mem-bers of the audience. Rather, we should picture music hall atten-dance for the child or youth as containing different meanings at different times. As a child, the music hall was a treat to be enjoyed in the company of one's parents or relatives – part of a festive family occasion. In the teenage years, the music hall gallery was more properly an extension of the street "click," characterized by boister-ous good fun and the solidarity of the male gang. In later adoles-cence, as a kind of cyclical return, it became common to treat girls met on the street or in the gallery to the music hall – "because in those days, if you had a shilling – say if you had sixpence – you could take your girl out [to] theatre of varieties – tuppence for her and tuppence for yourself up in the gallery, you know, the gods. Tuppence each, and the two pennies that was left you could buy two banburys or cakes or one banbury between you and a bottle of pop between you."[71]

A certain etiquette seems to have operated in treating; for older and more serious suitors, "it was *de rigueur* to go to the pit," which cost from sixpence to a shilling for a seat.[72] Presumably such a decision would form one of the marks of approaching manhood, when the older youth left the gallery boys to join the mature couples and families in the quieter sections, in much the same way as the time-expired apprentice left his fellows behind in their lunch break groups to sit with the journeymen. There, in the pit, the songs about working-class love prepared the courting couple for the acceptance of the "peevish cry of the child," the importuning of the rent collector, and the long, shared struggle before them.

Working-class art has traditionally been a "'showing' rather than an 'exploration'," a "presentation of what is already known."[73] The observation that, among boys, most moral judgements, opinions and witticisms came from the halls[74] was probably not strictly true. What the music hall did was to feed upon the vast body of working-class axioms and saws, often contradictory in themselves, that formed the ethical guidelines of this group and projected them back to the audience in neatly encapsulated and catchy forms. In doing so, of course, it acted not only as a repository of working-class culture, but also as a medium for its propagation and reinforcement. It did so, moreover, in an increasingly national rather than regional mode. Whatever regional tradition could be claimed for the North-East or Lancashire, it is apparent that most areas soon fell under the sway of the syndicates and the touring system of stars;[75] by the Edwardian years even the former regions were succumbing. The Lancashire spinner who had "seen all the big turns as come to Bolton,"[76] and the Salford and Preston boys who enjoyed George Formby, Vesta Tilley, Fred Barnes, Marie Lloyd, Florrie Ford, Gertie Gitana, Little Tich, George Elliot, Ella Shields, and George Robey – "all the old troupers who made the theatre live"[77] – were witnesses and participants in the creation of a popular art form that sought out and exploited the common elements within its audiences at a national level. The late Victorian and Edwardian youths who crowded the galleries of the music halls were perhaps the main group affected by these processes and by this institution – one that, for all its conservatism and vulgarity, stressed the worth of the working class and its values, and in so doing acted as a solvent of intra-class and inter-regional barriers.

Toward the end of the Edwardian period, the music hall began to be challenged as the premier site of working-class entertainment by the new "cinematographs" that appeared at the end of the century and that, from the beginning, catered mainly to a working-class clientele.[78] Yet the cinema did not spring full grown into life as an independent art form. It appeared first as a novelty, taking its place as one of the "turns" in the music hall, along with other scientific and magical demonstrations. From the beginning, it captured the imagination and affections of the populace. "The house holds its breath till it is over: cheers lustily the moment it is done."[79] The cinema also soon became a staple item in the travelling fairs that provided entertainment to rural areas.[80] At first, the films were understandably crude, and in their subject matter tended to follow the magic lantern shows so popular among children. The king opening a bridge, a storm at sea, or the Derby were the type of scene displayed, emphasizing the novelty aspect of the new machine. Within a few years, however, permanent cinemas began to be built as proprietors and film-makers discovered both the commercial possibilities and the storytelling potential of the medium. For one or two pennies, several hours of amusement could be had, and the low cost prompted hordes of women and children to attend. Wives who would never be seen in a pub were now observed dragging their husbands to the picture palace, while children crowded the Saturday matinées.[81] Youths were the other major group to patronize the cinema. The Birmingham boys studied by Freeman in 1913–14 usually went at least once or twice a week, and this figure is borne out by oral history respondents.[82] Cinemas were cheap, informal, and accessible. In 1912 in Birmingham, forty-seven cinemas provided seating for 32,836 customers, or twice the capacity of the city's music halls, while, by 1913, Salford offered thirteen cinemas to the area's four music halls.[83] Many of the new establishments were small and located in the heart of the working-class districts, making them easier to get to than the music halls. In addition, they did not require the youth to put on his best clothes, which were "a *sine qua non*" for the Saturday night music hall visit.[84] It would appear that for the youth the cinema was regarded as a weekday diversion, its special attractions in cost, proximity, and informality making it a logical choice for after-work entertainment. In its early years, then, the cinema should perhaps be regarded as a supplement to other forms of leisure rather than as a direct competitor.

The success of the cinema nonetheless provoked a quick reaction from moral watchdogs and from those with vested interests elsewhere. Pub owners complained that the new art form hurt trade; the picture palace was a powerful element in the "positive temperance movement."[85] Moralists, on the other hand, deplored the crude plots, the passive nature of the entertainment, and, perhaps, most of all, the darkness of the venue. This was not without foundation; in 1909 the commissioner of police noted that "indecent assaults have somewhat frequently occurred at entertainments of this kind" and advised that separate seating be provided for unaccompanied children.[86] Cinema owners and film-makers did their best to ward off both these kinds of complaints and those about the nature of the films. In 1912 the film-makers voluntarily formed the British Board of Film Censors to screen material, categorize films, and suggest cuts where appropriate.[87] Early films, despite their depiction of lurid and improbable adventures, also tended to follow the traditions of the melodrama; virtue always got its reward, vice its punishment.[88]

Middle-class observers of working-class life nevertheless remained disquieted by the cinema. Many saw a connection between the cinema and juvenile crime, since boys (especially younger ones) often stole in order to obtain the price of admission.[89] One author correlated youth unrest to the cinema, conjecturing that the "the 'school-boy strikes' of 1911 were directly caused by the exhibition of strike scenes in various parts of the country."[90] The cinema was also drawing people away from the religious organizations that had played a major role in the community's social life; this was particularly the case in the smaller towns and mining villages where previously the "only entertainment one had in those days ... was made by the chapels."[91] This comment, by a lad from a Cornish tin-mining village, whose only commercial recreation was the cinema, is echoed by a Rhondda collier. "There was nothing else ... in the valleys in them days – no amusements, nothing at all, only the religion ... but when the cinema came out and the couple of clubs opened out, well, then the menfolks ... was going here, going there ... Instead of going to the chapel, they were ... going to the clubs."[92] In a larger urban centre such as Salford, the effects of the new form of entertainment were even more telling; there, the first "Kinema" was housed in the abandoned premises of the Primitive Methodist chapel.[93]

All this worried speculation is reminiscent of the similar debate on the effects of television several decades ago, and it is a measure of the potential impact of the cinema upon working-class lives that this was so. Yet what these effects in fact were is much harder to determine than in the case of the music hall. Whereas the music hall had been, so to speak, mainly their property, the cinema, through its newsreels portraying events in England and overseas and its elaborate sets depicting other (especially American) cultures, opened up to the working class a world they had up til now only glimpsed. That this world was inevitably distorted by its passage through the medium was relatively unimportant. The working class actually saw, or thought they saw, how the rich, the foreign, and the unfamiliar lived. By providing this window through which the working class could look, the cinema probably acted as a further catalyst in the breakdown of local loyalties and of a life revolving around factory, home, and street. It also may have begun eroding that class-centred popular culture that had emerged before World War I. In this sense, the youths of the Edwardian period may have been a transitional generation, growing up in the presence of both a series of leisure institutions (music hall, football, betting) that reinforced class lines and reflected (however indirectly) their culture, and a series of institutions (cinema, wireless, dance hall) that in their outlook, clientele, and, perhaps most important, mode of consumption, may be more properly termed institutions of mass, or at least classless, culture. As such, the role of popular culture in producing the "classic" working-class life way of life, which emerged in the late Victorian period and persisted until about World War II, was both historically conditioned and provisional. By the 1930s, it was noted that the shrinking music hall audience "in the main to-day is composed of middle-aged people, and men predominate ... [The music halls] seem however to have little appeal to the present generation of young people."94 The Edwardian youths who were the first generation of film-goers were also the last generation of the gallery boys, lingering on as an audience in later years in interwar revues such as "Thanks for the Memories" and providing the only mainstay of the few music halls left by 1940; their younger siblings and children would grow up in a world whose cultural horizons were formed more by the products of Hollywood than by anything even remotely resembling their own class. That this transition did not immediately lead to a mass culture in the American mode is, one could argue, evidence of the cultural impact of the late Victorian and Edwardian leisure institutions in helping to form a distinctly working-class point of view.

Turning from more passive to more active forms of commercial entertainment, we come inevitably to sport and hence to football [soccer]. That football was, as it is now, one of the consuming interests of English working-class youth is borne out by the evidence of various observers. The talk of the group at the street corner was mainly about football, the members of the "click" showing a great and detailed knowledge of teams and players.[95] One writer stated unequivocably that the sport was a boy's "single greatest interest."[96]

The growth of football from an ad hoc and unorganized game to one of the great spectator sports of the nation was another development of the period, and is a further illustration of the vitality of working-class leisure forms during the second phase of industrialization. The professional teams often had their origins in church or chapel clubs (Aston Villa, Bolton, Everton, Birmingham) or trade unions (Stoke City, Manchester United, Arsenal, West Ham) and, from the 1880s, began to wrest control of the game, both on and off the field, from the public school men who had dominated it until then.[97] Rugby began to take the same route, until a clash in the 1890s over professionalism led to the formation of two separate, and class-based, associations.[98]

Many boys attended the new professional matches on a regular basis. For some, this interest began at an early age, when their fathers or brothers took them to a game on a Saturday afternoon.[99] Later, when working, these boys would go by themselves or with friends to cheer on their local favourites.[100] Such a practice was not cheap; although a less prestigious team such as Lancaster Town charged 3d. per match for admission, the better teams usually charged 6d. in the regular season and as much as 1s. for a league championship or an International.[101] Despite these prices, youths seem to have constituted an important element of the crowd. At the Ibrox Park disaster in Glasgow in 1902, 15 per cent of the casualties were teenagers – close to their proportion of the total population. Skilled tradesmen made up 67 per cent of the total casualties, illustrating the wealthier nature of the working-class football crowd and again confirming the leisure resources of boys, who could manage to attend a fixture that most of their unskilled adult counterparts could not. This was, moreover, a 1s. International and would have involved travelling expenses for some.[102] It is impossible to estimate what degrees of financial sacrifice were necessary for some of these boys to attend, but it is clear that many youths were to be found on the terraces. Judging from the oral evidence, such youths were more likely to come from the families of skilled workers – engineers, spinners, warp dressers – than from those of unskilled or semi-skilled workers; the continuing connections between football and the economic, religious, and cultural institutions of the skilled may be responsible in part for this.

The advent of professional football brought with it the usual denunciations from working-class critics, who saw parallels with Roman gladiatorial shows in the modern game: mob passions, inordinate and slavish praise of "stars," and an increased tendency to watch rather than to do.[103] Yet youths, at least, were rarely merely passive spectators. Many of the most avid fans played on the street or on any ground they could find, and there is a close correlation in the oral evidence with regard to playing and watching. In August and September, neighbourhoods would be canvassed for money to buy a ball by teams of boys who took upon themselves the task of organizing local leagues.[104] There is also little doubt that one of the greatest attractions of boys' clubs was the opportunity to play on a regular basis and on a proper ground with proper equipment.

Youths were therefore connoisseurs rather than merely consumers, and the weekly trek to the professional match was primarily the homage of an enthusiastic amateur to highly developed skill. Professional football, however, also had other attractions to the youth, through its linkage to betting, its consolidation of local loyalties, and the dissemination of its news through a vast sporting press.[105] Perhaps most of all, after a week of work, the football stadium offered excitement, noise, and variety. Any attempt to gauge the overall cultural effects of football must recognize the dangers of reading too much into what was, after all, a game, but it is surely permissible to characterize many football crowds as mass working-class meetings, complete with rituals, songs, colour, and folk heroes, recreating in a delimited time and place some of the characteristics of the union meeting, Sunday school outing or Wakes Week parades.[106] In this sense, an undue emphasis on the role of football in promoting regional or intra-class rivalries would be misplaced; no one would seriously suggest that a rugby game between two public schools promoted rivalries within the upper middle class. What is important in both cases is the participation of the whole crowd in a common experience of friendly competition and the way that this sets the participants apart from others in society who do not share, either directly or vicariously through the press, this interest or experience.

To the child or youth, football had a further attraction – the sight of former colliers, dockhands, or lathe operators making an average of £4 per week to kick a football around.[107] A proficiency at football must have seemed to many youths to be the quickest and surest way out of the slum, and the "stars" in this sense were a living and identifiable focus of aspirations to a better and easier life. In the popular imagination, a professional player was someone who had beaten the system and who resided in some Land of Cockaigne, where he lived well by playing an enjoyable game before settling down with honour as the landlord of a pub. The reality, of course, was very different, since very few players could support themselves on their pay or purchase an inn with their savings.[108] Yet the fables contained a grain of truth. Employers were more likely to hire a man if he had brought credit to the locale, as a Lancaster respondent recalls. "Bob Dillworth, if he knew of a lad that was going in the army, he'd buy him out to come and play for the City. He'd give him a job labouring in t'building.[109] A Bolton youth recalls one boy who "got on" through football, first getting a better job in the mill, then becoming a municipal councillor, and ending his days as a justice of the peace.[110] Clearly, if football did not lead to riches, it at least opened a few doors. For these reasons, football became the leading sport of the working class. Its attractions operated on all levels of competition, from the street to Wembley Stadium and from the desire for physical exercise to the desire for a better life. Although boxing, cricket, and racing had their devotees, no other sport could match football in its capacity to meet the physical and emotional needs of its participants and fans.

A leisure pursuit on the brink of change at the end of the Edwardian period was dancing. In the Victorian period, dancing was considered vulgar by most of the working class. Parents would often insist that their children avoid dance halls completely, believing them to be a danger not only to their morals but to their health as well, although the precise nature of the possible diseases to be found there were never spelled out.[111] Most boys heeded these warnings, even in their teenage years. "There were only one dance hall, and if you went there you were a member of the fast set. ... I never went. No, ... [n]either me nor her never went dancing."[112] Another remembers, "I still [kept] listening to these other lads ... they kept telling me about different girls in there and I said, I don't like it."[113]

For a small minority of both sexes, however, the attractions of the dancing saloon outweighed the fear of parental displeasure, and such places, though relatively few in number, did a good business.[114] Their patrons were usually older adolescents of about eighteen to twenty, and the staff often included a number of girls whose job it was to get people onto the floor. It was at these establishments that youths were apparently most likely to start drinking, since the dance halls were often close or attached to pubs and dancing was hot work. Many older boys gave up every other pastime once they had become a "hopper," and the reputation of the saloons was such that to be "dancing mad" was to be going downhill fast. Often, however, a boy became a dancer for two seasons or so, then gave it up; presumably the required partner had been found.[115] The dancing saloon thus operated as a subsidiary Monkey Parade, usually for older adolescents and, if oral respondents are correct, usually for the looser members of this age group.

Even at the end of the Edwardian years these halls had an evil reputation, being places where only "the most vicious of the two sexes gather."[116] Yet, by the end of the next decade, dancing had become a national craze. World War I and larger cultural trends were partly responsible for this; the recreational desires of soldiers on leave were a good deal more frenetic than those that could be satisfied by the music halls and cinemas alone. Among teenagers, parental control had been further relaxed through the absence or long working hours of many fathers, and wages for adolescents were exceptionally high.[117] Moreover, after the war, a numerical disjunction between the sexes created, for a time, an abnormal marriage market. Even the most respectable girl knew that the dancing hall, now echoing to the youthful strains of ragtime and Dixieland jazz, was the most likely place to find a potential husband.[118] The formerly widespread suspicions about such places crumbled under these more compelling factors, and by the 1920s the dancing halls had become one more site of the penetration of American leisure modes acceptable to the working class as a whole.

During these years, the working class was building its major modern leisure institutions, and its youthful component was one of the primary groups affected. While it is difficult to reach any hard and fast conclusions on the effects of cultural change, the broadening of social horizons and the breakdown of intra-class barriers would appear to be among them. In short, it seems that the cultural institutions of the working class in the decades before 1914 were moving in the same direction that the industries were from which this class drew its sustenance – toward the creation of a more homogeneous group. The music hall's main topic was always its own audience and its audience's trials, hopes, and comic moments. Its final effect, after all the profits and losses have been calculated, was probably to act as a powerful agency in the creation and consolidation of this class's value system, but these values were themselves both assertive and accepting. As such, its role in the creation of the class consciousness that was recognizably emerging before World War I was undoubtedly profound, and, although this consciousness may have been essentially passive, it was there nevertheless, to be an important factor in the political and social developments of the interwar years.

Football may have had contradictory effects, in that it stressed local loyalties at the same time that it provided an arena for all levels of the working class to meet with a common purpose. In this sense, it may have acted as a solvent of craft and occupational loyalties by stressing the essential unity of a region. More important than this, however, football provided a vivid example of the working class meeting and beating the best of their social superiors. The defeat of the Old Etonians by the working-class Blackburn Olympics in 1883 was the death knell of aristocratic dominance of the game and ensured that the players rather than the gentlemen would control it from then on.[119] Although football may have diverted the workers from more important issues of class contention, it set an example to this class of their ability to fight for control over one aspect of their lives, and it formed yet another activity that divided them from other sections of the national community.

The effects of the cinema are rather harder to define. Never truly working class in subject matter or control, the final effect of the cinema may well have been mostly a broadening of social horizons, as that portion of the working class who did not read regularly or who had never been in service were introduced to the modes of thought and behaviour of other strata of society. If nothing else, the cinema certainly helped to break down the parochiality of much of working-class life, giving people a vision of life beyond their home, locale, or factory. Yet the full impact of the cinema is probably more properly to be found in the late interwar period, acting upon a later generation of adolescents who grew up under its spell.

Of all the members of the working class, its youth were probably most affected by these new cultural factors. Youths attended music halls, cinemas, and sports grounds regularly and in large numbers. This fact alone points up the large leisure resources that working boys possessed, since an average teenager could easily spend one and a half to two shillings per week on entertainment, and often much more.[120] In a very real sense, these commercial venues rested on the willingness of youth to patronize them. Such institutions may have acted as a new opiate for the masses, with their emphasis on having a good time at all costs.[121] Yet what is most striking about such cultural forms is the extent to which they recapitulated or recreated – even if in an exploitative way – the values and experiences to be found in the working-class home and neighbourhood. In the end, the youth in the music hall gallery and on the stadium terraces was a participant in a process that would lead, after World War I, to a relatively unified and consolidated working-class point of view.

CHAPTER SEVEN

Organized Youth Movements

The apparent aimlessness and anarchic quality of street lounging and music hall going alarmed many middle-class observers, who saw these activities as factors working toward the creation of an undisciplined and irresponsible working class. One of the responses to this perceived trend was the creation of alternative youth recreation, solidly based upon middle-class ideals of patriotism, service, and responsibility. The period 1890 to 1914 saw an efflorescence of such organizations and institutions, catering to a successively broader range of youths and using increasingly subtler and more sophisticated methods to attract and hold the loyalty of boys.

This development has drawn the attention of various scholars in recent years, who have been intrigued by the combining of such concepts as religious zeal, national efficiency, social control, and fears of physical and moral deterioration.[1] These scholars have examined in detail the aims, methods, and underlying philosophies of the founders and organizers of youth movements and uncovered the movements' main chronological framework. The standard interpretation has tended to conclude that such organizations as the Boys' Brigade, the Church Lads' Brigade, and the Boy Scouts were powerful agents of social conformity in the years leading up to World War I. The aims of the movements were twofold: negatively, to exercise a preventive check on the behaviour of boys and thus keep them from the harm that they might come to on the unsupervised streets and, positively but covertly, to mould their attitudes – to enlarge their mental and spiritual outlook, to carry on as far as possible the work of the elementary schools, and to replace the lost peasant and artisan culture of the past with an appropriate urban one.[2] Young people's lives would be so ordered that a better community and, ultimately, a better nation would result. In this period, adolescence was increasingly recognized as a stage in life in which the patterns of subsequent conduct and fortunes were set for the individual.[3] The primary function of these organizations, then, consistent with the theory of social control, was the development of institutions that imposed restrictions on the behaviour of a group that threatened the equilibrium of society. At the same time, their long-term aim is seen as the propagation of the hegemonic values of the élites among this target group. Although in the beginning the emphasis on this ordering was primarily religious, in the 1890s and 1900s there appeared another major motivation, which can be summarized under the heading of "national efficiency." Under this umbrella term may be grouped all the concerns about eugenic deterioration, industrial inefficiency, and military weakness that were such a prominent feature of the literature of the day. These motives can be seen most clearly in such authentically Edwardian creations as the Boy Scouts and the Church Lads' Brigade, both of which were seen as substitutions for the politically impossible scheme of compulsory military service.[4] By the inculcation of a spirit of self-sacrifice, corporate feeling, and obedience in the youth of the nation, the leaders of these movements hoped to reverse the slow slide of Britain's position in relation to its continental rivals. One might almost say that the youth workers were as envious and fearful of Germany's compulsory continuation schools and flourishing youth movements as the admiralty was of that country's naval program.[5] Far from being altruistic in intent, then, these paramilitary organizations had the primary aim of inculcating habits of obedience, hard work, and unthinking patriotism in the boys whom they attracted, so as to reproduce and strengthen a class society and ready it for future European economic and military conflicts. In this light, the hundreds of thousands who flocked to join Kitchener's Army in the best Boy Scout spirit, or the 50,000 ex-Boys' Brigade members and officers killed in World War I can be seen as the vindication and crowning achievement of these groups' work.[6] One scholar, summing up the ultimate effect of these groups, states, "It is no exaggeration to say that Kitchener's Army depended on a Boy-scout spirit and resourcefulness for its morale, and on the dissemination of public school loyalties and values among lower middle class and working men. This had been, to a large extent, accomplished by the patriotic youth movements."[7]

Though valuable, these studies have been incomplete and, hence, perhaps misleading. They have based themselves mainly upon the archival material at headquarters, thus getting an eagle eye's view of the processes at work below, and have concentrated upon philosophical and organizational differences at the top to the detriment of grass roots development at the bottom. They have also tended toward an a priori argument, in which the aims and methods of the giants, such as Sir William Smith and Lord Baden-Powell, become the dominant aims and motives, not only of the lower officers but also of the boys themselves. Moreover, the boys' clubs, the most truly working-class youth institutions in terms of clientele, have tended to be ignored. Often unfederated, sometimes short lived, the boys' clubs are a hard subject for institutional examination, while the aims and methods of their founders – often local clergymen or professionals – were more various and are harder to explore. Finally, missing from these analyses is any serious attempt to examine the actual effects of such institutions on the boys themselves. As Paul Wilkinson has noted, in these movements "there was a ... complex and subtle inter-generational dialectic of pressure, response, leadership, and collaboration."[8] Too often, however, the boys' side of this process has been lost in a morass of headquarters memoranda.

Any attempt to understand these effects must look more closely at the actual numbers of boys drawn in and must consider not only the organizers' but also the boys' attitudes and motives, as well as the specific conditions of life that affected their leisure choices. The various brigades and the Boy Scouts essentially limited their membership to schoolboys by their agency of recruitment, which was usually the Sunday school or local school (especially if this was a Church of England establishment). When working life began, school was left behind, as were those things associated with the educational regime – Sunday school and membership in any attached youth organization.[9] The boys' clubs, however, were for working youths, who were engaged in labour for fifty to seventy hours per week. After a day of nine to twelve hours, boys were simply not interested in organized leisure that ran counter to their tastes, and most forms offered by adults fell into this category. Even less appealing were any educational or religious programs offered. Beyond these factors, a more complete treatment must recognize that leisure consumption on the part of the target group was less a matter of passive absorption than it was an active choosing, which may well involve a reworking of the value system being articulated.[10] An examination of the work of these organizations from the vantage point of the working-class boy leads to a very different analysis of their appeal and their effects.

Long before the years of adolescence, in fact, working-class people had developed a highly pragmatic attitude to social agencies, arising from their experiences in childhood and from their need to obtain resources wherever and however possible. This can be seen clearly even at an early age, when children flocked to such religious organizations as the Band of Hope or Christian Endeavour. While enjoying the songs and entertainment provided, "which was all free mind you,"[11] children retained a rooted scepticism toward the aims of the organizers. "You never went to the Band of Hope to sign the pledge, you went because it was a magic lantern slide, but you signed the pledge 'cos it was part of the rituals ... Kids about eight and nine signing the pledge ... I mean to say its fantastic ..."[12] A Lancastrian concurs. "I belonged to the Band of Hope. It was very popular because it showed slides."[13] Other children had even less pure motives. "You only went to have a bit of fun ... pinching one another, getting turned out";[14] "all the lads in the street attended the Band of Hope, the Christian Endeavour, the Confirmation Class – in fact, everywhere that there were possibilities of getting up to mischief."[15]

The choice of church or Sunday school was likewise often influenced by considerations other than those of doctrine or religion. As one Londoner rather cynically observed, most of the adults who went to church were "what I consider mumpers and cadgers that used to go for what they could get ... I think half the working class who went to church only went to get what they could out of it."[16] Most children went because their parents sent them, so that the elders, who very rarely attended themselves, could have an hour or so of privacy and quiet. As to which organization to join, "it would depend on what we got from these places for special treats ... we always went where they give the most away."[17] A contemporary joke summed up the tactic.

Deacon: Do you attend Sunday School regularly now?
Boy (with supreme contempt): No! not now. I've got all I can git out of it until next Christmas.[18]

Churches that stopped actively tempting boys soon saw their attendance fall, "and so the schools go on, bidding against each other with increasing promises of prizes, treats, and clothing, until they are lowered in the eyes of their scholars to the level of mere adjuncts, more or less endurable, to the bribes they offer."[19]

An enterprising "cake-sniffer" would belong to two or more Sunday schools, collecting "doles, rewards, gifts, or benefits" at each one.[20] A Preston respondent described the day when he made good his year's work. "I've taken as many as four breakfasts home on Christmas morning. As I've gone into the places for them and we brought them out in a paper bag, I've had my mother meeting me and taking them home while I've gone to the next place and then when I came out of the next place she met me and took them home ... Not only me but scores of kiddies used to do the same thing."[21]

In short, most children attended Sunday school, Bands of Hope and similar educational or religious groups for the sake of their parents, who wanted them to go, and for the sake of the treats, prizes, and amusements offered. The working-class attitude to established religion was generally one of "simply utter indifference"[22] when it was not self-serving, as an exasperated cleric complained at the time. "Respect for religion and its ministers form no part of the boy's home training, unless we may include under this head that grovelling subservience often forced on the children with the hope of obtaining a speedy reward in the shape of coal tickets, soup, and other material goods."[23] This is not to say that the working class was irreligious or atheist, but only, as one author stated, that "their ethical views, taken as a whole, can be more justly described as different from those of the upper classes than as better or worse."[24] The moral feelings of the working class were more "antique Roman" than Christian, slanted as they were toward actions and the fulfillment of practical needs and interested in positive results rather than introspection.[25] Theological and doctrinal niceties rarely interested the working class, still less their children. Thus, one finds a promiscuity in the choice of church or Sunday school, which made nonsense of the doctrinal and liturgical differences so important to religious leaders. The son of a Primitive Methodist attended the local Church of England Sunday school, and later changed to the fiercely Anglican Church Lads' Brigade because his chapel provided no social amenities;[26] a boy whose father was "more or less an atheist" joined the Band of Hope, went to Sunday school twice a week and joined the church youth club;[27] and in "a parish where a Church Sunday School was discontinued ... most of the children went to the Baptist School sooner than have none."[28] A boy from Barrow-in-Furness, nominally Anglican, attended the gym class at his church twice a week (a class composed in large part by Roman Catholics), went to the Primitive Methodist concerts and played football on their team, and was a member of the Baptist Band of Hope.[29] As another Barrow lad (who went to the Gospel Hall for services, the Methodist chapel for Christian Endevour, and the Church of England for other activities) pointed out, "Each was a denomination to themself, apart from the children, which was all one."[30] The final choice of Sunday school was therefore influenced more by availability and amenities than by denominational affiliation or doctrine or even basic Christian belief, and, long before the twentieth-century movement among Church leaders, working-class children and teenagers had developed an ecumenism based on their own value system – one that emphasized community and good fellowship in a leisure setting and a pragmatic concentration on tangible benefits. It may well be that the decline in sectarian animosities that characterized the religious history of the early twentieth century owes something to the passage into adulthood of working-class children who spent so much of their leisure hours sampling the offerings of the various churches in their neighbourhoods.

Within these parameters and according to these values, the Bands of Hope and Sunday schools that catered to the children of the working class across the nation had a great appeal. Two accounts from opposite ends of the country illustrate the similarities in experience and outlook of the Sunday school attenders. A lad from Hackney remembers with great detail his Tuesday night Band of Hope meeting and the annual Sunday school outing to Epping Forest or Loughton. "Tuesday night, well you start off with the hymns you know. And then perhaps the parson'd give you a talk and then you'd have games up and down the hall and on ropes – things like that. Couple of hours. I think we used to have to take a farthing or ha'penny, put it in the basin. Then also they had an outing once a year you know somewhere ... off on the brakes ... You'd have a big meat pie for dinner, I remember that vividly. It was really a good meal, and you'd have a bag of sweets, orange, apple and you'd have races in the afternoon ... I suppose really that's why we went, just for these outings you know."[31] For the son of a Barrow joiner, the Band of Hope

was one of the main attractions when we were kids. Practically the whole of Barrow Island went to the Band of Hope. It used to be run by a Minister called Mr. Whitely, he was the curate of St. John's. There'd be a hall full of kiddies and bedlam and you couldn't have anything like law or order. They used to have a bit of a concert, or someone come up and sing or do a turn or just amuse yourselves generally. It lasted for about an hour each week. There was no competition, no pictures, no television, and the church was your life. Everything that happened socially, dances, Band of Hope, Close Brethren Society, everything flocked around the church. You'd be surprised at numbers, it was always a full house ... We were told about the evils of drink. Of course, talking about evil in general, that being a church organisation, but I think the whole purpose was a Temperance Society. It got kiddies off the street and tried to teach them a little bit of Christianity.

How far they succeeded one will never know. You started off with a hymn or a prayer and hand up anyone who'll come and sing, or do a dance. Just now and again he'd get some of the elder ones together and organize a little concert and give it to the kids in the hall but it's difficult to say what purpose it served.[31]

Likewise, the memory of the annual Sunday school outing is stripped of virtually all of its religious content and remains, in the man's memory, as it undoubtedly was, a festive occasion.

The thrill of our young days was the Sunday school trip. Our Sunday school trip was once a year, and there would be about probably 400 scholars from St. John's and we assembled at the Church hall, outside the Church. I think we took our own enamel mug or they gave us one, I'm not sure which, and we'd process three or four abreast all the way down Ramsden Dock Road, way down to Ramsden Dock Station. They'd get in front of you and there was a train and you all got in and off you went. You'd go perhaps to Rampside or Kirkby, we only went about half an hour away and we'd walk into a field and have our tea. The teachers brought you a bag with your tea and you had a good tuck in and then you'd sports, racing, running and jumping, and you got prizes and then at the end of the day when you were tired out they brought you back home. That was the event of the year.[33]

With the passage of schooldays went the power of parents to insist on a child's attendance at such gatherings, while the boy's newly earned wages also tended to lessen the need for that "grovelling subservience" so detested by middle-class authors and resented in turn by many of its practitioners. At the same time, the boy's wages provided the means to indulge in commercial forms of entertainment. What did not change was the attitude of the youth toward organized and "improving" leisure. Moreover, with parental compulsion largely removed, these movements were now truly voluntary, and the youth was thus a buyer in a buyer's market.

The Boys' Brigade was the first successful attempt to form a voluntary uniformed youth movement. Founded in Glasgow in 1883 by William A. Smith, a Sunday school worker with pronounced military leanings, it had as its objects "the Advancing of Christ's Kingdom among Boys, and the promotion of habits of Reverence, Discipline, Self-Respect, and all that tends towards a true Christian Manliness."[34] A further virtue, Obedience, was added in 1893, presumably as a result of a decade's experience with working class boys. Smith formulated the basic idea that was to impel most subsequent attempts: "boys could be won over by appealing to the 'boy mind.'"[35] It was found that by putting a pill-box cap on a boy's head and calling him a soldier, wonders could be performed in the fields of discipline and deportment. Indeed, "no lion-king making his wild beasts jump through hoops could be prouder of himself. You order them about like an emperor. You criticize their hands, their faces, their feet – even their boots – without a murmur of dissent."[36]

The Boys' Brigade combined military trappings and drill with non-conformist religious teaching in an effort to protect, guide, and socialize the boy in an acceptable middle-class manner. The boys enjoyed playing at soldiers, and the movement grew rapidly from 30 boys in 1884 to 18,052 in 1890.[37] By 1913 the figure had risen to over 65,000.[38]

Although the Boys' Brigade successfully enlisted the voluntary support of many boys, it suffered from the same problems that would beset all other attempts; it could not mould boys that it could not attract, and it could not attract the largest portion of the working class, whose activities it viewed with the most alarm. Though specifically set up to deal with the "ruder class of boys," the rank and file in many companies consisted in fact of the "sons of the respectable working class."[39] In the First Glasgow Brigade in the years 1890–95, 72 per cent of the boys were from the families of skilled workers, 27 per cent from lower middle class families, and only 1 per cent from the unskilled or semi-skilled working class.[40] From the beginning of the venture, the attitude of the latter boys was far from welcoming. "The local gangs tried hard to disrupt this new movement, and Boys and Officers alike had often to run the gauntlet of abuse and violence. The tall hats of the Officers formed a ready target for the sticks and stones of the wild lads, and for many nights there were running fights between the B.B. and the gangsters."[41] The Brigade boys were also often greeted by the "wild lads" with the famous refrain,

> Here comes the Boys' Brigade
> All smovered in marmalade
> A Tu'penny-a'penny pill box
> And 'arf a yard of braid.[42]

Of the boys who did in fact join, many dropped out if attendance at drill and Bible class was strictly enforced.[43] As well, the Sunday school boy who joined during his schooldays was very likely to drop out when he began to work.[44] Even the first Brigade company, under its charismatic founder, had these difficulties. "Fifty-nine names were taken during the opening weeks, though as it turned out some had come in from curiousity, quite a few perhaps with the idea of 'ragging' this new authority ..."[45] The Anglican response to the Boys' Brigade, the Church Lads' Brigade, fared even worse in recruiting members, especially in urban areas. It was by and large a rural and small-town movement. Always more militaristic and nationalist than its nonconformist rival, it set the seal on this aspect of its work by formally affiliating with the War Office cadet scheme in 1911. With two field marshals and nine generals among its vice presidents, its nature as a vehicle for the propagation of imperialistic and conscriptionist ideas was quite plain.[46]

The influence on youths of any or all types of the brigades, however, pales in comparison with that of the Boy Scouts. This organization, formally founded only in 1908, literally took the country by storm and, after a lapse of only half a decade, had a national membership of 152,333, or nearly two and a half times that of the thirty-year-old Boys' Brigade in the same year.[47] Baden-Powell took his original inspiration from the Brigade, but displayed a far greater understanding of the interests of boys. In place of the rigid drill and discipline of the Brigades, the Scouts substituted a seemingly looser program concentrating on the development of initiative and cultivating a sense of adventurous independence, while their system of badges and gradations was designed to cater to many different interests and to open up to the boy a widening world of woodcraft and lore. Baden-Powell understood that the military image that appealed most to a boy's mind in an age of "little wars" and imperial expansion was the outrider or scout rather than the well drilled, Wellingtonian guardsman.

Such was the immediate appeal of the scouting movement that in many areas boys organized themselves into troops before looking around for a scoutmaster and seeking formal affiliation.[48] Again, however, the Scouts failed to attract boys from the lower social strata; the overwhelming majority of early Scouts were from the middle and lower middle classes.[49] Unlike the Boys' Brigade, the movement failed to penetrate even the upper reaches of the working class. Both financial and ideological reasons can be put forward for this. With a much more elaborate uniform than the Brigades', and an onerous system of dues, the Scouts were usually beyond the financial reach of schoolboys from the working class.[50] As a Liverpool respondent remembers, "I was in the scouts ... but I wasn't in it long – couldn't afford the uniform actually."[51] As well, the militaristic nature of the early Scout movement, while often denied, was quite apparent. Particularly in heavily unionized areas such as iron and steel, mining, and textile districts, the Scouts were frowned upon, while radicals and labourites everywhere viewed with mistrust an organization run largely by ex-officers and National Service League members.[52] The Liverpool boy's father, a Lib-Lab adherent, "thought the scouts was a military organization. And of course it was ... the scouts were turned to military purposes."[53] For these reasons, the organization in the pre-war era remained solidly middle and lower middle class, though undoubtedly its appeal reached down to many individual working-class boys.

Those boys who did join often left by the age of fifteen in any case, since the Scouts, like the various brigades, essentially limited themselves to schoolboys by their agency of recruitment, which was usually the Sunday school or local school. Similarly, when working life began for the boy, Scouts was left behind.[54] It was not until the foundation of the Rover Scouts in 1923 that the problem of retaining the older teenager was even partially solved.[55] Because the Scout movement failed to hold[56] or even attract working-class boys, its socializing and indoctrinating effects on this group were likely minimal. On the evidence of numbers alone, it is difficult to see how public school loyalties and values could be disseminated among a group who never joined.

The boys' club proved to be the most successful institution in catering specifically to working-class youths. Although youths had often joined the early working men's clubs (in some cases virtually taking them over), the first true boys' club was probably the Bayswater Boys' Club, founded by Charles Baker in 1858. This and other early clubs were not very well equipped on the sporting side and, with their high subscriptions, tended to limit their intake to the sons of clerks and artisans.[57] Another, continuing problem was that of retaining the allegiance of boys while attempting to instil discipline. The pitfalls associated with this balancing act are well illustrated by the case of one of the earliest London clubs and night schools.

The Honourable Maude Stanley began a Sunday school in February 1873 in the Five Dials district of London, out of which grew both a night school and a boys' club. From the beginning, many of the local youths demonstrated their hostility to the venture. "Cabbage stalks and winkles picked up from the street were often thrown through the apertures. Occasionally a boy would come and spit at us through the openings, or make noises that were answered by the boys within, with such powers of ventriloquism that it was impossible to discover the culprit." One night-school teacher was driven away by the taunts of the boys in the class, while an older boy who helped to teach eventually quit rather than run the nightly gauntlet of mud and stones. The night school eventually had to arrange to have a constable on duty outside while sessions went on within.[58] In 1875 a boys' club was started by Stanley on Saturday nights, which provided such amenities as boxing, fencing, bagatelle, draughts (checkers) and dominoes. At 1d. admission, it attracted an average of 140 boys per week.[59] In the meantime, however, the school and club had twice moved from their original location in the poorest street of the quarter – first to a better schoolroom nearby and then to a better neighbourhood altogether. In the process, wrote Stanley, "the worthless boys have ceased to come to our school. We have a regular attendance and perfect order and quiet ... But the natural consequences of the improved discipline is to attract only the better class of working boys. To meet the rest a school must begin again in the worst neighbourhood ..."[60]

It is not clear here what the author thought she had accomplished. The tone of the work seems to claim that a proportion of youths were rescued from their life of indiscipline and lawlessness and that a similarly labourious and expensive procedure would rescue a few more. If this was in fact the case, it should have been enough to call into question the efficacy of such efforts. What is more likely, however, and is indicated by the successive moves, is that, finding the poorer area's youths unamenable to control, she had located an area where boys from the more respectable part of the working class could be attracted and where discipline could be enforced. These were, of course, precisely those boys in least need of this type of social work. It may well have been this club, or a similar one, that drew the comment in 1884, "But, as is always the case, the success of the club has attracted a higher class of boys than those who first joined it, and for whom it was originally intended; the club house has been moved out of the district into a more respectable street, and street arabs ... would not now be admitted to it."[61] The more perceptive club workers soon realized that organizational and disciplinary success often entailed the defeat of their primary objective.

This proved to be the perpetual dilemma of the boys' club movement. A club that enforced rules too strictly – in other words, attempted to fulfil its function of social control – either became starved of boys or else attracted only the more fastidious adolescents of the area. If the latter, the members would object strenuously to the inclusion of the "rougher element" in its activities.[62] But a club with relaxed rules could hardly be said to satisfy the perceived need for control and discipline. In short, "the tragedy of the Club movement lies in the fact that in so far as it fails to provide amusement it will not attract boys; while in so far as it provides amusement, it is not assisting, except incidentally, in the moral and mental unfoldment of the boy."[63]

In the main, after the early years, boys' club managers opted – or were forced to opt – for the second alternative of amusement and tolerant rules, and the movement rapidly spread from London throughout the urban areas of the country. Relying largely on local and individual initiative, the clubs presented a wide range of characteristics; [o]ne is military, another is educational, a third athletic and gymnastic, a fourth social, with a strong religious basis."[64] Of the thirty-one boys' clubs affiliated to the London Federation in 1889, eighteen were parish clubs, eight were attached to public school or university missions, three were educational, and two were independent.[65] By the turn of the century, this number had grown to fifty, few with more than two hundred members. In the north, especially in Manchester, the taste was for considerably larger clubs of up to two thousand boys, such as the Adelphi and the Hulme boys' clubs.[66] These provided a wide range of classes, games, and activities, usually in a nondenominational setting. Specifically targeted for working youths, the clubs attracted members by providing amenities that reflected the boys' own interests. Thus, draughts, dominoes, and billiards made their appearance in order to counter the popularity of gambling. The clubs catered to the boys' love of football and, in general, emphasized entertainment rather than educational or moral development, these being seen as by-products. Amateur theatricals competed with the music halls, while dances for the older boys, properly chaperoned, vied with the dangerous dancing saloons.[67] By keeping the boys off the street and, through sports and activities, instilling in them a team and club spirit, the boys' clubs hoped to fulfil a double function: to keep youths out of trouble and to mould them in a purposeful way into useful members of society. These grand aims often boiled down to a simple strategy – "[o]bligatory attendance at Bible class ... administered medicinally, with cricket and football to take the taste away."[68] Yet the boys' club managers sincerely believed that the influence of wholesome surroundings and activities would have a real effect on the attitudes of members. "It is a fine thing, reflects the boy, to swagger at a street corner in a pearl-buttoned waistcoat, and name the odds on each horse in the St. Leger with indifference, but it is a finer thing still to pace up the street in shorts and striped jersey at the head of a panting line."[69] That a few boys might want to do both, and would see no ethical contradiction between them, does not seem to have occurred to these men.

The boys' clubs tried to solve the problem of retaining the "rough" youths by developing a tolerance and indulgence toward bad behaviour and by the tactic of co-opting boys onto the management of the club. Tolerance could not have been easy; the boys were often unruly, especially when they "broke the windows, blew down the gas pipes, and pommelled and pelted their officers in the darkness."[70] The new premises and equipment of many late Victorian clubs often simply gave the boys "a further scope for indulging in their favourite pastime of destruction of property."[71] Bagatelle boards were used "for the breaking of heads," cues were "employed for the perforation of lath and plaster walls instead of for the propulsion of the ivory balls," and draughts, dominoes, boards, and boxes were thrown by the youths at club workers and at each other.[72] When not tormenting the officers, boys could be entirely oblivious and indifferent to them, as reported one manager when his club was visited by the local toughs. "They seemed ... quite at their ease, took no notice of my existence, ignored the original members of the club, and retired upstairs to spend the evening, in what was evidently their wonted pastime, viz. boxing ... they certainly could box. I thought that I should be rather in a fix if I had to chuck any of them out."[73] This manager, seeing diamonds in the rough, let them carry on. Soon the original members of the club left, "remarking that the new-comers were too rough for them." Henceforth, with the club full, the manager "had to be very discriminating in choosing boys, and keeping the club *down* to a proper standard. If once a club likes this gets into a sort of respectable groove, it is done for." (my italics)[74]

The tactic that this and other club managers used to limit material damage was to be as self-effacing as possible – to allow the boys themselves to regulate discipline, to have some say in the choice of amenities offered, and to involve themselves in the management of the club.[75] The formula for the success of a boys' club was thus a prescribed one, and any large deviation from it spelled disaster. A club that became too respectable quickly lost either its clientele or, if appealing only to the more respectable working-class boy, its *raison d'être*. In reality, only a small minority of boys joined to begin with, this proportion estimated at 5 per cent in London in 1904 and 12 per cent in Birmingham in 1913.[76] Since fees were very low (usually one or two pennies per week) and well within the means of most working boys, one can speculate either that even the limited discipline of the clubs was repugnant to the majority or that the amenities were insufficiently attractive. If the latter was the case, this was in spite of the fact that the London clubs, for example, "jostle one another in their anxiety to provide attractions for the boys of their neighbourhood, and it is the frequent complaint of the local clergy that their boys are continually straying from the fold, tempted by some newer, or more interesting, or more costly form of amusement ... it makes the East-end boy luxurious, fanciful, and a trifle blasé, a good deal spoilt, and very independent: censure him and he will leave you and join the club around the corner."[77] In 1907–8, excluding the costs of camping, receipts from boys in eighty-nine clubs in England and Scotland totalled £3,830, while actual outlay amounted to £18,574.[78] A host of churches, public schools, and private benefactors subsidized nearly 80 per cent of the expenditure of the boys' clubs in order to provide sufficient facilities to attract the youths of the street. In addition, attendance was usually voluntary on any given night, and although continuation classes were often offered, these were recognized impediments and rarely compulsory. Still, most youths were never drawn in.

The failure to capture the "roughest" and lowest segment of the working boys (that is, 90 to 95 per cent!) was recognized and regretted but never remedied; even in 1930, the National Association of Boys' Clubs reported that "for half the boys in our land the street gang is the one possible club, and the street corner the one possible continuation school."[79] This doleful estimate was probably itself an understatement; in 1935 only 9.4 per cent of London youths aged ten to twenty belonged to either the Boys' Brigade, the Church Lads' Brigade, the Boy Scouts or a boys' club.[80] The valiant and, in many ways sensible, attempts of the boys' club managers to attract, hold, and subtly influence working youth had little effect among the great majority of this group, because the great majority simply refused to join.

Most boys, surveying the games, amusements, and benefits offered, continued to pass them by. Those who did join the various youth organizations seem to have done so for the same reasons they went to Sunday school – for the sake of access to recreational resources. The oral material shows very little evidence that boys joined for other than these pragmatic reasons. A Liverpool resident mentions his church club only in the context of the snooker available there; a Bolton apprentice went to his local youth club for the football, cricket, and running.[81] A Manchester respondent says of the Church Lads' Brigade, "They used to have a clubroom of their own, they used to have football team and things of that. They used to go to camp … [which] was the first time I really stayed at the seaside, and it was at Scarborough."[82] Another boy tried to join the Church Lads' Brigade. "We were supposed to be a rough lot and we didn't get in … we weren't allowed to join the Lads' Brigade." Instead he joined a youth club, gaining access to billiard tables, bowls, and dominoes.[83] The reasons for church or club attendance are most explicitly stated by a Salford respondent. "I just belonged to the football club and that was … why I went to the church – … so I could play football." This youth stayed in Sunday school until the unusually late age of eighteen in order to play, but when the minister insisted that attendance at the Empress music hall was incompatible with membership in his classes, the youth gave up the game.[84]

Nor was it only those clubs sponsored by the middle class or by religious bodies that were used in these ways by youths, and in which the ideological or programmatic content was regarded as secondary by the clientele. A Preston respondent was an early member of both the Independent Labour Party (ILP) and the Clarion movement. Why did he join? "It was more a matter of company, and the ILP had a room in the middle of Preston and it had a decent floor, and they used to run dancing classes on a Saturday afternoon, and it got quite a reputation as a place to go learn dancing. I spent quite a number of years there, very enjoyable for the company. I joined the Clarion Cycle Club, which, of course, was based on the *Clarion* paper. The Clarion never got credit for what it did. The Clarion organized clubs, rambling clubs, cycling clubs, the Clarion Vocal Union, years in advance of other movements ... So the ILP provided me with a number of very pleasant years."[85] This man became a sincere and lifelong socialist, but his socialism was the non-doctrinaire, pragmatic version common among the English working class, one that emphasized bread and butter issues and the simple creed of helping people overcome real problems, making their lives happier, more fulfilling, and more secure. In this context, the left-wing leisure associations were no different from their bourgeois counterparts – each had to adapt itself to what the workers themselves considered important. Indeed, *Clarion* followed the typical leisure movement trajectory. "During the mid-1890s *Clarion* moved to London, dropped the important 'Notes from the Front' feature where branch life had been covered, and gradually became what it is now remembered as – a recreational society."[86]

The boys' clubs, then, like the Sunday schools before them, seem to have reacted to their perpetual dilemma by forgoing much of the overt proselytizing and character-forming that were their primary motives. They tended to fall back on a simpler, negative goal, wherein if one "provided [boys] with footballs and made them kick footballs, they would not be so inclined to kick policemen in the street."[87] So boys were provided with footballs, billiard tables, and table tennis; educational and religious work was toned down or omitted altogether; and hopes were placed in the "atmosphere" and "spirit" of the club, fostered by the resident gentry of the club workers, to produce the desired results. Much good faith, effort, and money were placed in these tactics, yet one must question the final results of a group of institutions that often enough became little more than providers of recreational services.

Still more must one examine the applicability of terms such as social control or cultural hegemony to the results, rather than the aims, of these movements as a whole. There may not be much doubt that the ulterior motives of the founders and leaders were consistent with theories of social control; the briefest survey of the connections of the Boy Scout or Church Lads' Brigade executives would be enough to bring the disinterestedness of these men into question. It is, however, another thing to go beyond these aims in an attempt to gauge their effects on the boys themselves. Given the bare membership rolls of these organizations, it is surely an exaggeration to state, as one scholar has, that "British youth in the Edwardian era found its energies harnessed only to causes approved of by adult leadership,"[88] or that, as another puts it, "the work of organised youth was fully realised" in the Unionist successes of the pre-war years and in the mass enlistments of 1914–15.[89] This harnessing was only true of the middle and lower middle class boys who flocked to join Baden-Powell's Scouts, and, even in this case, a simple cause and effect relationship between participation and indoctrination is difficult to prove. In any case, the vast majority of working-class youths completely escaped adult control in their leisure time, and those in the boys' clubs who did not escape essentially forced adults to organize leisure on the boys' own terms. An overly demanding Boys' Brigade offficer, or a boys' club manager who ran too tight a ship, would quickly be faced with mass desertion. Opposition to social control, then, can take many forms; the boys who pelted Brigade bands exhibited one form, the majority of boys who simply stayed away presented another. Boys' club members who lobbied successfully for a relaxation in rules and in compulsory classes, and for a greater emphasis on amusement, presented perhaps the subtlest form of all.

The Boy Scouts and Boys' Brigade generally limited themselves to younger and, on the whole, wealthier boys, and an estimate of their influence on working and earning teenagers is too easily exaggerated when drawn from *Punch* cartoons, headquarters papers, and contemporary articles, especially when these are tinged with the xenophobia of the immediate pre-war or early war years. The boys drawn into these movements generally proved to be as manipulative as the leaders were with regard to aims and methods, and, underneath the rhetoric of social improvement and behavioural modification, one can see a gradual abandonment of overt indoctrination and gradual development of recreational rather than strictly ameliorative aims. In the boys' clubs especially, where the largest recruitment of working-class boys took place, the intergenerational dialectic seems to have produced a synthesis more nearly approaching the boys' concept of amusement and leisure than the organizers' one of control. In this struggle, the youth held nearly all the cards; with money in his pocket and comparative freedom from family restrictions, he had to be actively tempted into the club from a street life containing a multitude of other leisure options. Once in the club, there is evidence of a continued resentment of condescension and continued assertion of independence from the behavioural dictates of the officers. The attempt by the leaders of youth movements to recreate the "total" environment of the public school, and thus extend its value system to boys of the lower orders, was doomed to failure. Leisure consumerism rather than social control is thus perhaps a more useful concept with which to interpret the effects of the clubs and brigades.

If we go beyond the fascination with the Scouts and brigades as illustrations of the political, economic, and social concerns of the Edwardian élites, we can see, in fact, that the major cultural development of the period is not as much the imposition of an artificial popular patriotic culture, as it is the consolidation of a working-class culture that emphasized the value of its own customs, needs, and point of view. This process took place as much in the purposeful youth movements as in the commercially driven institutions such as the music hall. The culture of working youths exhibits similarities with that of their elders in the same period – defensive, impermeable, and self-contained, yet willing to take advantage of certain middle-class offerings if these were attractive and easy to procure. The working class, including its youthful component, had its own internal norms and its own cultural and ethical standards, and this cultural cohesion was being strengthened rather than weakened throughout this period. Such a reading might place the work of the organized youth movements in a more proper perspective as institutions that had a limited appeal and that were shaped and influenced by their clientele at least as much as the reverse. It would be from such a position, as well, that we could start to write a more authentic history of popular patriotism – one, for example, that might begin by replacing such a label as "Kitchener's Army," with its hegemonic implications, with the alternative and perhaps more accurate title of the time: the Pals' Battalions. The men who marched off to war in 1914 did not do so primarily for King and Country; they were not blind and pitiable victims of militaristic indoctrination; they were chums from the same club, the same neighbourhood, or the same team, who joined out of a sense of shared community and fellowship that they themselves had largely created.

Conclusion

Among the main aims of social history are those of recreating, as far as possible, the patterns of life of the past and of seeking a deeper understanding of the process of change by the exploration of the actions of ordinary people. In so doing, the part played by individually obscure people in the shaping of their world can be rescued from the anonymity to which it is consigned by more traditional history, while a fuller picture can be drawn of historical forces and their interactions. The present work has been impelled in large part by these objectives, with youth as its subject. Until recently, most historical work, even in social history, tended to concentrate on adult males and to ignore other groups – children, youth, women – that do not operate within the formal organizations most amenable to study and analysis. In addition, in a reversal of the psychological truism, historically significant experiences are generally thought to occur only in the years of adulthood; the key to major shifts in economic and social structures, in political values, and in cultural developments are thus most often sought by historians within the adult world itself. In the late Victorian and Edwardian period, however, it could be argued that change was most significantly felt by, and showed itself through, children and youths rather than adults. The creation of a universal educational system, the breakdown of apprenticeship and its widespread substitution by non-vocational teenage labour, the emergence of mass commercial entertainment, and the foundation of organized youth movements all impinged directly on youths, and all had major influences on the type of society and polity that was produced in the early twentieth century. The dynamic element of social change contained within the simple act of growing up should be recognized; in many cases, changes noted as occurring in the working class as a whole were first felt by successive generations of children and youth, who, passing into adulthood, carried with them new norms, new attitudes, and new ways of approaching problems. As such, the specific experiences and actions of youth are a legitimate subject for historical inquiry, which may yield information necessary for a full understanding of overall social, cultural, and political trends.

The experiences and the choices made by children and youths in the late Victorian and Edwardian period were, as a whole, helping to create a more homogeneous working class, less fragmented by occupational or regional differences and more conscious of itself as a distinct stratum of society. The factors that impelled this process were in part educational, in part work related, and in part effected through leisure, as they were filtered through the individual lives of millions working-class youths.

The educational system established after 1870 acted as an effective consolidator of the working class. Instead of an interlocking system of universal education from the elementary school to the university, by which large numbers of workers' children could rise into another class, the school system, in its clientele and curriculum, made class barriers all too plain and, hence, tended to dissolve the still existing differences within the lower strata. While token efforts were made to permit the very brightest of the elementary school products to advance, the educational system and its ethos generally helped to emphasize rather than to disguise the gulf between classes and thus probably lessened the barriers within the lowest. The 1902 education act, moreover, whatever its true intentions, was widely interpreted to be an attack upon a grassroots movement to provide challenging and appropriate secondary education to a wider section of the working class. In the end, however, neither the "élitist" nor the "democratic" side of the educational debate in these years held much practical significance for the majority of those it purportedly concerned. Most working-class children displayed a great indifference and cynicism toward elementary education, and their approach to vocational and continuing education stressed purely pragmatic and often rather limited benefits; this attitude probably offset and rendered futile the social propagandizing carried on within the classroom.

Changes within the workplace that particularly affected youths also pointed the way to a new and less stratified working class. The workforce was becoming much less rigid and differentiated, as industry moved in a direction that would result in less demand for the highly skilled artisan and a greater demand for a new type of adaptable semi-skilled worker. Many of the technological and organizational changes of these years allowed this substitution of the semi-skilled for the skilled to be accomplished. Such a development posed a direct threat to the craft unions, whose power was in many cases founded upon the limited availability of a necessary skill, controlled by a system of apprenticeship. A new type of industrial organization would be necessary if the working class were to be able to impose some degree of control on the labour market. The general and industrial unions that first appeared in the 1880s and that established a solid base of membership in the Edwardian period were, in part, an attempt to come to terms with this problem. Their emphasis on class solidarity and their political complexion pointed the way to a future in which the gulf between skilled and unskilled would be narrowed and would be bridged by a large contingent of semi-skilled workers. At the same time, the older craft unions were being forced to acknowledge and welcome into their ranks lower grades of workers and to recognize in many cases that their "skilled" members were no longer as sharply differentiated from others as they had been in the past. On a more individual level, the adolescent industrial careers of late Victorians and Edwardians show a new type of vocational training coming to the fore – one more open than that of the past, less restricted by formal apprenticeship, more haphazard and variegated in form, and much more reliant on individual initiative, as well as, for some, on community and state resources.

This buoyant and increasingly mobile adolescent market carried with it various corollaries and results. It placed the boy in a central position within the family economy, enabling him to gain considerable freedom from family restrictions; it allowed him to take advantage of a growing number of commercialized leisure pursuits, and it called into being a large movement of middle-class social reformers fearful of the consequences of these developments. These often contradictory and competing forces provide some of the main themes and tensions that shaped the lives of youth in this era.

It seems fairly clear from the evidence that, of these forces, those appealing to diversion were stronger and more fateful than those attempting to inculcate youths with habits of thrift, diligence, and obedience. The music hall, the cinema, and sports probably had a greater impact on forming the attitudes of working-class youths than did the boys' movements in all their forms, yet this impact was itself contradictory. Music hall art as a whole was an examination and celebration of the norms, foibles, and sense of community of its main clientele, producing a populist rhetoric and imagery that all could share; this celebration is reflected in the music hall songs, an examination of which reveals political and social conservatism mixed with a quite confident assertion of the worth of working-class values. Likewise, football, while playing up regional diffferences, was still in itself a celebration of local and class loyalties. When one considers the disappearance of older popular leisure forms during the period of industrialization, the appearance of new working-class leisure forms dedicated to working-class problems and concerns is all the more remarkable. The youths who made up such a large portion of the music hall gallery and football terrace were probably the group most affected by this renewed and reinvigorated sense of community and class solidarity. Parallel to this commercially influenced consolidation is the emergence of a recognizably national youth street culture. The conventions of the Monkey Parade, the infatuation with football, the custom of collecting, and so on, are as typical of the metropolis as they are of a Lancashire mill-town, while the transition from the fighting gangs to the more dandified Edwardian street lads can be chronicled contemporaneously in most of the towns and cities of England. Despite the continuing industrial and demographic differences among the various regions of urban England, it is apparent that by the early years of the twentieth century a certain similarity had come into the unsupervised leisure time and street life of working-class youths. This was not the result, however, of an imposed uniformity, but the spontaneous response to a similar set of conditions and pressures. The effects of universal education, mass circulation periodicals, touring music hall companies, and the cinema were combining with widespread economic changes to produce a street culture that, across the nation, shared common customs, common symbols, and common aspirations.

In contrast to these developments, the organized youth movements have received more attention from both contemporaries and historians. This is in its way understandable; the institution of the Boy Scouts, for instance, was a quite startling phenomenon, and its emergence and methods are useful points of entry for an examination of the political, social, and cultural concerns of the pre-war years. Yet the effects of this and other youth movements, including the boys' clubs, on working-class youth are overestimated. In the first place, working-class boys were attracted to these movements only in small numbers, and even this limited success was achieved only by constantly catering to the leisure desires rather than to the perceived behavioural or attitudinal needs of the youths. If any co-optation was taking place in such organizations, it was the reverse of that intended by the leaders, and the more successful an institution was in attracting working-class boys – such as the boys' clubs – the truer this was. The Boy Scouts and, to a lesser extent, the

Boys' Brigade, proved themselves to be generally unattractive to working-class boys, especially after the school-leaving age had been passed. The role of these clubs as agents of patriotism, obedience, and social passivity was at all times seriously hampered by their failure to attract those boys who were seen as the major problem to be combatted.

Furthermore, beyond the limited success of these attempts at cultural co-optation looms the emergence of class politics in the years immediately before and after World War I. This transition was a similar development to what, in another context, has been called "one of those facts of history so big that it is easily overlooked, or assumed without question; and yet indicates a major shift in the inarticulate, 'sub-political' attitudes of the masses."[1] Whatever the strength of the continuing differences in occupational, wage, status, or regional characteristics of the workers, whatever the hidden agendas of educational and leisure agencies in propagating hegemonic values, it is worth remembering that it was precisely this generation, born between the 1880s and the 1900s, that led the decisive shift toward Labour politics, itself less a theoretical socialist construct than a populist movement built upon an assumed solidarity of the nationwide community of workers with common social problems and interests. Thus, through a study of the experiences of youths in this period, we may begin to get some idea, not only of the deeper and longer-term causes of the growth of Labour loyalties, but also a better idea of the chronology of this phenomenon – a chronology masked to a great extent by World War I and the massive electoral changes of 1918 and 1928.

Political socialization begins at a young age and usually most strongly in the home, yet the factors investigated in this study that were operating during the childhood and youth of late Victorians and Edwardians would turn them away from the political loyalties of their parents. The empirical evidence for a major haemorrhaging of support for the traditional parties before World War I has existed for some time and has tended to show that the major factor has been a change not in individual but in generational loyalties.[2] Labour grew, in other words, not only as the unions grew, but as labourites grew up. Indeed, this feeling of social and cultural solidarity, rather than ideological conviction or programmatic intent, is probably the major reason for Labour's successes among ordinary working-class voters in the 1920s. A London clicker, who went to work in a suit and tie and, like his late Victorian peers, thought himself a cut above the unskilled in their corduroys and handkerchiefs, still voted Labour all his life and was illustrating, when a choice was to be made, where he felt that his true interests and loyalties lay – "Well, I should think the conditions we lived in, you know, poor conditions. And we thought naturally that Labour would do more for us."[3] A Vickers engineer from Barrow echoes this belief in an almost reflexive connection between social experience and political choice. "I think they feel the same as they do today that the people who represent them as Labour are more concerned, having come from their way of life, than a person who's never lived that life – rightly or wrongly. I'm not saying that's correct but that's the view. He's one of us and knows our circumstances and knows what we're up against, and there is a better chance of him looking after our interest than a man who hasn't had to work for his living."[4] The oral history sample taken from the Essex archive shows that these were feelings not confined to a few; of the fifty-one respondents whose political views are known, twenty-nine professed different beliefs from their fathers, and twenty-one of these shifts were toward Labour.[5] Increasingly similar educational levels and leisure pursuits, coupled with increasingly similar problems in finding a secure place in the labour market, moved these youths toward a more inclusive and less hierarchical identification of their class and its particular needs. Labour, in its very name and non-doctrinaire approach, was the political expression, and hence the beneficiary, of a wider change in social, cultural, and industrial attitudes.

A full history of the social developments of these years, then, must take into account the experiences of children and of youths, and the responses of individuals of these groups to the pressures and problems confronting them. Social history often has been the history of social problems perceived by élites and of the institutions and strategies developed to deal with these. Not only must the response of those to be "educated," "helped," or "controlled" be considered, but so also must the institutions and strategies developed by the working class itself to provide security, amusement, and fellowship as intrinsically good things. The outcome of these struggles and processes for the group under discussion was a heightened and more cohesive feeling of class culture and class identity. This would prove to be a major source of working-class solidarity in its political and economic offensive after World War I.

Appendix A

ORAL HISTORY MATERIAL

In choosing to use oral history material as one of the major sources for this study, I was aware of certain methodological problems that might arise. The main one was that, working from Canada in the mid-1980s, it would be impossible to organize the collection of my own sample and to use an interview schedule of my own devising. Neither the funding nor, of course, the Victorians and Edwardians were available. Because of this, I would be relying on interview transcripts produced by other scholars, who had collected this evidence up to fifteen years beforehand, according to their own selection procedures and with their own particular interests in mind. Each of the two archives used was, in fact, constructed upon rather different principles, and it is worthwhile discussing these in some detail, as well as giving the reader an idea how the present study used them.

In building the University of Essex Archive, Paul Thompson attempted to construct a true "quota sample" of 444 people proportionally distributed according to the categories of the 1911 census with regard to sex, region, class, and locale. (When some samples did not fit these categories Thompson expanded the sample, holding twenty to thirty further interviews.) The classifications used at Essex are listed as follows:

Family and
Respondent: C – middle- and working-class borderline (foreman, small shopkeeper, clerical worker, and so on)
              D – skilled worker
              E – semi-skilled worker
              F – unskilled or casual worker
              G – unemployed (usually but not always a schoolchild)

Region: A – Greater London
              B – Bedford, Hertford, Buckingham, Surrey, Kent, Sussex
              C – Essex, Suffolk, Norfolk, Cambridge, Lincoln
              D – Cornwall, Devon, Dorset, Somerset
              E – Shropshire, Hereford, Worcester, Gloucester, Oxford, Berkshire
              F – Derby, Nottingham, Stafford, Leicester, Warwick, Northampton
              G – Lancashire, Cheshire
              H – Yorkshire
              I – Northumberland, Durham, Cumberland, Westmoreland
              J – Glamorgan, Monmouth
Locale: A – Conurbation
              U – Urban
              R – Rural

My attempt to collect a sample that reflected a cross section of Edwardian society was largely achieved; nonetheless, for my own purposes, certain problems arose. Each respondent was classified according to his or her occupation in 1911; if the respondent was still a schoolchild, I used the main breadwinner's social grouping as the first determinant of the respondent's position. This sometimes led to my listing the family as Class C (middle/working class borderline) when in fact the family was more accurately Class D (skilled worker) through most of the respondent's childhood. Or, if a young teenager was working in 1911 as a van boy, the classification would be F (unskilled worker), although the family might be in a considerably higher class, while the youth himself might well end up as a skilled worker. In addition, information as to the respondents' experiences and occupation after 1918 was not solicited, so that in many cases it is difficult to determine the adult respondent's eventual occupational status. Because of these potential problems, I decided that the family's (usually the father's) occupational classification would be the one used to construct my own sample, with some modifications. I listed colliers as semi-skilled rather than skilled, largely on the basis of the regularity and size of their income and on the belief that they did not fit in very well with the artisanal lifestyle of many of the other skilled trades. I also treated some Class C families as Class D, if it was clear that the main breadwinner was a skilled worker who had become a foreman.

In using the Essex archive, I attempted to construct a quota sample from the larger sample. Of Thompson's expanded sample, 126 fit into my subject area – working-class males in urbanized England and Wales. Of these, I chose half, according to the ratios found in the full sample regarding region, community, and class. A perfect fit was not possible, however, since, for example, some regions had working-class females but not males, or had males but of the wrong class. The final sample chosen was as follows:

Interview No.	Family	Respondent	Region	Locale
8	F	E	A	C
12	D	G	C	U
14	F	G	C	U
24	D	C	F	U
25	C/D	E	F	U
27	D	D	F	U
31	D	D	F	U
32	D	G	G	U
34	F	D	E	U
43	D	G	G	C
47	C/D	G	G	C
48	E	D	B	U
52	D	F	G	C
54	D	E	G	U
55	E	D	G	U
58	F	D	A	C
74	C/D	E	G	C
86	E	G	G	C
88	D	F	G	C
96	E	E	A	C
99	F	G	G	C
102	E	F	G	C
103	D	F	G	C
104	E	E	G	U
106	E/D	D	G	C
118	C/D	E	G	U
121	E	G	G	C
122	D	D	G	U
124	F	E/F	A	C
131	G	D	G	U
134	D	G	G	U
140	F	G	G	U
146	D	G	H	U
150	E	E	H	U
170	D	E	H	U
176	D	G	H	U
177	F	D	E	U
190	D	E	F	U

Interview No.	Family	Respondent	Region	Locale
208	F	E	A/B	C/U
214	E	G	A	C
222	E	G	E	U
236	F	G	A	C
237	D	E	F	U
240	E	G	A	C
241	E	E	F	U
246	E	E	I	U
252	D	D	F	U
266	D	D	I	U
296	E	D	A	C
302	F	G	A	C
314	D	E	I	U
334	E	G	A	C
341	E	G	H	U
356	D	E	J	U
368	F	G	A	C
373	E	G	D	U
380	D	D	J	U/R
383	E	E	J	U
416	E	G	B	U
417	E	G	A	C
453	D	G	J	U
457	D	G	E	U/R

A comparison of my sample with the full Essex sample of urbanized working class males gives the following percentages:

	Essex Sample (percentage)	My Sample (percentage)
Class		
D	43.6	44.2
E	39.6	34.4
F	16.6	19.7
Region		
A	23.0	19.4
B	7.4	4.8
C	9.8	3.2
D	4.1	1.6
E	4.1	6.5
F	16.4	12.9

	Essex Sample (percentage)	My Sample (percentage)
Region		
G	22.2	32.2
H	9.1	8.1
I	6.1	4.8
J	5.7	6.5
Locale		
C	43.6	37.7
U	56.3	62.3

In building up the Centre for North-West Regional Studies Oral History Archive, Elizabeth Roberts took a more eclectic approach to classification, narrowing the geographic range and widening the chronological span. Dr Roberts defined the working class in broader terms, including small shopkeepers and clerical workers who lived in working-class neighbourhoods or who came from working-class backgrounds. Her archive concentrates on people living in Barrow, Lancaster, and Preston in the years up to World War II and is heavily accented on women, the family, and daily life within the home. Because of the nature of the archive, when choosing the transcripts to study I did not attempt to create a sample, but simply read all the pertinent transcripts derived from males, leaving aside those respondents who were born after 1903; those who were clearly not working class or who did not live in working-class neighbourhoods; those who lived in rural areas before the World War I and who moved into one of the three cities afterward; and, in one or two cases, those who were uncommunicative. This gave me a total of thirty-four transcripts out of a total male count of seventy-five.

The interviews in both archives were recorded using similar procedures. An interview schedule was prepared listing a long series of questions to be asked, sometimes over two or more sessions. Answers to the full schedule were usually provided although digressions were common. In most cases, the information was elicited as much by judicious direction or invitations by the interviewer to expand on a point as it was by rigid adherence to the set schedule. One of the major methodological criticisms of oral history – that it directs and leads the respondent according to the interests of the interviewer – was thus largely negated by allowing the respondent a wide latitude in answering questions and expanding on points he or she thought important. Anyone who uses either of these archives soon realizes that the material has not been unduly weighted by the preoccupations or agenda of the researchers.

My method of using the archives was to read the chosen transcripts in their entirety, although the Essex archive, for example, also provides scholars with a series of subject-linked excerpts. Although I began reading these excerpts, I soon realized that it was necessary to form a full impression of the circumstances and situation of the individual respondent in order to place the experiences themselves in context. When going through the transcripts, I had my own schedule of subjects and areas of experience, which I took particular note of as I read. These included:

- Father's occupation – regularity of employment; the father at home; respondent's view of
- Mother's occupation – daily tasks; respondent's view of
- Type of home and neighbourhood
- Housework – by children and how this changed
- Bedtime – in childhood and adolescence
- Food – how distributed; in childhood and in adolescence; table manners; gardening, poaching, or other sources of food
- Family discipline – how enforced; what was permitted or banned; in childhood and adolescence; who administered punishment
- Leisure and free time – reading, in home and on street; sports, organized and impromptu; membership in youth organizations; view of Sabbath; church attendance in childhood and youth; family's view of religion; relations with females; theatre, music hall, and cinema attendance; socializing in neighbourhood and street leisure activities
- Politics – views on; how deeply held; reasons for; views about social structure
- School – how long; why left behind; discipline at school; views on education; continuation education, if applicable
- Work – preadolescent work; job history in adolescence and early manhood – wages, hours, experiences, how jobs were found, why they were left; apprenticeship; how wages were spent; pocket money; changes in relations with parents and siblings; views on labour force, e.g., skilled and unskilled.

As anyone who has used this type of material can attest, however, rarely is equally full information given by all respondents to all questions, a situation that in itself attests to the latitude given to and discretion possessed by the respondents. Facts, events, and experiences that struck a chord with one respondent may be passed over in silence or be merely the subject of a simple comment by another. Given this, it was difficult to employ the archives as a quantitative data base, using the full list of respondents to measure norms and deviations by category on such things as nourishment, wages, pocket money, and educational levels. Such statistics are better found in, or derived from, the reports and censuses of various official or voluntary bodies, which, in addition, are based a much larger group. Beyond this, I was primarily interested in the reasons why people acted the way they did when confronted with various options, and these reasons could be investigated only when respondents chose to talk about them at some length. For this reason, the conclusions I have drawn about attitudes and behaviour are often based on a few examples rather than on the full list of respondents. Such conclusions are, nonetheless, based on the answers of all the respondents who felt that subject was important or worth commenting on at length, and reflect, as far as can be judged, either the general consensus or the major differences of the group on that subject. An example might be the reasons given for leaving school, where a number of problems kept appearing: finances, failure to see any long-term benefit from staying on, desire to escape a rigid regime, and so on. Although not all respondents expanded on these reasons, simply noting that they left school as early as possible, it is safe to assume that these considerations applied to them as well.

Such an approach is not, of course, the only one. An alternative method would be to find a series of "representative" respondents, according to such factors as region, social position, and locale. This was the method adopted by Paul Thompson himself in central sections of *The Edwardians,* where it was used most effectively. A number of considerations prompted me to take a different approach. This method relies at base on a small number of talkative, expressive respondents, rather than on a larger number of respondents who are expressive about different things. Further, although it allows the drawing out of differences among the respondents, these differences are established and shaped to a large extent by the original selection; for example, differences in nourishment between a skilled worker with four children and an unskilled worker with four children might come out if occupational status was an overt category, but the similarities in nourishment between a skilled worker with four children and an unskilled worker with one child would not, unless family size was also used as a criterion for selection. The desire to bring out the full diversity of English working-class life, in other words, might well end in overemphasizing that diversity at the expense of common experiences, structures, and experiences across the spectrum. Attempts to correct this, by including a full range of "representative" respondents with a full range of selection criteria, would soon become excessively unwieldly. With these problems in mind, I decided that the best method to proceed would be to get a sense of both differences and commonalities among the group investigated and to document these with testimony from the respondents. This has been admittedly a subjective process to some degree, yet it is based on a full reading of a large number of transcripts, where common patterns or major differences have become apparent as a result of the slow accretion of evidence. As such I believe it is a valid and worthwhile approach, and no different in aim and method from that of scholars working with more traditional source material. Certainly many of the conclusions drawn about attitudes and reasons for behaviour would have been very different had the oral testimony not been used and had I relied exclusively upon the writings of adult, usually middle-class, observers.

Appendix B

ORAL HISTORY RESPONDENTS

Oral History Archive on Family, Work and Community Life Before 1918, Department of Sociology, University of Essex. All respondents are male. TI refers to Thompson Interview. The number of siblings noted includes the respondent and is intended as only a rough indication of family size since respondents were often unclear about the number of children (understandable given the high infant mortality rate at the time). The religious affiliations of the family are noted where obtainable. If they were different for different family members, or if they changed, more than one is given: CE = Church of England; NC = Nonconformist (unaligned to a particular sect); RC = Roman Catholic.

TI   #8: Rook: b. 1887 London NW. Father: navy (Class F). Respondent: butcher's assistant (Class E). 9 siblings (6th). CE/NC.

TI   #12: b. 1903 Halstead, Essex. Father: ironmoulder (Class D). Respondent: schoolboy. 8 siblings. NC (agnostic?).

TI   #14: b. 1899 Chelmsford. Father: silk factory labourer (Class F). Respondent: schoolboy. 2 siblings. NC.

TI   #24: b. 1882 Normacott, then Stoke. Father: ovenfireman and dipper in potteries, (Class D), d. 1893. Respondent: clerk (Class C). 4 siblings (4th). Primitive Methodist.

TI   #25: b. 1896 Stoke. Father: stonemason/foreman (Class C). Respondent: warehouse labourer (Class E). 7 siblings. CE.

TI   #27: b. 1895 Wolstanton. Father: brickmaker (Class D) d. 1900; stepfather: collier (Class D). Respondent: collier (Class D). 8 siblings. NC.

TI   #31: b. 1893 Stoke. Father: carpenter (Class D). Respondent: carpenter (Class D). 8 siblings (1st). CE.

TI #32: b. 1898 Liverpool. Father: shipwright (Class D). Respondent: schoolboy. 2 siblings. CE/NC.

TI #34: b. 1879 Oxford. Father: builder's labourer (Class F). Respondent: printer (Class D). 8 siblings. CE.

TI #43: b. 1901 Liverpool. Father: bootmaker (Class D) d. 1908? Respondent: schoolboy. 4 siblings (3rd). RC/CE.

TI #47: b. 1902 Salford. Father: railway goods checker (Class C). Respondent: schoolboy. 5 siblings. RC.

TI #48: b. 1894 Guildford, Surrey. Father: railway toolman (Class E). Respondent: apprentice mechanic (Class D). 3 siblings (3rd). CE.

TI #52: b. 1897 Manchester. Father: iron planer (Class D). Respondent: errand boy (Class F). 4 siblings (1st). NC.

TI #54: b. 1895 Bolton. Father: iron: moulder (Class D). Respondent: shop assistant (Class E). 6 siblings. CE.

TI #55: b. 1882 Salford. Father: iron fettler (Class E). Respondent: leather craftsman (Class D). 4 siblings. RC.

TI #58: b. 1889 London. Father: soldier (Class F), d. 1893? Mother: charwoman (Class F). Respondent: merchant AB seaman (Class D). 9 siblings. NC.

TI #74: b. 1898 Liverpool. Father: dock crane driver and sometime clerk (Class D/C). Respondent: shop assistant (Class E). 8 siblings (2nd). RC.

TI #86: b. 1900 Liverpool. Father: carter (Class E). Respondent: schoolboy. 5 siblings (1st). NC.

TI #88: b. 1895 Liverpool. Father: slaughterer (Class D), d. ca 1905; stepfather: engineer shipbuilder (Class D). Respondent: biscuit factory worker (Class E). 5 siblings (2nd). RC.

TI #96: b. 1881 Westminster, London. Father: postman (Class E). Respondent: postman (Class E). 5 siblings (1st). NC.

TI #99: b. 1902 Liverpool. Father: textile factory labourer (casual) (Class F). Respondent: schoolboy. 3 siblings (1st). CE/athiest.

TI #102: b. 1899 Manchester. Father: tram driver (irregular) (Class E). Respondent: paper-boy (Class F). 9 siblings. Agnostic.

TI #104: b. 1890 Bolton, then Westhoughton. Father: collier (Class E). Respondent: cough medicine mixer (Class E). 5 siblings (5th). CE.

TI #106: b. 1887 Bolton. Father: printer, then gas meter inspector (Class D/C). Respondent: fitter (Class D). 2 siblings (1st). CE.

TI #118: b. 1880 Liverpool. Father: dock cargo checker (Class C). Respondent: shop assistant (Class E). 8 siblings (4th). Methodist.

TI #121: b. 1903 Liverpool. Father: tram driver (Class E). Respondent: schoolboy. 5 siblings. CE.

TI #122: b. 1895 Manchester. Father: mule spinner (Class D). Respondent: mule spinner (Class D). 11 siblings (3rd). CE.

TI #124: b. 1879 London. Father: builder's labourer (Class F). Respondent: soapmaker (Class E). 8 siblings (5th). CE.

TI #131: b. 1881 Farnsworth. Father: mule spinner (Class D). Respondent: mule spinner (Class D). 4 siblings. NC.

TI #134: b. 1901 Bolton. Father: fitter and turner (Class D). Respondent: schoolboy. 6 siblings (6th). NC

TI #140: b. 1901 Salford. Father: labourer (Class F). Respondent: schoolboy. 5 siblings (6th). Methodist.

TI #146: b. 1899 Keighley. Father: stationary engineer (Class D). Respondent: schoolboy. 3 siblings (1st). NC.

TI #150: b. 1888 Barnsley, then Rotherham. Father: collier (Class E). Respondent: collier (Class D). 5 siblings (1st). CE.

TI #170: b. 1892 Keighley. Father: machine moulder (Class D). Respondent: shop assistant (Class E). 9 siblings (1st). Methodist.

TI #176: b. 1899 Keighley. Father: warp dresser (Class D). Respondent: schoolboy. 6 siblings (6th). Methodist.

TI #177: b. 1894 Reading. Father: soldier, then casual labourer (Class F). Respondent: apprentice blacksmith (Class D). 9 siblings (5th). NC.

TI #190: b. 1894 Eastwood, Nottingham. Father: carpenter (Class D). Respondent: shop assistant (Class E). 7 siblings (4th). Baptist.

TI #208: b. 1892 Blackfriars, London. Father: docker (Class F). Respondent: mineral water case maker (Class E). 9 siblings (9th). CE.

TI #214: b. 1903 London WC. Father: coal carter (Class E). Respondent: schoolboy. 4 siblings (2nd). CE.

TI #222: b. 1904 New Basford, Notts, then Peterborough 1906, then Nottingham 1908. Father: hosiery finisher (Class E). Respondent: schoolboy. Only child. Baptist.

TI #236: b. 1899 London. Father: soldier, then labourer (Class F). Respondent: schoolboy. 3 siblings (1st). NC.

TI #237: b. 1884 Nottingham. Father: foreman lace dyer (Class C), d. 1897. Respondent: bleacher (Class E). 6 siblings (2nd). CE?

TI #240: b. 1902 Camden Town, then Hackney, London. Father: carpenter (Class D), died 1905; mother: shirt factory worker (Class E). Respondent: schoolboy. 5 siblings (5th). CE, then agnostic.

TI #241: b. 1896 Nottingham. Father: collier (Class E). Respondent: wheeltruer's mate (Class E). 4 siblings (1st). CE.

TI #246: b. 1894 Carlisle, then Darlington 1903. Father: gardener (Class E). Respondent: plater's labourer (Class E). 4 siblings. NC.

TI #252: b. 1893 Arnold, Nottingham. Father: frame work knitter (Class D). Respondent: caneworker (Class E). 4 siblings (3rd). Congregationalist.

TI #266: b. 1891 Stanhope, Durham. Father: railway guard (Class E). Respondent: shunter (Class E). 7 siblings (7th). Primitive Methodist.

TI #296: b. 1892 Tottenham, London. Father: cabinet maker (Class E/D). Respondent: wood machinist (Class D). 7 siblings (6th). NC.

TI #302: b. 1900 Canning Town, London. Father: gasworks labourer (Class F). Respondent: schoolboy. 8 siblings (3rd). CE.

TI #314: b. 1894 Darlington. Father: railway guard (Class E). Respondent: engine cleaner (Class E). 9 siblings (8th). CE.

TI #334: b. 1901 Canning Town, London. Father: crane driver on docks (Class E). Respondent: schoolboy. 5 siblings (1st). CE.

TI #341: b. 1899 Keighley. Father: coachman (Class E). Respondent: schoolboy. 4 siblings (3rd). CE.

TI #356: b. 1890 Port Talbot, S. Wales. Father: engine driver (Class D). Respondent: carder in flannel mill (Class E). 10 siblings (5th). Church of Wales.

TI #368: b. 1897 Wapping, London. Father: dockworker (Class F). Respondent: van boy (Class F). 7 siblings (7th). CE.

TI #373: b. 1901 Helston, then Redruth, Cornwall. Father: tin-miner (Class E), abandoned family 1904. Respondent: schoolboy. 6 siblings (6th). Primitive Methodist.

TI #380: b. 1890 Tongwynlais, near Cardiff. Father: tinworker (Class D). Respondent: tinworker (Class D). 6 siblings (2nd). Baptist.

TI #383: b. 1896 Rhondda. Father: pit winder (Class E). Respondent: collier (Class D). 9 siblings (3rd). CE.

TI #416: b. 1901 Rushden; moved to Luton 1903. Father: packer in flour mill (Class E). Respondent: schoolboy. 11 siblings (11th). NC.

TI #417: b. 1899 City of London. Father: master chimneysweep (Class C), died 1900. Mother: cook (Class E). Respondent: messenger (Class F). 6 siblings (6th). CE.

TI #453: b. 1899 Southampton; moved to Cardiff 1904. Father: sailor (Class D): mother: boarding house keeper (Class C). Respondent: delivery boy (Class F). 6 siblings (2nd). NC.

TI #457: b. 1902 Oxford. Father bootmaker (Class D). Respondent: schoolboy. 9 siblings (6th). CE.

Oral History Archive – Working Class in Barrow, Lancaster and Preston, Centre for North-West Regional Studies, University of Lancaster. All respondents are male. The last letter in each respondent's code gives the initial of one of the three towns studied (Barrow, Laancaster, and Preston). Religious affiliation is indicated by the same codes used for the University of Essex archive respondents (see p. 171).

B.1.B.: b. 1897 Barrow. Father: coachman, then, with wife, caretakers/cooks at a Masonic Lodge (£2 for both). Respondent: trainee baker. 7 siblings (7th). NC.

B.4.P.: b. 1896 Adlington, near Bolton. Father: bleachworker (22½–25 s.), died 1911; mother fowl dresser after marriage. Respondent: bleachworker. 10 siblings (2nd). CE.

B.8.P.: b. 1896 Preston. Father: mule spinner (£2.10 s.). Respondent: mule spinner. 6 siblings from 2 marriages (3rd). Evangelical CE until 1914–18, then athiest.

C.1.B.: b. 1900 Barrow. Father: joiner's labourer. Respondent: office boy, then engineering apprentice. 4 siblings (4th). CE.

C.1.P.: b. 1884 Preston. Father: goods porter on railway (18 s. in 1880s). Respondent: weaver. 4 siblings (1st). Methodist, later atheist.

C.3.L.: b. 1898 Lancaster. Father: soldier. Respondent: junior clerk. 6 siblings (6th). CE.

E.1.P.: b. 1895 Preston. Father and mother: pub keepers, died when respondent was very young. Brought up by mother's relatives. Respondent: textile worker, then after World War I, hotel porter. 4 siblings. RC (lapsed).

F.3.B.: b. 1881 Barrow. Father: iron moulder (£2). Respondent: boiler maker. 6 siblings (5th). NC.

G.2.L.: b. 1879 Galgate, near Lancaster. Father: clerk (but lost job ca 1890?). Respondent: joiner. 6 siblings (6th).

G.4.P.: b. 1895 Preston. Father: spinner, then fish and chip shop owner, then publican. Respondent: weaver, then tackler (overseer). 3 siblings (3rd). CE.

H.6.P.: b. 1896 Preston. Father: blacksmith. Respondent: weaver, then collier. 4 siblings. CE.

I.1.L.: b. 1902 Lancaster. Father: railway fireman, then boilerman in textile factory (£1). Respondent: cabinetmaker. 3 siblings.

L.1.P.: b. 1894 Preston. Father: stablehand, then injured; family on poor relief. Respondent: weaver. 11 siblings.

M.1.B.: b. 1892 Barrow. Father: railway labourer (20 s.) Respondent: Apprentice in Co-op. 10 siblings (5th). Methodist.

M.2.B.: b. 1898 Barrow. Father: sailor, died 1901; mother: housekeeper. Respondent: office boy, then apprentice fitter. 3 siblings.

M.2.P.: b. 1901 Preston. Father: cranedriver at docks (25 s.). Mother: weaver up to third child. Respondent: furniture worker, then cranedriver. 4 siblings (1st). CE. Author of an unpublished manuscript, "Edwardian Preston: Give or Take a Year or Two."

M.7.B.: b. 1897 Barrow. Father: fish and chip shop owner. Respondent: apprentice draughtsman. 10 siblings (4th).

M.8.B.: b. 1901 Barrow. Father: shopkeeper. Respondent: rent collector, then shopkeeper. 2 siblings.

P.1.B.: b. 1900 Barrow. Father: steel works labourer (18–24 s.). Respondent: office boy, then apprentice fitter/turner. 6 siblings (4th). CE.

P.1.L.: b. 1894 Lancaster. Father: clerk in textile mill (quite comfortable). Respondent: engineer in textile mill. 3 siblings (2nd). CE.

P.2.L.: b. 1899 Lancaster. Father: mill labourer (20 s.). Respondent: mill labourer. 9 siblings.

R.1.L.: b. 1894 Lancaster. Father: carter, d. ca 1900. Mother, washerwoman. Respondent: apprentice stonemason. 5 siblings (3rd).

R.3.L.: b. 1890 Freehold, then Lancaster. Father: cabinet maker/wood machinist (30–32 s.). Respondent: apprentice cabinetmaker. 3 siblings (1st).

S.1.B.: b. 1896 Barrow. Father: stonemason (36 s.), d. 1913. Respondent: apprentice joiner and pattern maker. 5 siblings. Methodist.

S.1.P.: b. 1900 Preston. Father: horseman (21 s.). Mother: charwoman. Respondent: weaver, then railway worker. 4 siblings (1st). Methodist.

S.3.L.: b. 1884 Lancaster. Father: carter (18 s.). Respondent: apprentice blacksmith, then blacksmith. 13 siblings (13th). RC/CE.

T.1.L.: b. 1888 Lancaster. Father: electric wirer in coachworks (25 s.). Respondent: apprentice painter in wagon works, then textile worker. 7 siblings. CE.

T.1.P.: b. 1897 Preston. Father: dock labourer (28 s.). Mother: kept sweet shop. Respondent: weaver, then loom sweeper; after World War I irregularly employed. 13 siblings (ca 7th). CE

T.3.P.: b. 1886 Preston. Father: farmworker (lived in town) (16–17 s.). Mother: took in washing. Respondent: apprentice, then journeyman shuttlemaker; lost arm 1908, then clothing club and insurance collector. 4 siblings. CE.

W.6.P.: b. 1887 Flintshire, then Preston. Father: itinerant preacher, d. 1891; stepfather: general labourer. Respondent: delivery boy, post office messenger, then nurseryman. Only child. Baptist.

Notes

INTRODUCTION

1 Thompson, *The Making of the English Working Class*, 8.
2 Morris, *Class and Class Consciousness*, 27–31.
3 Thompson, *The Making of the English Working Class*, 10.
4 An example is that of census material, which uses five-year cohorts. The years of adolescence overlap two of these.
5 See Thompson, *The Voice of the Past*, for a discussion of this source by one of its pioneers in England. A discussion of the principles and methods that governed my own use of this material may be found in Appendix A.
6 See for example Johnson, "Educational Policy and Social Control," 96–119. The essentials of the social control model also form the basis of a more recent work: Simon, "Systematisation and Segmentation in Education." For other areas, see Donajgrodzki, *Social Control*.
7 Humphries, *Hooligans or Rebels?*
8 Gray, *The Labour Aristocracy in Victorian Edinburgh*.
9 Wilkinson, "English Youth Movements."
10 Springhall, *Youth, Empire and Society*.
11 Stedman Jones, "Working Class Culture"; Meacham, *A Life Apart*.

CHAPTER ONE

1 Particularly important for this period and the interwar years – the era of the "classic" working class – are Roberts, *A Woman's Place*; Gittens, *Fair Sex*; and Ross, "'Fierce Questions and Taunts.'" Although concentrating largely on the position of women, these works all have much to say about family structure in general.
2 Booth, *Life and Labour, First Series: Poverty*, vol. 2, 21.

3 Whether these findings surprised Booth or not is still a matter of debate. Certainly a poverty rate of 30.7 per cent would not seem to afford grounds for the complacency on Booth's part that now is generally accepted. See the preface to the 1984 edition of Stedman Jones, *Outcast London*, xviii.

4 Rowntree, *Poverty*, 117. Primary poverty signified that earnings were insufficient for the maintenance of physical efficiency. Secondary poverty resulted when earnings were sufficient but income was absorbed in some other way.

5 Bowled and Burnett-Hurst, *Livelihood and Poverty*, 46–8.

6 Ibid., 48.

7 Bosanquet, *Rich and Poor*, 78.

8 Oral History Archive, University of Essex Thompson Interview (hereafter TI) #27, 27–8. A list of the respondents, with their biographical data, can be found in Appendix B.

9 TI #417, 5. Presumably one of the respondent's three elder sisters took over the household-tasks.

10 TI #237, 50–1.

11 TI #8, 4.

12 Mearns, *The Bitter Cry of Outcast London*, 55–6, 61. See also Wohl, "Sex and the Single Room," where it is argued that the fears of reformers may not have been exaggerated.

13 Sims, *How the Poor Live*, 15.

14 Files at the Public Record Office, Kew, HO45.10198.B31375: *Housing the Working Classes Up to 1903*, 7–10.

15 *Inter-Departmental Committee on Physical Deterioration: Report* 14.

16 Bowley and Burnett-Hurst, *Livelihood and Poverty*, 21.

17 Burnett, *A Social History of Housing*, 143.

18 Bray, "The Boy and the Family," 51–2.

19 Hobson, *Problems of Poverty*, 11.

20 *Inter-Departmental Committee on Physical Deterioration: Minutes*, 24–5.

21 *Inter-Departmental Committee on Physical Deterioration: Report*, 66.

22 Oddy, "Working-Class Diets in Late Nineteenth-Century Britain," 318–20.

23 Greenwood, *The Health and Physique of Schoolchildren*, 80–1.

24 Ibid., 60.

25 Oral History Archive, Centre for North-West Regional Studies, Interview B.8.P., 7. Hereafter referred to by the individual reference code. A list of the particulars may be found in Appendix B.

26 Turner, *About Myself*, 42.

27 McLaren, *Birth Control in Nineteenth-Century England*.

28 Ibid., 81.

29 Ibid., 219–20.

30 Ryder and Silver, *Modern English Society*, Table 2, 311; Table 6, 315.

31 Thompson, *The Edwardians*, 78.

32 Wright ("A Journeyman Engineer"), *Our New Masters*, 54; Roberts, *The Classic Slum*, 52.

33 McLaren, *Birth Control*, 81.

34 Roberts, *The Classic Slum*, 127.

35 Davin, "Child Labour," 633–52.

36 Roberts, *A Woman's Place*.

37 Gittens, *Fair Sex*, especially chap. 5. Gittens calls these joint role-relationships rather than segregated role-relationships.

38 Compare, for example, Roberts, *A Woman's Place*, 110–21. with Ross, "'Fierce Questions and Taunts,'" 575–602.

39 Ross, "'Fierce Questions and Taunts,'" 576.

40 C.I.P., 12.

41 M.1.B., 30.

42 TI #48, 22.

43 TI #341, 10, 30.

44 TI #214, 31, 19.

45 T.1.P., 12.

46 White, *Rothschild Buildings*, 149–52.

47 F.3.B., 14.

48 This was especially the case in London, where it proved to be fertile ground for marital strife. See Ross, "'Fierce Questions and Taunts,'" 584–5.

49 Roberts, *The Classic Slum*, 50.

50 TI #122, 3.

51 TI #102, 5.

52 TI #48, 12; TI #190, 16.

53 TI #214, 12–13.

54 TI #122, 11.

55 TI #31, 8; TI #32, 8.

56 TI #48, 7; TI #222, 6; M.1.B., 14; C.1.P., 8.

57 TI #170, 9; TI #314, 14; M.1.B., 13; F.3.B., 10; Roberts, *A Woman's Place*, 22–3; White, *Rothschild Buildings*, 156.

58 TI #8, 40; TI #31, 7; TI #32, 5; TI #241, 8; M.2.B., 129; Turner, *About Myself*, 38.

59 S.1.P., 5. Preston, as a textile town, was likely to exhibit lower gender-based differences than normal.

60 TI #27, 21.

61 Ibid, 48.

62 Ibid, 28.

63 TI #31, 49.

64 TI #8, 41; TI #177, 51; TI #246, 50.

65 TI #296, 18.
66 TI #8, 41; TI #296, 18.
67 TI #302, 57; Burnett, *Useful Toil*, 92.
68 TI #302, 8.
69 TI #31, 50. The boy's father marched him down to the post office and expropriated the £2 saved from his part-time job as a lather boy. Another example is that of TI #96, 21, whose money box was taken by his parents when a sister was born. Both of these respondents were eldest sons.
70 TI #34, 13.
71 TI #296, 26.
72 C.1.P., 54.
73 TI #99, 31.
74 Rowntree, *Poverty*, 83–4.
75 Paterson, *Across the Bridges*, 15.
76 Burnett, *Destiny Obscure*, 298.
77 TI #240, 21.
78 M.1.B., 4.
79 B.4.P., 5.
80 T.1.L., 9.
81 TI #150, 36.
82 TI #170, 5.
83 TI #121, 7.
84 TI #96, 20.
85 TI #176, 70.
86 B.8.P., 2.
87 C.1.P., 11.
88 B.4.P., 1.
89 C.1.P., 30.
90 T.1.L., 12.
91 Burnett, *Useful Toil*, 103.
92 TI #27, 14.
93 TI #31, 6.
94 M.2.P., 125–6.
95 TI #241, 15.
96 Bosanquet, *Rich and Poor*, 111.
97 TI #48, 7, 38.
98 TI #54, 52.
99 TI #236, 85.
100 TI #296, 70.
101 TI #252, 44, 53.
102 TI #356, 74.
103 TI #334, 80.

104 Meacham, *A Life Apart*, 161.

105 G.4.P., 1.

106 TI #240, 46.

107 Roberts, *The Classic Slum*, 52.

108 Burnett, *Destiny Obscure*, 99.

109 Willis, *A Book of London Yesterdays*, 170.

110 TI #8, 38. The one case examined where swearing was not frowned upon and punished is TI #208, whose parents were "two of the biggest drunkards in Blackfriars and Waterloo."

111 Roberts, *The Classic Slum*, 57.

112 TI #52, 14.

113 TI #356, 21. Both parents were regular church goers, as well as teetotalers.

114 TI #31, 11; TI #8, 8.

115 TI #47, 53.

116 Russell, *The Problem of Juvenile Crime*, 11.

117 TI #8, 59; TI #124, 42; TI #134, 70–1; TI #177, 58, 60; T.1.L., 16.

118 TI #122, 10.

119 TI #8, 38; TI #48, 42; TI #74, 65; TI #140, 48; TI #240, 6; TI #74, 65; TI #106, 6; TI #453, 26; P.1.B., 21.

120 TI #453, 16.

121 Russell, *The Problem of Juvenile Crime*, 10–11.

122 Paterson, *Across the Bridges*, 84.

123 Bray, "The Boy and the Family," 83.

124 Murphy, *New Horizons*, 24; TI #302, 99–100.

125 Paterson, *Across the Bridges*, 15.

126 TI #106, 11; M.1.B., 24.

127 Bray, *Boy Labour and Apprenticeship*, 124.

128 Freeman, *Boy Life and Labour*, 124.

129 Bray, *Boy Labour and Apprenticeship*, 101.

130 Findlay, *The Young Wage-Earner*, 40–1.

131 TI #31, 18; TI #43, 48; TI #74, 55; TI #99, 45; TI #214, 41–3; TI #246, 52. This fixed sum varied between 6d. and 3s., with 1s. the norm.

132 TI #106, 48; TI #122, 22; TI #140, 2; TI #241, 45.

133 TI #296, 66; B.1.B., 52; Rowntree, *Poverty*, 391; Russell, *Manchester Boys*, 16–17.

134 Booth, *Life and Labour*, Second Series: Industry, vol. 5, 319–20.

135 Rowntree, *Poverty*, 86.

136 TI #266, 77–82; TI #334, 91, 122–3; Russell, *Manchester Boys*, 17.

137 TI #314, 9; B.1.B. 52; TI #334, 83.

138 For example, the son of a London dockworker kept most of the 15s. 6d. he made as a rivet carrier during World War I. By the age of

eighteen he was earning over £3 per week as a fireman, but in the meantime his father had returned home from the war, gassed and unable to work. The young man now once more gave most of his wages to his parents so they "would not worry about how they were to get on" (TI #334, 96, 122–3).

139 TI #236, 85.
140 This can be seen particularly in the oral testimony collected in Barrow, Lancaster, and Preston by E.A.M. Roberts. See Appendices A and B.
141 Roberts, *The Classic Slum*, 45–6.
142 For example, one respondent (TI #134, 22–4) was an apprentice moulder in Bolton in a shop where both grandfathers worked and only given a house key at age twenty-one; another respondent (T.1.L., 83) was an apprentice engineer in the Lune Mills of Lancaster, where his father was a clerk; a strict bedtime of 9 P.M. was enforced even at eighteen years of age.
143 Ross, "'Fierce Questions and Taunts,'" 578.
144 T.1.L., 10.
145 Thompson, *The Edwardians*, 180.
146 B.8.P., 20, 3, 11. The father was a highly paid spinner.
147 TI #31, 18.
148 Thompson, *Edwardian Childhoods*, 98–100.
149 TI #222, 54, 56; P.1.B., 55.
150 Thompson, *The Edwardians*, 80, 71.

CHAPTER TWO

1 Williams, *The Long Revolution*, 141.
2 Simon, *Education and the Labour Movement*, 115.
3 See the important work by Gardner, *The Lost Elementary Schools of Victorian England*, which fills in this gap in our knowledge on education in the earlier period.
4 Rubinstein, *School Attendance in London*, 36.
5 Simon, *Education and the Labour Movement*, 219–20.
6 Searle, *The Quest for National Efficiency*, 208–9. For the political motivation of the Conservatives, see also Banks, *Parity and Prestige*, 26.
7 Searle, *The Quest for National Efficiency*, 213.
8 Banks, *Parity and Prestige*, 37–50. Banks argues persuasively that this change was welcome even to progressive educators, but neglects to discuss its effects on elementary schoolchildren passing into the new secondary system.
9 Reeder, "The Reconstruction of Secondary Education," 147.

10 On the response of the Trades Unions to this "reactionary" restructuring, see Griggs, *The Trades Union Congress*, 163–73.

11 Hurt, *Elementary Schooling and the Working Classes*, especially 52–74.

12 *Board Teacher*, 1 May 1886, 129.

13 Rubinstein, *School Attendance in London*, 24.

14 *Board Teacher*, 1 May 1886, 128.

15 Files at the Public Record Office, Kew, ED10/11: National Union of Teachers, "Report on School Attendance in England and Wales," 1891, 3.

16 Reeves, *Recollections*, 34–5.

17 Rubinstein, "Socialization and the London School Board," 248.

18 Reeves, *Recollections*, 16.

19 Files at the Public Record Office, Kew: ED10/10: Memorials from Various School Boards to the Board of Education, 1882–84.

20 Rubinstein, *School Attendance in London*, 47.

21 *Royal Commission on the Elementary Education Acts: Final Report*, 105. See also TI #373, 46; the respondent worked part time as an errand boy for a Mr. Wilton while still at school. "Then if there was an errand to go I had to run this errand before I go to school ... strange as it may seem, but Mr. Wilton was one of the governors over there ... if it should happen that I had an errand to go, and was late – well I never used to have anything said."

22 *Royal Commission on the Elementary Education Acts: Final Report* 104.

23 Rubinstein, *School Attendance in London*, 67–8.

24 Files at the Public Record Office, Kew, ED11/78: A.J. Mundella, "The Fight for the Child."

25 Files at the Public Record Office, Kew, ED14/20: Memorials from various London unions and parishes to the Board of Education, 1880–90. See Rubinstein, *School Attendance in London*, 30–1, for the 1891 "Piano" Election.

26 Ibid, 38. In 1883 in London, one-fifth of the total salary of an assistant teacher and one-third that of the head teacher depended on the size of the grant.

27 Holmes, *What Is and What Might Be*, 110.

28 Ibid., 110.

29 Ibid., 111.

30 *Board Teacher*, 1 May 1886, 119.

31 TI #58, 24.

32 TI #102, 56.

33 TI #236, 75.

34 Burnett, *Destiny Obscure*, 197.

35 Greenlee, "Imperial Studies and the Unity of the Empire," 321–35.

36 Fletcher and Kipling, *A School History of England*.

37 Murphy, *New Horizons*, 22.

38 TI #43, 31.

39 TI #32, 27.

40 Gorst, *The Children of the Nation*, 202.

41 Files at the Public Record Office, Kew, ED11/246: Internal minutes and decisions of the Department of Education on curriculum and book selection, 1908–12.

42 Thompson, *The Edwardians*, 73.

43 Humphries, *Hooligans or Rebels?*, especially 62–89.

44 TI #237, 37.

45 TI #8, 43; TI #140, 39; TI #58, 23–4; TI #214, 36–7.

46 M.2.P., "Edwardian Preston," (unpublished MS), 7; TI #190, 56.

47 P.1.B., 31.

48 Pritchett, *A Cab at the Door*, 103.

49 Holloway, *A London Childhood*, 66.

50 Burnett, *Destiny Obscure*, 194.

51 TI #208, 14.

52 *Board Teacher*, 1 November 1883, 45.

53 M.2.P., "Edwardian Preston," 8.

54 Bell, *Pioneering Days*, 17.

55 Ibid., 18.

56 TI #453, 84. See also Marson, "Children's Strikes in 1911," for an analysis of the wave of school strikes, which are a little known aspect of the "Edwardian Crisis."

57 Hodges, *My Adventures as a Labour Leader*, 6.

58 *Board Teacher*, 1 September 1883, 16; 1 May 1886, 119.

59 Ibid., 1 June 1895, 133–4. The elementary teachers, of course, were not totally disinterested in the higher grade controversy. The higher grade schools served many elementary teachers as an avenue for their own career advancement. If they were to be reorganized along liberal arts lines and connected to the post-secondary system they would require a different set of educational qualifications for their faculty than that possessed by most elementary school teachers.

60 Simon, *Education and the Labour Movement*, 114.

61 *Board Teacher*, 1 May 1886, 117.

62 TI #302, 48.

63 *A People's Autobiography of Hackney*, 25.

64 Pritchett, *A Cab at the Door*, 105–6.

65 TI #31, 5; McGeown, *Heat the Furnace*, 35.

66 *The Poor Law Officers Journal*, 25 February 1892, 5; TI #58, 23–5; TI #43, 15, 31.

67 TI #122, 5.

68 TI #27, 41.

69 TI #176, 70.

70 *Board Teacher*, 1 September 1895, 176.

71 TI #86, 23.

72 TI #99, 40.

73 Files at the Public Record Office, Kew, ED11/78: Notes following a deputation of cotton spinners (employers and operatives) to the Home Office and the Department of Education, September, 1915.

74 TI #190, 59.

75 TI #32, 39.

76 *Royal Commission on the Elementary Education Acts: Third Report*, 411. Evidence of Rev. J.B. Paton.

77 For the bewildering variety of these clauses, see Hey, *Development of the Education of Wage-Earners*, 4–6.

78 TI #240, 36.

79 Files at the Public Record Office, Kew, ED11/77: Letter of West Riding Education Authority to the Department of Education, May 1914. See also TI #27, 11; this boy left at twelve when he should have remained at school until thirteen. He simply had to avoid factory work for one year, as the factory acts required the production of a birth certificate.

80 *Departmental Committee on Juvenile Education: Report*, 3. Statistics refer to 1911.

81 TI #341, 79.

82 Rowntree, *Poverty*, 334.

83 Files at the Public Record Office, Kew, ED24/38: "Historical Note on Higher Grade Schools," 1897. This was written by R.L. Morant, a vociferous critic of these schools and the chief architect of the 1902 education act. See also Fitch, "The Higher Grade Board Schools," 321–31.

84 Files at the Public Record Office, Kew, ED12/91: "Letter of Association of School Boards to Lord President of Council," March 14, 1900.

85 *Royal Commission on Elementary Education Acts: Final Report*, 169. Fees in the H.G. Schools were rarely higher than a few pennies per week.

86 Files at the Public Record Office, Kew, ED11/91: *Royal Commission on Secondary Education: Report*, 144.

87 Reeder, "The Reconstruction of Secondary Education," Table, 144.

88 Files at the Public Record Office, Kew, ED24/38: "Historical Note on Higher Grade Schools," 1897.

89 Files at the Public Record Office, Kew, ED12/91: Letter of Rev. E.C. Maclure, President, Association of School Boards, to the Duke of Devonshire, Lord President of the Council, March 14, 1900.

90 Files at the Public Record Office, Kew, HO45.10424.RB15884A.1: Notes on the Royal Commission on Secondary Education.

91 Files at the Public Record Office, Kew, ED10/13: Memorials from Chelmsford Trades Council and Various School Boards to the Board of Education, February, 1901.

92 Simon, *Education and the Labour Movement*, 240–4.

93 Files at the Public Record Office, Kew, ED24/185: "Report of the Consultative Committee on Higher Elementary Schools," 1906. This report was savagely attacked by the National Union of Teachers for its "anti-democratic" and "reactionary" tone and conclusions.

94 *Board Teacher*, 1 June 1895, 134.

95 *Royal Commission on Elementary Education Acts: Final Report*, 170. Although referring to an earlier period, these comments are perhaps even more pertinent for the post-1902 period, at least until the advent of the free place system.

96 TI #24, 11.

97 TI #314, 70.

98 TI #31, 6, 12–14.

99 S.1.B., 5.

100 TI #190, 60.

101 TI #383, 21.

102 TI #222, 42.

103 TI #74, 51.

104 Files at the Public Record Office, Kew, ED12/114: Letters of parents to the Department of Education, and minutes of the department, 1906–7. Whether a binding contract to receive a benefit was enforceable at law is doubtful, but this point would have been lost on most parents.

105 Personal interview with George Henry Childs; Pritchett, *A Cab at the Door*, 103–6.

106 Thompson, *Edwardian Childhoods*, 92–3.

107 McGeown, *Heat the Furnace*, 38. McGeown, born in 1897 in the Glasgow area, spent two years at a higher grade school. His parents were delighted with this, but the headmistress was openly sceptical of his finishing the course. This was proved in his second year, when a required French course became a hurdle he could not overcome. At sixteen, therefore, instead of going further, he found himself bound for the destination he had tried to avoid – the local steelworks; 37–40.

108 Pritchett, *A Cab at the Door*, 103–4.

109 Escott, *Social Transformations of the Victorian Age*, 132.

110 Files at the Public Record Office, Kew, ED11/78: Mundella, "The Fight for the Child," 208.

111 Pritchett, *A Cab at the Door*, 113.

112 The problem of overcoming the very different educational and cultural milieu of the grammar schools seems to have remained a problem well into the twentieth century; see Jackson and Marsden, *Education and the Working Class*.

113 Introductory Note, Sadler, *Continuation Schools*, 52–64.

114 The technical education boards, like their school board counterparts, disappeared in 1902, but, in fact, their personnel and outlook were largely absorbed by the local education authorities.

115 Bruce, "Evening Schools in London," 130–1.

116 Sadler and Beard, "English Employers," 306–7.

117 Hyde, *The Boy in Industry and Leisure*, 68.

118 Sadler, *Report on Secondary Education*, 124–30.

119 *Departmental Committee on Juvenile Education: Report* 3. The verbal estimate given in the report is 15 per cent, but this is too low, as can be seen from the statistics in Sadler, *Continuation Schools*, 111.

120 Beard, "Results of an Inquiry," 246.

121 Paterson, *Across the Bridges*, 110.

122 Sadler, *Report on Secondary Education*, 125–7.

123 *Consultative Committee on Attendance: Report*, 29. This figure, of course, includes teenagers of all social groups. The percentage of working-class youths not under instruction must have been considerably higher.

124 *Royal Commission on the Elementary Education Acts: Third Report*, 409.

125 Findlay, *Young Wage-Earner*, 54; Hey, *Education of Wage-Earners*, 7; Braithwaite, "Boys' Clubs," 178–80.

126 TI #296, 59; M.2.P., 148.

127 B.8.P., 7.

128 Russell, *Manchester Boys*, 11.

129 TI #106, 40–41; TI #106, 56; B.4.P., 8; C.1.B., 45; P.1.B., 33; R.3.L., 2.

130 TI #341, 78; C.1.P., 29; G.4.P., 13.

131 TI #170, 70–1; TI #190, 60; TI #417, 60; M.1.B., 82–3.

132 TI #190, 48.

133 Simon, "Systematisation and Segmentation," 92.

134 Ibid.

135 In less theoretical garb, this was the view of radicals and socialists at the time; in recent decades it can be found in a straightforward Marxist formulation in the works of Brian Simon; given a Gramscian slant by Johnson, "Educational Policy and Social Control"; and used as a starting premise by Humphries, *Hooligans or Rebels?*

136 Donajgrodzki, *Social Control*, 9. This point is also made in Silver, "Aspects of Neglect," 60; it leads to "a discussion not ... of authority and power, but of the *intentions* of those in authority."

137 Silver, "Aspects of Neglect," 62.

138 See especially Humphries, *Hooligans or Rebels?*, chap. 1.

139 None of the oral history respondents examined ever completed the full four year course at a secondary school.

140 Of the eighteen boys who took extensive night courses, for example, ten came from the families of semi-skilled or unskilled labourers.

141 Burnett, *Destiny Obscure*, 135. Burnett is drawing upon and universalizing an atypical group – working-class autobiographers – for this conclusion.

CHAPTER THREE

1 See the recent work by Springhall, *Coming of Age*, especially 65–108. Springhall tends to examine the boy labour "problem" as a case study in social imperialist thought rather than as a factor of social change. Moreover, although the debate between age and class as the main determinant of historical development is useful, the object perhaps should be to combine the two, if possible, and to analyze how age-specific experiences may affect the wider social structure over time.

2 See especially Hobsbawm, *Workers: Worlds of Labour*, chaps. 10 and 11; Stedman Jones, "Working Class Culture and Working Class Politics"; and Meacham, *A Life Apart*. Both the proponents of growing homogeneity and its critics can be found in Mommsen and Husung, *The Development of Trade Unionism*, especially the articles by Price and Hyman among the former, and Reid and Zeitlin among the latter.

3 Hobsbawm, "The 'New Unionism' Reconsidered," 18; Price, "The New Unionism and the Labour Process," 136–37; Zeitlin, "Industrial Structure," 326–8.

4 For a general discussion, see More, *Skill and the English Working Class*, 43–59.

5 Howell, "Trades Unions, Apprentices," 835.

6 Hawkins, *Norwich*, 194.

7 Fox, *Smoky Crusade*, 48.

8 More, *Skill and the English Working Class*, 82.

9 Howell, "Trades Unions, Apprentices," 835.

10 Fox, *A History of the National Union*, 10–17.

11 Ibid., 21.

12 *Commission on Labour: Minutes, Group "c,"* vol. 2, 595.

13 Webb and Webb, *Industrial Democracy*, 483–4.

14 *1871 Census*, 1; *1911 Census: Occupations*, 22.

15 Child, *Industrial Relations*, 66.

16 Ibid., 173–9.

17 *General Report on the Wages of the Manual Labour Classes*, 117, 119, 121. Figures are for 1886. *1871 Census, xxxix*.

18 *Royal Commission on Labour: Minutes Group "c,"* vol. 3, 171–2.

19 Ibid., 195.

20 Ibid., 197.

21 Fyrth and Collins, *The Foundry Workers*, 59.

22 Dearle, *Industrial Training*, 45–8.

23 Booth, *Life and Labour, Second Series: Industry*, vol. 5, 49.

24 Ibid., 251.

25 *Royal Commission on Labour: Minutes, Group "C,"* vol. 2, 794.

26 Ibid., 805–7.

27 *Royal Commission on Labour: Minutes, Group "C,"* vol. 3, 81.

28 Dearle, *Industrial Training*, 45, 380.

29 Ibid., 380.

30 Booth, *Life and Labour, Second Series: Industry*, vol. 1, 198–201, 316.

31 *Royal Commission on Labour: Minutes, Group "A,"* vol. 2, 565.

32 *Royal Commission on Labour: Minutes, Group "B,"* vol. 1, 137–8.

33 Ibid., 365–6.

34 *Royal Commission on Labour: Minutes, Group "B,"* vol. 2, 67–9.

35 See Richards, "Women in the British Economy," 337–57, which argues for a drop in women's employment in the first phases of industrialization, followed by a rise after the mid-century, when service and tertiary industries became prominent.

36 *Royal Commission on the Poor Laws*, "Report on Boy Labour," 12.

37 Dearle, *Industrial Training*, 381; Booth, *Life and Labour, Second Series: Industry*, vol. 2, 123.

38 Dearle, *Industrial Training*, 381.

39 Ashworth, *An Economic History*, 194.

40 *1861 Census*, xlv; *1911 Census*, 14.

41 *Departmental Committee on the Employment of Children Act 1903: Minutes*, 534.

42 Hawkins, *Norwich*, 209.

43 *Royal Commission on the Poor Laws*, "Report on Boy Labour," 42.

44 *Royal Commission on Labour: Minutes, Group "B,"* vol. 1, 375.

45 *Royal Commission on Labour: Minutes, Group "B,"* vol. 3, 42, 47.

46 Webb and Webb, *Industrial Democracy*, 482.

47 Booth, *Life and Labour, Second Series: Industry*, vol. 2, 13.

48 Askwith, *Industrial Problems and Disputes*, 8–9.

49 Ashworth, *An Economic History*, 200.

50 Tawney, "The Economics of Boy Labour," 522.

51 Bradby and Durham, "Apprenticeship," 312.

52 Tawney, "The Economics of Boy Labour," 521.

53 Reeves, *Recollections*, 521.

54 Cloete, "The Boy and His Work," 12.

55 Ibid., 111; Russell, *Manchester Boys*, 35–9.

56 Files at the Public Record Office, Kew, MT9/680/M9903/1901; this is to be distinguished from the high-premium apprenticeship still applicable to those who wished to become officers.

57 Files at the Public Record Office, Kew, POWE8/24/H/S164/155: Deputation of Lancs. colliery owners to Chief Inspector of Mines, 20 July 1911.

58 *Report of the Cambridge Juvenile Employment Agency for 1911*, 11; *Report of the Cambridge Juvenile Employment Exchange for 1913*, 2.
59 Gibb, *Boy Work*, 100; Bray, *Boy Labour and Apprenticeship*, 70.
60 Booth, *Life and Labour, Second Series: Industry*, vol. 5, 297.
61 *Royal Commission on the Poor Laws*, "Report on Boy Labour," 41.
62 Bowley and Burnett-Hurst, *Livelihood and Poverty*, 29. 1900 was an average year for adult unemployment, while in 1913 trade was very good.
63 *1871 Census*, xii, xliii; *1911 Census*, 1, 24. This calculation is based on the total male population over 10 years of age.
64 Dearle, *Industrial Training*, 254.
65 Ibid.
66 Cloete, "The Boy and his Work," 113.
67 *General Report on the Wages of the Manual Labour Classes*, xxxviii-xl; *Report of an Enquiry of the Board of Trade*, vol. 6, 8.
68 Bray, *Boy Labour and Apprenticeship*, 125.
69 Paterson, *Across the Bridges*, 135; Booth, *Life and Labour, Second Series: Industry*, vol. 5, 271.
70 Russell, *Manchester Boys*, 158.
71 Tawney, "The Economics of Boy Labour," 530.
72 Hawkins, *Norwich*, 201.
73 Russell, *Manchester Boys*, 12; Roberts, *The Classic Slum*, 158.
74 *1911 Census*, xxxv.
75 Paterson, *Across the Bridges*, 130.
76 Hawkins, *Norwich*, 187.
77 Tawney, "Economics of Boy Labour," 534–5.
78 Booth, *Life and Labour, Second Series: Industry*, vol. 5, 292.
79 Paterson, *Across the Bridges*, 80.
80 Dearle, *Industrial Training*, 379.
81 Russell, *Manchester Boys*, 11.
82 Askwith, *Industrial Problems*, 8.
83 More, *Skill and the English Working Class*, 71.
84 *Royal Commission on the Poor Laws*, "Report on Boy Labour," 20.
85 Ibid., 23.
86 Dearle, *Industrial Training*, 383–4.
87 Tawney, "Economics of Boy Labour," 526–8.
88 Webb and Webb, *Industrial Democracy*, 811.
89 Bradby and Durham, "Apprenticeship," 303–4.
90 Gibb, *Boy Work*, 18–20.
91 Greenwood, *Juvenile Labour Exchanges*, 3.
92 Ibid., 24–5.
93 Paterson, *Across the Bridges*, 83.
94 Greenwood, *Juvenile Labour Echanges*, 48–51.

95 Ibid., 43–4.
96 Ibid., 62–3.
97 Ibid., 100.
98 Russell, *Manchester Boys*, 160–1.
99 Files at the Public Record Office, Kew, LAB2/19/TB217/1922: Memorandum on system of learnership certificates established by Trade Boards, 1914.
100 *Royal Commission on Labour: Final Report, part I*, 16.
101 Webb and Webb, *Industrial Democracy*, 479.
102 Ibid., 476.
103 Howell, "Trades Unions, Apprentices," 851.
104 Webb and Webb, *Industrial Democracy*, 481.
105 Howell, "Trades Unions, Apprentices," 855–7.
106 *Minutes of the London Trades Council*, 19 July 1883; Webb and Webb, *Industrial Democracy*, 481.
107 More, *Skill and the English Working Class*, 199–202.
108 Fox, *National Union*, 96, 135–6.
109 Ibid., 148–52, 276–7.
110 Mortimer, *History of the Boilermakers' Society*, vol. 1, 122.
111 Ibid., 155–6.
112 Child, *Industrial Relations*, 173–6.
113 Fyrth and Collins, *The Foundry Workers*, 121.
114 *Royal Commission on Labour: Minutes*, Group "c," vol. 1, 746. The spinners are an example of a group that relied heavily themselves on a large supply of boy labour. For their concurrence with employers on this and on other industrial questions, see Joyce, *Work, Society and Politics*.
115 *Royal Commission on Labour: Minutes*, Group "A," vol. 3, 195.
116 See Burgess, *The Challenge of Labour*, 53–6, and Hobsbawm, *Labouring Men*, 179–203. These unions relied more on numbers and on political action than on the scarcity value of their members' skills.
117 *Royal Commission on Labour: Minutes*, Group "B," vol. 2, 169–71; vol. 1, 34.
118 Hobsbawm, *Industry and Empire*, 172–94.
119 Pelling, "The Concept of the Labour Aristocracy," 52.

CHAPTER FOUR

1 *Report of the Departmental Committee on the Employment of Children Act 1903: Minutes*, 533, 546.
2 Paterson, *Across the Bridges*, 104–5.
3 *Inter-Departmental Committee on the Employment of School Children: Report*, 170.

4 Burnett, *Destiny Obscure*, 91.

5 Pollitt, *Serving my Time*, 26.

6 Files at the Public Record Office, Kew, HO45.10378.16273.4: Notes on the results of employment of children, if full time was enforced, 1908.

7 Turner, *About Myself*, 36.

8 G.2.L., 9; see also Turner, *About Myself*, 36, and TI #106, 40.

9 Pollitt, *Serving my Time*, 29.

10 Files at the Public Record Office, Kew, HO45.10378.162723.4: Notes on the results of employment of children, if full time was enforced, 1908.

11 *Labour Gazette*, vol. 1, no. 4, August 1893, 86.

12 Greenwood, *The Health and Physique of Schoolchildren*, 58.

13 C.1.P., 10–11.

14 TI #341, 81; G.4.P., 2.

15 Files at the Public Record Office, Kew, HO45.10378.162723.5: Labour Department to the Board of Education, 11 May 1908.

16 Simon, *Education and the Labour Movement*, 290.

17 *Departmental Committee on the Employment of Children Act 1903: Report*, 12.

18 Files at the Public Record Office, Kew, HO45.9813.B7311A.45: Memorial of Salford School Board to H.H. Asquith, Home Secretary, 1893.

19 Burke, "The Street-Trading Children of Liverpool," 720–2.

20 Ibid., 725, *Royal Commission on the Poor Laws*, "Report on Boy Labour," 24.

21 Ibid., 23.

22 Files at the Public Record Office, Kew, HO45.9813.B731A.21: Notes on the Proposed Employment of Schoolchildren Act, 1903.

23 *Departmental Committee on the Employment of Schoolchildren Act 1903: Report*, 9.

24 TI #88, 4.

25 *Departmental Committee on the Employment of Schoolchildren Act 1903: Report*, 10.

26 Russell, *Manchester Boys* 45–6. Fourteen year olds earning 15s. per week were said to be common.

27 TI #88, 4; H.6.P., 5.

28 TI #52, 38; TI #88, 29; H.6.P., 5.

29 Murphy, *New Horizons*, 21; Bell, *Pioneering Days*, 21; TI #32, 37; TI #214, 25; TI #240, 32; C.1.B., 16.

30 TI #177, 51.

31 *Report of the Departmental Committee on the Employment of Schoolchildren Act 1903: Minutes*, 212.

32 TI #314, 74; TI #373, 29; I.1.L., 2.

33 Burnett, *Useful Toil*, 92–8.

34 Roberts, *A Woman's Place*, 51.

35 Hawkins, *Norwich*, 202.
36 Webb and Webb, *Industrial Democracy*, 476.
37 Ibid., 474.
38 Booth, *Life and Labour, Second Series: Industry*, vol. 1., 255, 299, 312, 332.
39 TI #140, 1; S.1.B., 5.
40 Dearle, *Industrial Training*, 61.
41 TI #146, 47.
42 Ibid., 47–8.
43 *Royal Commission on the Poor Laws*, "Report on Boy Labour," 10.
44 P.1.L., 126.
45 TI #341, 82.
46 M.1.B., 19.
47 Cloete, "The Boy and his Work," 115.
48 Dearle, *Industrial Training*, 216.
49 More, *Skill and the English Working Class*, 70.
50 TI #106, 40–5; TI #176, 72–8.
51 TI #296, 60–4; TI #31, 15–17.
52 More, *Skill and the English Working Class*, 69.
53 TI #106, 40–1; TI #176, 73; TI #140, 44; Pollitt, *Serving My Time*, 31.
54 TI #48, 39.
55 Ibid., 31; Murphy, *New Horizons*, 23.
56 R.3.L., 8.
57 TI #106, 34.
58 TI #140, 20, 3.
59 Fox, *Smoky Crusade*, 17.
60 R.3.L., 21–2.
61 TI #31, 53.
62 TI #140, 51.
63 TI #134, 65–6.
64 Ibid., 24.
65 Goldman, *Breakthrough*, 4.
66 McGeown, *Heat the Furnace*, 80–1.
67 Haw, *From Workhouse to Westminster*, 4.
68 Wright, *Some Habits and Customs*, 84, 107.
69 Ibid., 87–8; Fox, *Smoky Crusade*, 16–17.
70 TI #140, 1.
71 M.2.B., "Edwardian Preston," 60.
72 Fox, *Smoky Crusade*, 16–17; Wright, *Some Habits and Customs*, 85.
73 TI #140, 1.
74 Williams, *Life in a Railway Factory*, 76.
75 Wright, *Some Habits and Customs*, 106.
76 TI #134, 64–6.

77 Wright, *Some Habits and Customs*, 105.
78 Haw, *Life of Will Crooks*, 40.
79 P.1.L., 127.
80 TI #106, 48; Burnett, *Useful Toil*, 332.
81 S.1.B., 5–6.
82 Pollitt, *Serving My Time*, 58; TI #140, 21.
83 Dearle, *Industrial Training*, 20–8.
84 TI #314, 83.
85 TI #417, 60.
86 TI #122, 24.
87 TI #131, 6.
88 TI #150, 42.
89 TI #380, 75–7.
90 TI #241, 47.
91 TI #252, 49.
92 Askwith, *Industrial Problems and Disputes*, 15.
93 Dearle, *Industrial Training*, 99.
94 Collet and Robertson, *Family Budgets*, 10.
95 Dearle, *Industrial Training*, 100.
96 B.1.B., 35, 55–6.
97 TI #417, 60.
98 Pollitt, *Serving my Time*, 28.
99 TI #457, 63.
100 TI #96, 54.
101 Williams, *Life in a Railway Factory*, 40. The boys in question were coach and engine cleaners.
102 TI #122, 24; TI #131, 9.
103 Hodges, *My Adventures as a Labour Leader*, 10.
104 TI #380, 76.
105 More, *Skill and the English Working Class*, 103. The figure is taken from a 1906 Wage Census.
106 TI #24, 15.
107 TI #124, 39; TI #266, 74.
108 TI #368, 18.
109 Burnett, *Destiny Obscure*, 99.
110 TI #8, 15.
111 TI #43, 48; TI #99, 45–6.
112 TI #266, 73–4.
113 TI #74, 54–9.
114 TI #236, 5, 54.
115 M.1.B., 19.
116 See Cardus, *Autobiography*.
117 TI #118, 28–9.

118 TI #24, 5, 12, 15.

119 TI #74, 37.

120 TI #240, 23–4.

121 McGeown, *Heat the Furnace*, 73.

122 TI #124, 26.

123 TI #368, 74.

124 *Departmental Committee on Van Boys and Warehouse Boys: Report*, 12.

125 This is recognized among scholars as diverse as Hobsbawm, *Labouring Men*, and Joyce, *Work, Society and Politics*.

126 *Report of an Enquiry by the Board of Trade*, vol. 1, 14–16; vol. 2, 12; vol. 7, xxv.

127 *Departmental Committee on Van Boys and Warehouse Boys: Report*, 12.

CHAPTER FIVE

1 M.2.P., *Edwardian Preston*, 55.

2 Bray, *Boy Labour and Apprenticeship*, 98; M.7.B., 7. For the history of children's games, see Opie and Opie, *Children's Games*.

3 P.1.L., 10.

4 TI #240, 17.

5 TI #236, 45; TI #296, 37–8.

6 P.1.B., 47.

7 T.3.P., 44; TI #296, 11; B.1.B., 41.

8 TI #236, 47; TI #240, 17; Fox, *Smoky Crusade*, 33.

9 TI #236, 48.

10 C.1.B., 14.

11 TI #252, 27; C.3.L., 5.

12 T.3.P., 41.

13 Paterson, *Across the Bridges*, 114–15.

14 Shadwell, *Industrial Inefficiency*, 62.

15 Cardus, *Autobiography*, 62.

16 TI #236, 79; Booth, *Life and Labour, Final Volume*, 52.

17 Russell, *Manchester Boys*, 113.

18 P.1.B., 9; Paterson, *Across the Bridges*, 139–40.

19 TI #8, 59.

20 *Ibid.*, 9–10.

21 M.2.P., 141; S.1.P., 41.

22 Roberts, *The Classic Slum*, 27. Roberts' closest friends were a case in point; Sydney, the "low class," and Ig, the "no class," were both neighbours of the more respectable Roberts.

23 Paterson, *Across the Bridges*, 96.

24 Roberts, *The Classic Slum*, 157.

25 Goldman, *Breakthrough*, 30.

26 *Inter-Departmental Committee on Physical Deterioration: Minutes*, 83; Files at the Public Record Office, Kew, HO45.10319.127693.20: Material submitted by the British Anti-Tobacco and Anti-Narcotic League, August, 1906. Russell, *Manchester Boys*, 98–9.

27 Paterson, *Across the Bridges*, 95.

28 Thompson, *Edwardian Childhoods*, 23; S.1.B., 12.

29 Paterson, *Across the Bridges*, 170.

30 TI #122, 33.

31 Paterson, *Across the Bridges*, 104–5; Booth, *Life and Labour, Final Volume*, 56.

32 Ibid., 58; S.1.B., 13.

33 Hawke, "The Extent of Gambling," 21–7.

34 Ibid., 35.

35 Roberts, *A Ragged Schooling*, 183–4.

36 Paterson, *Across the Bridges*, 115.

37 McGeown, *Heat the Furnace*, 21.

38 Russell and Russell, *Lads' Clubs*, 210–13.

39 M.2.P., *Edwardian Preston*, 79–80.

40 Morrison, "Lizerunt," 29.

41 Burke, *The Streets of London*, 134. The author here is referring to the turn of the century.

42 TI #236, 87.

43 TI #240, 48.

44 Fox, *Smoky Crusade*, 31–2.

45 Paterson, *Across the Bridges*, 149–50.

46 Hyde, *Boy in Industry and Leisure*, 64.

47 TI #124, 45.

48 TI #122, 29.

49 Ibid., 29; TI #302, 74; T.1.L., 16.

50 M.1.B., 25.

51 Hoggart, *The Uses of Literacy*, 83.

52 Paterson, *Across the Bridges*, 150; Russell and Rigby, *The Making of the Criminal*, 210; TI #96, 56.

53 TI #48, 42.

54 Paterson, *Across the Bridges*, 132; Bell, *At the Works*, 254. Bell's study deals with Middlesbrough.

55 Paterson, *Across the Bridges*, 132–3.

56 Loane, *The Next Street But One*, 107.

57 Fox, *Smoky Crusade*, 30.

58 TI #236, 56; TI #240, 30; TI #341, 52.

59 Roberts, *The Classic Slum*, 169.

60 TI #58, 16.

61 TI #296, 17.

62 M.1.B., 24.

63 TI #134, 71.

64 TI #8, 59–60.

65 TI #24, 43–4; TI #106, 27–8.

66 TI #150, 23.

67 T.3.P., 35.

68 Williams, *The Long Revolution*, 167–8, 199.

69 See the comments of Roberts, *The Classic Slum*, 129–32.

70 Williams, *The Long Revolution*, 166.

71 Bell, *At the Works*, 224–30.

72 TI #240, 14; T.1.P., 16.

73 Roberts, *The Classic Slum*, 160; see also Bell, *At the Works*, 207 and M.1.B., 33–4.

74 Files at the Public Record Office, Kew, H045.10295.114564.3: Penny Dreadful file, 1903–4.

75 Russell, *Manchester Boys*, 109.

76 Files at the Public Record Office, Kew, H045.10295.114564.1: Williams, *Life in a Railway Factory*, 77.

77 Files at the Public Record Office, Kew, H045.10295.114564.1.

78 Pritchett, *A Cab at the Door*, 110–11. Pritchett's family oscillated between lower middle class comfort and penury throughout his childhood.

79 Personal interview with George Henry Childs, born 1894.

80 Roberts, *The Classic Slum*, 160–1.

81 TI #99, 17, 27; C.1.P., 61; TI #32, 16.

82 TI #236, 18.

83 Roberts, *The Classic Slum*, 161.

84 TI #240, 21; see also Ross, "'Fierce Questions and Taunts.'"

85 Rowntree, *Poverty*, 315; TI #236, 71–2.

86 T.3.P., 4.

87 Morrison, *A Child of the Jago*, 63–9, 145–9. Although a fictional account of a London slum, the veracity of Morrison's scene setting is hard to doubt, based as it was on detailed research in the notorious Old Nicol area.

88 TI #214, 34.

89 Roberts, *A Ragged Schooling*, 118.

90 TI #43, 33; TI #32, 29–30.

91 Ibid., 36.

92 TI #55, 8.

93 TI #106, 15.

94 TI #96, 19.

95 TI #334, 52.

96 Hoggart, *The Uses of Literacy*, 53.

97 Roberts, *A Ragged Schooling*, 33.

98 TI #356, 63.

99 TI #296, 44.

100 Phelps-Brown, *The Growth of British Industrial Relations*, 60.

101 Russell and Rigby, *Working Lads' Clubs*, 8.

102 Roberts, *The Classic Slum*, 155.

103 Russell and Rigby, *Working Lads' Clubs*, 52.

104 Russell, *Manchester Boys*, 52–3.

105 "Howard Association Annual Report 1898," in Sanders, *Juvenile Offenders for 1000 Years*, 313.

106 *Board Teacher*, 1 October 1884, 21–3.

107 Roberts, *A Ragged Schooling*, 102.

108 TI #417, 27.

109 TI #302, 9–12.

110 TI #140, 14–15, 33.

111 TI #380, 15, 20.

112 Paterson, *Across the Bridges*, 185.

113 Russell and Rigby, *The Making of the Criminal*, 8.

114 Myers, "The Boy Criminal," 136.

115 TI #48, 12.

116 Rook, "Concerning Hooligans," 138.

117 Ibid., 141; *Inter-Departmental Committee on Physical Deterioration: Minutes*, 381–2.

118 Russell and Rigby, *The Making of the Criminal*, 77.

119 Chamberlain, "The Station Lounger,"153. The author was a nephew of Joe.

120 *Inter-Departmental Committee on the Employment of School Children: Minutes*, 211.

121 Russell and Rigby, *The Making of the Criminal*, 77.

122 Chamberlain, "The Station Lounger," 160.

123 Ibid.

124 Ibid., 154.

125 Ibid., 153.

126 Ibid., 156. See Russell *Young Gaol-Birds*, 111–24, for a discussion of the lodging house environment.

127 Chamberlain, "The Station Lounger," 156.

128 Humphries, *Hooligans or Rebels?*, 1.

129 Ibid., 4–25.

130 Tobias, *Crime and Industrial Society*, 14–21; Barrett, "The Treatment of Juvenile Offenders," 185.

131 Files at the Public Record Office, Kew, HO45.10332.136572.2: Letter and table of C.E.B. Russell to the Home Secretary, 1906; HO45.10332.136572.10: Letter of Wolverhampton Justices to the Home Secretary, 1906; Russell, *Manchester Boys*, 50.

132 Paterson, *Across the Bridges*, 126.

133 Gillis, "The Evolution of Juvenile Delinquency," 96–126.

134 Thompson, *The Edwardians*, 73.

135 TI #302, 43; TI #58, 21.

136 R.3.L., 32.

137 C.1.P., 51.

138 P.1.L., 39.

139 R.1.L., 46.

140 It is interesting to contrast here the very different response of working-class parents to violence perpetuated by schoolteachers, which often called forth vigorous protest. One can perhaps speculate that the relatively new educational system was seen as both more alien and more threatening than the police were to many working-class adults, and that it was much less closely identified with the needs of the working-class community, which itself had an interest in the maintenance of order and protection of property provided by police.

141 F.3.B., 15.

142 P.1.L., 50.

143 *Royal Commission on the Militia and Volunteers: Minutes*, vol. 2, 423.

144 *Spectator*, 27 August 1898; Haguch, "What to do with our Juvenile Paupers," 288. The latter is a classic example of eugenically influenced social Darwinism.

145 Russell, *Manchester Boys*, 53; Roberts, *The Classic Slum*, 156.

146 Russell, *Manchester Boys*, 54.

147 TI #140, 49.

148 TI #236, 85.

149 Gillis, *Youth and History*, 178.

150 Clarke, Hall, Jefferson, and Roberts, "Subcultures, Cultures and Class," 9. But the identification of youth subcultures in the post-war period rests upon a questionable theoretical definition. Youth subcultures, to qualify as such according to these authors, should be opposed to both the élite culture and the culture of the parents. But if this is the case, neither the Rockers and Skinheads, in their affirmation of lumpenproletarian values, nor the Mods, with their acceptance of middle-class consumerism, fit the model. What is needed, perhaps, is a wider definition of subculture that might not necessarily situate class and generational conflict at the centre, but treat them as two of a number of components of a distinct style or outlook.

CHAPTER SIX

1 Cunningham, *Leisure in the Industrial Revolution*.

2 See Bailey, *Leisure and Class*; Malcolmson, *Popular Recreations*.

3 For the following, see Bailey, "Making Sense of Music-Hall," viii-xxiii.

4 Hall, "Notes on Deconstruction," 239.

5 Mellor, *The Northern Music Hall*, 17. The best modern historian of the music halls gives different dates for both the Star and the Canterbury (1840 and 1851 respectively); see Bailey, "Custom, Capital and Culture," 182, 185.

6 MacInnes, *Sweet Saturday Night*, 135.

7 Mellor, *The Northern Music Hall*, 21; MacInness, *Sweet Saturday Night*, 13.

8 Pearsall, *Edwardian Popular Music*, 46–8.

9 Bristow, *Vice and Vigilance*, 211, 214. The licensing authorities were particularly severe when dealing with the smaller, "free" halls, where the popular content was probably most noticeable.

10 Mellor, *The Northern Music Hall*, 22.

11 Pearsall, *Edwardian Popular Music*, 47–8.

12 Ibid., 53; Wedmore, "The Music Halls," 129–30.

13 *The Music Hall*, 16 February 1889, 6. This weekly journal itself shows the effects of capitalization; starting as a fan magazine, by the mid-1890s it had become a trade paper, with information on shares and debentures, copyright law, and dividends, rather than on personalities or artistic trends.

14 Ibid., 25 May 1889, 6–7.

15 Bristow, *Vice and Vigilance*, 210.

16 Archer, "The County Council," 327.

17 Russell, *Manchester Boys*, 94.

18 Russell, *Manchester Boys*, 94; MacInnes, *Sweet Saturday Night*, 40.

19 "The Music Hall," 73.

20 MacInnes, *Sweet Saturday Night*, 30–1.

21 Bennett, "Music in the Halls," 9–10.

22 Senelick, "Politics as Entertainment," 155.

23 *The Music Hall*, 9 March 1889, 55.

24 Pearsall, *Edwardian Popular Music*, 58.

25 Traies, "Jones and the Working Girl," 23–48.

26 Mellor, *Northern Music Hall*, 59–60, 98.

27 Senelick, "Politics as Entertainment," 180.

28 MacInnes, *Sweet Saturday Night*, 75, 82–3.

29 Ibid., 80–1.

30 Davidson, *Songs of the British Music Hall*, 66.

31 Ibid., 113.

32 For instance, the Mafeking Night crowds appear to have been composed mainly of clerks and shop assistants; see Price, "Society, Status and Jingoism," 91.

33 MacInnes, *Sweet Saturday Night*, 91.

34 Bailey, "Champagne Charlie," 49–69.
35 See Stedman Jones, "Working Class Culture," 490–5, for an important discussion of these themes.
36 "The Music Hall," 74.
37 Pennell, "The Pedigree of the Music Hall," 580.
38 "Bertie Bright of Bond Street" in Gammond, *Best Music Hall and Variety Songs*, 170.
39 "My Beastly Eye-Glass" in Ibid., 165–6.
40 Examples are "Blue Ribbon Jane," about a glutinous teetotaler, and "The Vicar and I will be There," about two ministers who are always available when there is a party and when the silver is collected, in Ibid., 44, 144.
41 "Cuthbert, Clarence and Claude" in Ibid., 174–5.
42 Davidson, *Songs of the British Music Hall*, 36; Ibid., 174–5.
43 Wedmore, "The Music Halls," 134.
44 MacInnes, *Sweet Saturday Night*, 27–8.
45 Ibid., 133.
46 Bailey, *Leisure and Class*, 155.
47 Höher, "The Composition of Music Hall Audiences," 83.
48 Greenwood, *Odd People in Odd Places*, 64–5.
49 Ibid., 65.
50 *The Music Hall*, 16 March 1889, 71.
51 Freeman, *Boy Life and Labour*, 141–3; Paterson, *Across the Bridges*, 152.
52 Russell and Rigby, *Working Lads' Clubs*, 276.
53 TI #48, 25; TI #214, 50; TI #341, 55.
54 TI #52, 37.
55 TI #368, 7; TI #241, 26; TI #48, 25; TI #214, 50.
56 TI #236, 57–8.
57 TI #296, 45.
58 TI #380, 12.
59 TI #222, 41.
60 M.2.P., "Edwardian Preston," 91.
61 Bailey, "Making Sense of the Music Hall," xv.
62 Bosanquet, *Rich and Poor*, 124; M.8.B., 6.
63 Ibid., 1; MacInnes, *Sweet Saturday Night*, 136.
64 TI #296, 45.
65 TI #368, 7.
66 Ibid., 49.
67 Paterson, *Across the Bridges*, 154.
68 TI #122, 28.
69 TI #222, 31.
70 TI #334, 120–1.
71 TI #58, 15.

72 Hawkins, *Norwich*, 310; T.1.L., 20; TI #124, 44.

73 Hoggart, *The Uses of Literacy*, 100.

74 Paterson, *Across the Bridges*, 144.

75 Crump, "Provincial Music Hall," 53–72.

76 TI #131, 33.

77 M.2.P., "Edwardian Preston," 89–91; TI #47, 59.

78 Burke, *English Night Life*, 134.

79 Wedmore, "The Music Hall," 135.

80 Files at the Public Record Office, Kew, HO45.10593.186270: Cinematograph Bill, notes, 1909–1910.

81 Roberts, *The Classic Slum*, 175.

82 Freeman, *Boy Life and Labour*, 133; TI #31, 18; TI #74, 57; TI #86, 15; TI #99, 27; TI #104, 24; TI #134, 71; TI #214, 47; TI #236, 58; TI #240, 49; TI #314, 52; TI #334, 69; TI #341, 55; TI #383, 36; P.1.B., 12; T.1.L., 20.

83 Freeman, *Boy Life and Labour*, 133; Roberts, *The Classic Slum*, 176.

84 Freeman, *Boy Life and Labour*, 133.

85 Hyde, *The Boy in Industry and Leisure*, 23; Roberts, *The Classic Slum*, 175.

86 Files at the Public Record Office, Kew, HO45.10593.186270.18: Commissioner of Police to Home Office, Dec. 14 1909.

87 Bristow, *Vice and Vigilance*, 221; Files at the Public Record Office, Kew, HO45.10551.163175: Film Censorship, 1912–1914.

88 Hawkins, *Norwich*, 311.

89 Roberts, *The Classic Slum*, 175, note 7.

90 Freeman, *Boy Life and Labour*, 134. In September 1911 students in Hull and elsewhere walked out, demanding "less hours and no cane." What Freeman apparently forgot was that Hull had experienced a bitter dock strike in the summer of 1911. The schoolboys had fathers, brothers, and neighbours, not celluloid scenes, as models. See also Gillis, *Youth and History*, 174.

91 TI #373, 24.

92 TI #383, 42.

93 Roberts, *The Classic Slum*, 176.

94 Llewellyn Smith, *The New Survey of London Life*, vol. 9, 48.

95 Paterson, *Across the Bridges*, 144.

96 Freeman, *Boy Life and Labour*, 152.

97 Baker, "The Making of a Working-Class Football Culture," 243–4.

98 Ibid., 244. The exception, of course, is the continued adherence of Welsh working men to the Rugby Union.

99 TI #106, 14; TI #222, 18; TI #240, 16.

100 TI #48, 18; TI #74, 25; TI #131, 19; TI #176, 35.

101 R.3.L., 3; TI #134, 65.

102 Mason, *Association Football,"* 155, 192.

103 Baker, "The making of a Working-Class Football Culture," 244–5; one of Baden-Powell's main aims in promoting the Scouting movement was to get the thousands of "pale, narrow-chested, hunched-up miserable specimens" off the football terraces.

104 Russell, *Manchester Boys*, 62; TI #176, 35.

105 Mason, *Association Football*, 193.

106 Baker, "The Making of a Working-Class Football Culture," 248.

107 Shadwell, *Industrial Efficiency*, 490. The figure refers to the early 1900s.

108 Baker, "The Making of a Working-Class Football Culture," 246.

109 R.3.L., 3.

110 TI #122, 35.

111 Roberts, *A Ragged Schooling*, 205.

112 TI #122, 29. Neither the respondent nor his family was strongly religious, and the boy himself regularly gambled and went to the music hall and cinema. Prudery born of the urge to be respectable thus does not seem to operate in this value judgment.

113 TI #131, 34.

114 Statistics do not seem to exist for these saloons, but they were certainly not as common as music halls or cinemas, and the fact that most oral respondents do not even mention dancing seems to show that it was the pursuit of a minority.

115 Russell and Rigby, *Working Lads' Clubs*, 281.

116 Ibid., 281.

117 *Departmental Committee on Juvenile Education: Report*, 5.

118 Roberts, *The Classic Slum*, 234–5.

119 Baker, "The Making of a Working-Class Football Culture," 243.

120 This is based on one music hall, one football, and two cinemas attendances per week, extraneous of related expenses. Judging from surveys and oral testimony, such an entertainment regime was by no means unusual.

121 This is essentially the thesis of Richard Hoggart in *The Uses of Literacy*.

CHAPTER SEVEN

1 The respective works of Springhill, Wilkinson, and Blanch are particularly relevant here.

2 Percival, *Youth will be Led*, 103–12.

3 The influence in this connection of Hall's *Adolescence*, published in 1905, can hardly be overestimated. From this date, nearly every work on youth recapitulates the "recapitulation" theory and dutifully quotes extracts from the work.

4 Searle, *The Quest for National Efficiency*, 66–7.
5 First brought to the nation's attention in 1868 by Matthew Arnold, the German educational system served as a model for English educational reformers throughout the period, with commercial and industrial competitiveness used as a goad to action; see, for example, Sadler, "Compulsory Attendance," 514–30, and Ware, *Educational Reform*, 59.
6 Birch, *The Story of the Boys' Brigade*, 86.
7 Wilkinson, "English Youth, Movements," 23.
8 Ibid., 4.
9 TI #8, 29; TI #134, 71; M.2.B., 4–5.
10 See Bailey, *Leisure and Class*, 13–14.
11 TI #27, 29.
12 TI #296, 38.
13 C.3.L., 4.
14 TI #457, 50.
15 Pollitt, *Serving my Time*, 23.
16 TI #240, 25.
17 TI #52, 18, 41.
18 *Northern Gossip*, 3 January 1895.
19 Bosanquet, *Rich and Poor*, 46–7.
20 Hyde, *The Boy in Industry and Leisure*, 139.
21 T.3.P., 2.
22 Charles Booth, quoted in Thompson, *The Edwardians*, 204. This generalization is not meant to deny either the many working-class believers or their often important role in the political and social movements of the day.
23 Bray, "The Boy and his Family," 63.
24 Loane, *Next Street but One*, 106.
25 Ibid., 79.
26 TI #266, 38, 46.
27 TI #241, 20–1.
28 Anon. [Stanley], *Work about the Five Dials*, 150. The author, typically, ascribed this desire to a thirst for religion among little children. Her identity is given in Eagar, *Making Men*, 66.
29 P.1.B., 10–11.
30 B.1.B., 20.
31 TI #240, 18–19.
32 C.1.B., 12–13.
33 Ibid., 19.
34 Birch, *Story of the Boy's Brigade*, 13–21.
35 Wilkinson, "English Youth Movements," 5–6.
36 Drummond, "The Boys' Brigade," 94.
37 Ibid., 95.

38 Springhall, *Youth, Empire and Society*, 135.
39 Drummond, "The Boys' Brigade," 96.
40 Springhall, *Youth, Empire and Society*, 25.
41 Birch, *The Story of the Boys' Brigade*, 26.
42 Gillis, *Youth and History*, 130.
43 Roberts, *The Classic Slum*, 161.
44 Blanch, "Imperialism," 108.
45 Birch, *The Story of the Boys' Brigade*, 24.
46 Blanch, "Imperialism," 107–8.
47 Springhall, *Youth, Empire and Society*, 134.
48 Ibid., 90; Wilkinson, "English Youth Movements," 13.
49 Springhall, "The Boy Scouts, Class, and Militarism," 138.
50 Roberts, *The Classic Slum*, 161.
51 TI #99, 22.
52 Springhall, "The Boy Scouts, Class, and Militarism," 138.
53 TI #99, 22.
54 Blanch, "Imperialism," 112.
55 Wilkinson, "English Youth Movements," 17. Only one-third of Scouts went on to Rovers as late as 1951; see Percival, *Youth Will be Led*, 130.
56 Of the four Thompson respondents investigated who had been Scouts, three were in the organization for only a matter of weeks: TI #99, 22; TI #302, 68; and TI #453, 49.
57 Eagar, *Making Men*, 158–61.
58 Stanley, *Work about the Five Dials*, 175–9.
59 Ibid., 193.
60 Ibid., 204–5.
61 Notes, *Charity Organization Reporter*, July 1884, 223. The reference is to "a ten year old club."
62 *Inter-Departmental Committee on Physical Deterioration: Minutes*, 153.
63 Freeman, *Boy Life and Labour*, 128–9.
64 Paterson, *Across the Bridges*, 105.
65 Eagar, *Making Men*, 265–6.
66 Braithwaite, "Boys' Clubs," 186–8.
67 Russell and Rigby, *Working Lads' Clubs*, 19, 284.
68 *Inter-Departmental Committee on Physical Deterioration: Report*, 74.
69 Paterson, *Across the Bridges*, 115.
70 Russell and Rigby, *Working Lads' Clubs*, 14.
71 "'Home Rule' in a Club of Irish Boys" in *Charity Organization Reporter*, February 1886, 43.
72 Escott, *Social Transformations*, 119–20; "'Home Rule' in a Club of Irish Boys" in *Charity Organization Reporter*, ibid.
73 Legge, "The Repton Club," 138.
74 Ibid., 138, 142.

75 Ibid., 141–2; "'Home Rule' in a Club of Irish Boys," in *Charity Organization Reporter*, February 1886, 43; *Inter-Departmental Committee on Physical Deterioration: Minutes*, 153.

76 Ibid., 153; Freeman, *Boy Life and Labour*, 126–7.

77 *Charity Organization Review*, June 1912, 284.

78 From list in Russell and Rigby, *Working Lads' Clubs*, 402–35. Boys' receipts included payments for food and drink.

79 Russell, *Lads' Clubs*, 23.

80 Llewellyn Smith, *The New Survey of London Life and Labour*, vol. 9, 190–1.

81 TI #88, 13; TI #106, 21.

82 TI #122, 18.

83 B.4.P., 24–5. This reluctance on the part of the Church Lads' Brigade illustrates the more comfortable nature of its clientele.

84 TI #140, 26, 47.

85 C.1.P., 20–1.

86 Yeo, "A New Life," 38.

87 *Inter-Departmental Committee on Physical Deterioration: Minutes*, 156.

88 Springhall, "The Boy Scouts, Class, and Militarism," 157.

89 Blanch, "Imperialism," 118–120. What these "unionist successes" were is unclear.

CONCLUSION

1 Thompson, *Making of the English Working Class*, 85.

2 Butler and Stokes, *Political Change in Britain*, 250–9.

3 TI #240, 45, 47.

4 C.1.B., 45.

5 Of the fathers, 15 were Conservative, 25 were Liberal, 5 were Labour, and 6 were neutral; of the respondents, 5 were Conservative, 12 were Liberal, 25 were Labour, and 9 were neutral. The largest shifts in family politics were Conservative to Labour (7) and Liberal to Labour (11).

Bibliography

UNPUBLISHED SOURCES

Files at the Public Record Office, Kew:
Education Department, later the Board of Education, 1882–1916: ED9–ED12, ED14, ED23–ED24, ED35, ED77; Home Office, 1865–1911:HO45; Ministry of Labour, 1889–1915: LAB2, MT9, POWE8, ZPER45.
Minutes of the London Trades Council, 1883–85. McGill microfilm collection.
Oral History Archive on Family, Work and Community Life before 1918, Department of Sociology, University of Essex.
Oral History Archive – Working Class in Barrow, Lancaster and Preston, Centre for North-West Regional Studies, University of Lancaster.
Personal interview with George Henry Childs, August 1984.

PUBLISHED GOVERNMENT DOCUMENTS

1861 Census: Ages, Civil Condition, Occupations, and Birth-Places of the People, PP 1863 liii, Part 1 [5597].
1871 Census: Ages, Civil Condition, Occupations, and Birth-Places of the People, PP 1873 lxxi, Part 1 [C. 872].
1881 Census: Ages, Condition as to Marriage, Occupations, and Birth-Places of the People, PP 1883–84 lxxx [C. 3722].
1901 Census: Summary Tables, PP 1903 lxxxiv [Cd. 1523].
1911 Census: Ages and Condition as to Marriage, PP 1912–13 cxiii [Cd. 6110].
– *Occupations*, PP 1913 lxxvii [Cd. 7018].
Consultative Committee on Attendance, Compulsory or Otherwise, at Continuation Schools: Report, PP 1909 xvii [Cd. 4757].
Departmental Committee on the Employment of Children Act 1903: Minutes of Evidence, PP 1910 xxviii [Cd. 5230].

– *Report*, PP 1910 xxviii [Cd. 5229].

Departmental Committee on the Hours and Conditions of Labour of Van and Warehouse Boys: Report, PP 1913 xxxiii [Cd. 6886].

Departmental Committee on Juvenile Education in Relation to Employment after the War: Report, PP 1917–18 xi [Cd. 8512].

Factories and Workshops: Returns of Rates of Wages, PP 1871 lxii [440]; PP 1875 lxxi [303]; PP 1878–79 lxv [324]; PP 1884–85 lxxi [340]; PP 1890 lxvii [328].

General Report on the Wages of the Manual Labour Classes in the United Kingdom, with Tables, PP 1893–94 lxxxiii [C. 6889].

Inter-Departmental Committee on the Employment of School Children: Minutes of Evidence, PP 1902 xxv [Cd. 850]

– *Report*, PP 1902 xxv [Cd. 849].

Inter-Departmental Committee on Physical Deterioration: Minutes of Evidence, PP 1904 xxxii [Cd. 2210].

– *Report*, PP 1904 xxxii [Cd. 2175].

Report of an Enquiry by the Board of Trade into the Earnings and Hours of Labour of Workpeople in the United Kingdom: vol. 1: *Textile Trades in 1906*, PP 1909 xxx [Cd. 4545]; vol. 2: *Clothing Trades in 1906*, PP 1909 xxx [Cd. 4844]; vol. 3: *Building and Woodworking Trades in 1906*, PP 1910 lxxxiv [Cd. 5086]; vol. 4: *Public Utilities and Services in 1906*, PP 1910 lxxxiv [Cd. 5196]; vol. 6: *Metal, Engineering and Shipbuilding in 1906*, PP 1911 lxxxviii [Cd. 5814]; vol. 7; *Railway Service in 1907*, PP 1912–13 cviii [Cd. 6053]; vol. 8: *Paper, Printing and Misc. Trades in 1906*, PP 1912–13 cviii [Cd. 6556].

Return of Rate of Wages in the Mines and Quarries of the United Kingdom, PP 1890–91 lxxviii [C. 6455].

Return of Rate of Wages in the Principal Textile Trades of the United Kingdom, PP 1889 lxx [C. 5807].

Returns of Rates of Wages Published Between 1830 and 1886, PP 1887 lxxxix [C. 5172].

Royal Commission appointed to inquire into the Workings of the Elementary Education Acts (England and Wales): *Final Report*, PP 1888 xxxv [C. 5485].

– *Third Report*, PP 1887 xxx [C. 5158]

Royal Commission on Labour: Final Report, PP 1894 xxxv [C. 7421].

– *Minutes of Evidence taken before Group "A"*: vol. 1: PP 1892 xxxiv [C. 6708–iv]; vol. 2: PP 1892 xxxvi, part 1 [C. 6795–iv]; vol. 3: PP 1893–94 xxxii [C. 6894–vii].

– *Minutes of Evidence taken before Group "B"*: vol. 1: PP 1892 xxxv [C. 6708–v]; vol. 2: PP 1892 xxxvi, part 2 [C. 6795–v]; vol. 3: PP 1893–94 xxxiii [C. 6894–viii].

– *Minutes of Evidence taken before Group "C"*: vol. 1: PP 1892 xxxv [C. 6078–vi]; vol. 2: PP 1892 xxxvi, part 2 [C. 6795–vi]; vol. 3: PP 1893–94 xxxiv [C. 6894–ix].

Royal Commission on the Militia and Volunteers: Minutes of Evidence: vol. 1: PP 1904 xxx [Cd. 2062]; vol. 2: PP 1904 xxxi [Cd. 2063].
- *Report*, PP 1904 xxx [Cd. 2061].
Royal Commission on the Poor Laws and Relief of Distress: vol. 20: C. Jackson, "Report on Boy Labour," PP 1909 xliv [Cd. 4632].

PUBLISHED WORKS

Anderson, M. *Family Structure in Nineteenth Century Lancashire*. Cambridge: Cambridge University Press 1971.
- *Approaches to the History of the Western Family 1500–1914*. London: Macmillan 1980.
Archer, W. "The County Council and the Music Halls." *Contemporary Review* 67 (1895): 317–27.
Ashworth, W. *An Economic History of England 1870–1939*. London: Methuen and Co. 1960.
Askwith, G.R. [Lord] *Industrial Problems and Disputes*. London: John Murray 1920.
Bailey, P. "Champagne Charlie: Performance and Ideology in the Music Hall Swell Song." In *Music Hall: Performance and Style*, edited by J.S. Bratton. Milton Keynes: Open University Press 1986.
- "Custom, Capital and Culture in the Victorian Music Hall." In *Popular Culture and Custom in Nineteenth-Century England*, edited by R.D. Storch. London: Croom Helm 1982.
- *Leisure and Class in Victorian England: Rational Recreation and the Contest for Control*. Toronto: University of Toronto Press 1978.
- "Making Sense of Music Hall." In *Music Hall: The Business of Pleasure*, edited by P. Bailey. Milton Keynes: Open University Press 1986.
Baker, W.J. "The Making of a Working-Class Football Culture in Victorian England." *Journal of Social History* 13 (1979): 241–51.
Banks, O. *Parity and Prestige in English Secondary Education*. London: Routledge and Kegan Paul 1955.
Barnett, M.G. *Young Delinquents: A Study of Reformatory and Industrial Schools*. London: Methuen and Co. 1913.
Barrett, R.M. "The Treatment of Juvenile Offenders together with Statistics of their Numbers." *Journal of the Royal Statistical Society* 63 (1900): 183–261.
Beard, M.S. "Results of an Inquiry into the Working of Continuation Schools in England." In *Continuation Schools in England and Elsewhere*, edited by M.E. Sadler. Manchester: Manchester University Press 1908.
Bell, Mrs. H. [Lady]. *At the Works: A Study of a Manufacturing Town*. 2n ed. London: T. Nelson and Sons 1911.
Bell, T. *Pioneering Days*. London: Lawrence and Wishart 1941.

Bennett, A. "Music in the Halls." In *Music Hall: Performance and Style*, edited by J.S. Bratton. Milton Keynes: Open University Press 1986.

Beveridge, W.H. *Unemployment: A Problem of Industry*. 2d ed. London: Longmans, Green and Co. 1930.

Birch, A. *The Story of the Boys' Brigade*. Rev. ed., London: Frederick Muller 1965.

Blanch, M. "Imperialism, Nationalism and Organised Youth." In *Working Class Culture: Studies in History and Theory*, edited by J. Clarke, C. Critcher, and R. Johnson. New York: St. Martin's Press 1979.

The Board Teacher. (Journal of the Metropolitan Board Teachers' Association) London: 1883–1895.

Booth, C. *Life and Labour of the People of London*. Rev. ed. *First Series: Poverty*, 4 vols; *Second Series: Industry*, 5 vols; *Third Series: Religion*, 7 vols; *Final Volume*. London: Macmillan and Co. 1904.

Bosanquet, H. *Rich and Poor*. London: Macmillan and Co. 1898.

Bowley, A.L., and A.R. Burnett-Hurst. *Livelihood and Poverty*. London: G. Bell and Sons 1915.

Bradby, M.K., and F.H. Durham. "Apprenticeship." *Charity Organization Review* 13 (1903): 302–13.

Braithwaite, W.J. "Boys' Clubs." In *Studies of Boy Life in Our Cities*, edited by E.J. Urwick. London: J.M. Dent and Co. 1904.

Bray, R. "The Boy and the Family." In *Studies of Boy Life in Our Cities*, edited by E.J. Urwick. London: J.M. Dent and Co. 1904.

– *Boy Labour and Apprenticeship*. London: Constable and Co. Ltd. 1911.

Brehony, K. "Popular Control or Control by Experts? Schooling between 1880 and 1902." In *Crises in the British State 1880–1930*, edited by M. Langan and B. Schwarz. London: Hutchinson 1985.

Bristow, E.J. *Vice and Vigilance: Purity Movements in Britain since 1700*. Dublin: Gill and Macmillan 1977.

Bruce, G.L. "Evening Schools in London." In *Continuation Schools in England and Elsewhere*, edited by M.E. Sadler. Manchester: Manchester University Press 1908.

Burgess, K. *The Challenge of Labour: Shaping British Society 1850–1930*. London: Croom Helm 1980.

Burke, T. "The Street-Trading Children of Liverpool." *Contemporary Review* 68 (1900): 720–6.

Burke, T. *English Night Life*. London: B.T. Batsford 1941.

– *The Streets of London*. London: B.T. Batsford 1940.

Burnett, J. *A Social History of Housing 1815–1970*. Newton Abbott: David and Charles 1978.

– ed. *Destiny Obscure: Autobiographies of Childhood, Education and Family from the 1820s to the 1920s*. London: Allen Lane 1982.

– ed. *Useful Toil: Autobiographies of Working People from the 1820s to the 1920s.* London: Allen Lane 1974.

Butler, D., and D. Stokes. *Political Change in Britain: Forces Shaping Electoral Choice.* New York: St. Martin's Press 1969.

Cardus, N. *Autobiography.* London: Collins and the Book Society 1947.

Cecil, R. *Life in Edwardian England.* London: B.T. Batsford 1969.

Chamberlain, T.N. "The Station Lounger: A Study." In *Problems of Boy Life,* edited by J.H. Whitehouse. London: P.S. King and Son 1912.

Charity Organization Reporter. London: 1884–1890.

Charity Organization Review. London. 1890–1912.

Child, J. *Industrial Relations in the British Printing Industry.* London: George Allen and Unwin 1967.

Clarke, J., S. Hall, et al. "Subcultures, Cultures and Class." In *Resistance through Rituals: Youth Subcultures in Post-War Britain,* edited by S. Hall and T. Jefferson. London: Hutchinson and Co. 1976.

Cloete, J.G. "The Boy and His Work." In *Studies of Boy Life in Our Cities,* edited by E.J. Urwick. London: J.M. Dent and Co. 1904.

Collet, E., and M. Robertson. *Family Budgets: Being the Income and Expenses of Twenty-Eight British Households 1891–1894.* London: P.S. King 1896.

Crossick, G. *An Artisan Elite in Victorian Society: Kentish London 1840–1880.* London: Croom Helm 1978.

Crump, J. "Provincial Music Hall: Promoters and Public in Leicester 1863–1929." In *Music Hall: The Business of Pleasure,* edited by P. Bailey. Milton Keynes: Open University Press 1986.

Cunningham, H. *Leisure in the Industrial Revolution.* New York: St. Martin's Press 1980.

Davin, A. "Child Labour, the Working Class Family and Domestic Ideology in Nineteenth Century Britain." *Development and Change* 13 (1982): 633–52.

Davison, P., ed. *Songs of the British Music Hall.* New York: Oak [c. 1971].

Dearle, N.B. *Industrial Training: With Special Reference to the Conditions Prevailing in London.* London: P.S. King and Son 1914.

Desmond, S. *London Nights in the Gay Nineties.* New York: R.M. McBride and Co. 1928.

Drummond, H., "The Boys' Brigade." *Good Words* 32 (1891): 93–100.

Donajgrodzki, A.P., ed. *Social Control in Nineteenth Century Britain.* London: Croom Helm 1977.

Eagar, W. McG. *Making Men: The History of Boys' Clubs and Related Movements in Great Britain.* London: University of London Press 1953.

Escott, T.H.S. *England: Its People, Polity, and Pursuits.* London: Chapman and Hall 1885.

– *Social Transformations of the Victorian Age.* London: Seeley and Co. 1897.

Eyles, M.L. *The Woman in the Little House*. London: Grant Richards Ltd. 1922.

Fifteenth Annual Report of the Committee on Wage Earning Children. London: 1915.

Findlay, J.J. *The Young Wage-Earner and the Problem of his Education*. London: Sidgewick and Jackson 1918.

Fishman, W.J., *East End 1888: Life in a London Borough among the Labouring Poor*. Philadelphia: Temple University Press 1988.

Fitch, J.G. "The Higher Grade Board Schools." *Nineteenth Century* 49 (1901): 321–31.

Fletcher, C.R.L., and R. Kipling. *A School History of England*. Oxford: Clarendon Press 1911.

Ford, P., and G. Ford. *A Breviate of Parliamentary Papers 1900–1916*. Oxford: Basil Blackwell 1957.

Fox, A. *A History of the National Union of Boot and Shoe Operatives 1874–1957*. Oxford: Basil Blackwell 1958.

Fox, R.M. *Smoky Crusade*. London: The Hogarth Press 1938.

Freeman, A. *Boy Life and Labour: The Manufacture of Inefficiency*. London: P.S. King and Sons 1914.

Fyrth, H.J. and H. Collins. *The Foundry Workers: A Trade Union History*. Manchester: Amalgamated Union of Foundry Workers 1959.

Gammond, P., ed. *Best Music Hall and Variety Songs*. London: Wolfe Publishing 1972.

Gardner, P. *The Lost Elementary Schools of Victorian England*. London: Croom Helm 1984.

Gibb, S.J. *Boy Work: Exploitation or Training?* London: T. Fisher Unwin Ltd., 1919.

Gillis, J.R. "Conformity and Rebellion: Contrasting Styles of English and German Youth 1900–1933." *History of Education Quarterly* 13 (1973): 249–60.

– "The Evolution of Juvenile Deliquency in England 1890–1914." *Past and Present* 67 (1975): 96–126.

– *Youth and History: Tradition and Change in European Age Relations 1770–Present*. New York: Academic Press 1974.

Gissing, G. *The Nether World*. [London: Smith, Elder and Co. 1889], ed. J. Goode, Brighton: The Harvester Press 1974.

Gittens, D. *Fair Sex: Family Size and Structure 1900–39*. London: Hutchinson 1982.

Golby, J.M., and A.W. Purdue. *The Civilisation of the Crowd: Popular Culture in England 1750–1900*. London: Batsford 1984.

Goldman, R., ed. *Breakthrough: Autobiographical Accounts of the Education of Some Socially Disadvantaged Children*. London: Routledge and Kegan Paul 1968.

Gorst, J.E. *The Children of the Nation: How their Health and Vigour should be Promoted by the State*. London: Methuen and Co. 1906.

Gray, R.Q. *The Labour Aristocracy in Victorian Edinburgh*. Oxford: Clarendon Press 1976.

Greenlee, J.G. "Imperial Studies and the Unity of the Empire." *Journal of Imperial and Commonwealth History* 7 (1979): 321–35.

Greenwood, A. *The Health and Physique of Schoolchildren*. London: P.S. King and Son 1913.

– *Juvenile Labour Exchanges and After-Care*. London: P.S. King and Son 1911.

Greenwood, A., and J.E. Kettlewell. "Some Statistics of Juvenile Employment and Unemployment." *Journal of the Royal Statistical Society*, 75 (1911–12): 744–53.

Greenwood, J. *Odd People in Odd Places: or, The Great Residuum*. London: Frederick Warne and Co. 1883.

Griggs, C. *The Trades Union Congress and the Struggle for Education 1868–1925*. Lewes, Sussex: The Falmer Press 1983.

Haguch. "What to do with our Juvenile Paupers." *Westminster Review* 150, (1898): 282–8.

Hall, G.S. *Adolescence*. New York: D. Appleton and Co. 1905.

Hall, S. "Notes on Deconstructing the Popular.'" In *People's History and Socialist Theory*, edited by R. Samuel. London: Routledge and Kegan Paul 1981.

Hall, S., and T. Jefferson, eds. *Resistance through Rituals: Youth Subcultures in Post-War Britain*. London: Hutchinson and Co. 1976.

Harris, J. *Unemployment and Politics: A Study in English Social Policy 1886–1914*. Oxford: Clarendon Press 1972.

Haw, G. *From Workhouse to Westminster: The Life of Will Crooks, M.P.* London: Cassell and Co. 1911.

Hawke, J. "The Extent of Gambling." In *Betting and Gambling: A National Evil*, edited by B.S. Rowntree. London: Macmillan and Co. 1905.

Hawkins, C.B. *Norwich: A Social Study*. London: Philip Lee Warner 1910.

Heath, J. St. G. *The War and Some Problems of Adolescence*. London: Mowbray 1916.

Hey, S. *Development of the Education of Wage-Earners*, Oxford: Oxford University Press 1917.

Hobsbawm, E. *Industry and Empire*. Harmondsworth: Penguin Books 1969.

– *Labouring Men*. New York: Basic Books 1964.

– "The 'New Unionism' Reconsidered." In *The Development of Trade Unionism in Great Britain and Germany 1880–1914*, edited by W.J. Mommsen and H.-G. Husung. London: G. Allen and Unwin 1985.

– *Workers: Worlds of Labour*. New York: Pantheon 1984.

Hobson, J.A. *Problems of Poverty: An Inquiry into the Industrial Conditions of the Poor*. London: Methuen and Co. 1891.

Hodges, F. *My Adventures as a Labour Leader*. London: George Newnes Ltd. 1924.

Hoggart, R. *The Uses of Literacy*. London: Chatto and Windus 1967.

Höher, D. "The Composition of Music Hall Audiences." In *Music Hall: The Business of Pleasure*, edited by P. Bailey. Milton Keynes: Open University Press 1986.

Holloway, J. *A London Childhood*. New York: Charles Scribner's Sons 1966.

Holmes, E. *What Is and What Might Be: A Study of Education in General and Elementary Education in Particular*. London: Constable and Co. 1912.

Howell, G. "Trades Unions, Apprentices, and Technical Education." *Contemporary Review* 30 (1877): 833–57.

Humphries, S. *Hooligans or Rebels? An Oral History of Working Class Childhood and Youth 1889–1939*. Oxford: Basil Blackwell 1981.

Hurt, J. *Elementary Schooling and the Working Classes*. London: Routledge and Kegan Paul 1979.

Hyde, R. *The Boy in Industry and Leisure*. London: G. Bell and Sons Ltd. 1921.

Hyman, R. "Mass Organization and Militancy in Britain: Contrasts and Continuities." In *The Development of Trade Unionism in Great Britain and Germany 1880–1914*, edited by W.J. Mommsen and H.-G. Husung. London: George Allen and Unwin 1985.

Jackson, B., and D. Marsden. *Education and the Working Class*. London: Routledge and Kegan Paul 1962.

Johnson, R. "Educational Policy and Social Control in Early Victorian England." *Past and Present* 49 (1970): 96–119.

– "Three Problematics: Elements of a Theory of Working Class Culture." In *Working Class Culture: Studies in History and Theory*, edited by J. Clarke, C. Critcher, and R. Johnson. New York: St. Martin's Press 1979.

Joyce, P. *Work, Society and Politics: The Culture of the Factory in Later Victorian England*. Brighton: The Harvester Press 1980.

Keeling, F. *Child Labour in the United Kingdom: A Study in the Development and Administration of the Law*. London: P.S. King and Son 1914.

The Labour Gazette: The Journal of the Labour Department of the Board of Trade. London: 1893–1913.

Legge, H. "The Repton Club." In *The Universities and the Social Problem*, edited by J.M. Knapp. London: Rivington, Percival 1895.

Llewelyn Lewis, E. *The Children of the Unskilled*. London: P.S. King and Son 1924.

Llewellyn Smith, H., ed. *The New Survey of London Life and Labour*. vol. 9, *Life and Leisure*. London: P.S. King and Son 1935.

Loane, M. *The Next Street But One*. London: Edward Arnold 1907.

MacInnes, C. *Sweet Saturday Night*. London: MacGibbon and Kee 1967.

Macnamara, T.J. "Higher Education and the State." *Nineteenth Century* 45 (1899): 663–70.

Malcolmson, R. *Popular Recreations in English Society 1700–1850*. Cambridge: Cambridge University Press 1973.

Mander, R., and J. Mitchison. *British Music Hall*. Rev. ed. London: Gentry Books 1974.

Marsden, W.E. "Social Environment, School Attendance and Educational Achievement in a Merseyside Town 1870–1900." In *Popular Education and Socialization in the Nineteenth Century*, edited by P. McCann. London: Methuen and Co. 1977.

Marsh, D.C. *The Changing Social Structure of England and Wales 1871–1961*. London: Routledge and Kegan Paul 1965.

Marson, D. "Children's Strikes in 1911." *History Workshop Pamphlets*. Number 9, 1973.

Mason, T. *Association Football and English Society 1863–1915*. Brighton: The Harvester Press 1980.

McGeown, P. *Heat the Furnace Seven Times More*. London: Hutchinson and Co. 1967.

McLaren, A. *Birth Control in Nineteenth-Century England*. New York: Holmes and Meier 1978.

Meacham, S. *A Life Apart: The English Working Class 1890–1913*. Cambridge, Mass.: Harvard University Press 1977.

Mearns, A. *The Bitter Cry of Outcast London*. [1883]. ed. A.S. Wohl, Leicester: Leicester University Press 1970.

Meller, H.E. *Leisure and the Changing City 1870–1914*. London: Routledge and Kegan Paul 1976.

Mellor, G.J. *The Northern Music Hall*. Newcastle-upon-Tyne: Frank Graham 1970.

Mommsen, W.J., and H.-G. Husung, eds. *The Development of Trade Unionism in Great Britain and Germany 1880–1914*. London: G. Allen and Unwin 1985.

More, C. *Skill and the English Working Class 1870–1914*. London: Croom Helm 1980.

Morris, R.J. *Class and Class Consciousness in the Industrial Revolution 1780–1850*. London: Macmillan and Co. 1979.

Morrison, A. *A Child of the Jago*. [1896], ed. P.J. Keating, London: MacGibbon and Kee 1969.

– "Lizerunt." In *Working Class Stories of the 1890s*, edited by P.J. Keating. London: Routledge and Kegan Paul 1971.

Mortimer, J.E. *History of the Boilermakers' Society*. 2 vols. London: George Allen and Unwin 1973.

Murphy, J.T. *New Horizons*. London: John Lane 1941.

Musgrave, P.W. *Technical Change, the Labour Force, and Education*. Oxford: Pergamon Press 1967.

Musgrove, F. *School and the Social Order*. Chichester: John Wiley and Sons 1979.

The Music Hall. (Weekly). London: 1889–1895.

"The Music Hall." *Cornhill Magazine* 60 (1889): 68–79.

Myers, J.M. "The Boy Criminal." In *Problems of Boy Life,* edited by J.H. Whitehouse. London: P.S. King and Son 1912.

Neuman, B.P. "'It's Dogged as Does It': The Story of an Experiment in Boys' Clubs." *Charity Organization Review* 6 (1890): 189–93.

Northern Gossip. Newcastle-upon-Tyne: 1895.

Oddy, D.J. "Working-Class Diets in Late Nineteenth Century Britain." *Economic History Review* 23 (1970): 314–23.

Oliver, T. "Our Workmen's Diet and Wages." *Fortnightly Review* 56 (1894): 513–26.

Opie, I., and P. Opie. *Children's Games in Street and Playground.* Oxford: Clarendon Press 1969.

Orwell, G. "Boys" Weeklies." In *Dickens, Dali and Other Studies in Popular Culture.* New York: Reynal and Hitchcock 1946.

Osborne Jay, A. *Life in Darkest London.* London: Webster and Cable 1891.

Paterson, A. *Across the Bridges: or, Life by the South London River-Side.* London: Edward Arnold 1911; 2d ed. 1918.

Pearsall, R. *Edwardian Popular Music.* Madison: Fairleigh Dickinson University Press 1975.

Pearson, G. *Hooligan: A History of Respectable Fears.* London: Macmillan 1983.

Pelling, H. "The Concept of the Labour Aristocracy." In *Popular Politics and Society in Late Victorian Britain.* London: Macmillan and Co. 1968.

Pennell, E.R. "The Pedigree of the Music-Hall." *Contemporary Review* 63 (1893): 575–83.

A People's Autobiography of Hackney: Working Lives 1905–45. London: Hackney W.E.A. n.d.

Percival, A.C. *Youth will be Led: The Story of the Voluntary Youth Organizations.* London: Collins and Co. 1951.

Phelps-Brown, E.H. *The Growth of British Industrial Relations.* London: Macmillan and Co. 1965.

Pollitt, H. *Serving my Time.* London: Lawrence and Wishart 1940.

The Poor Law Officers' Journal. London: 1892.

Price, R.N. "The New Unionism and the Labour Process." In *The Development of Trade Unionism in Great Britain and Germany 1880–1914,* edited by W.J. Mommsen and H.-G. Husung. London: G. Allen and Unwin 1985.

– "Society, Status and Jingoism: The Social Roots of Lower Middle Class Patriotism 1870–1900." In *The Lower Middle Class in Britain 1870–1914,* edited by G. Crossick. London: Croom Helm 1977.

Pritchett, V.S. *A Cab at the Door.* New York: Random House 1967.

Reeder, D. "The Reconstruction of Secondary Education in England, 1869–1920." In *The Rise of the Modern Educational System,* edited by D.K. Muller, F. Ringer, and B. Simon. Cambridge: Cambridge University Press 1987.

Reeves, J. *Recollections of a School Attendance Officer*. London: Arthur H. Stockwell c. 1915.

Reid, A. "Intelligent Artisans and Aristocrats of Labour: The Essays of Thomas Wright." In *The Working Class in Modern British History: Essays in Honour of Henry Pelling*, edited by J. Winter. Cambridge: Cambridge University Press 1983.

– "The Division of Labour and Politics in Britain, 1880–1920." In *The Development of Trade Unionism in Great Britain and Germany 1880–1914*, edited by W.J. Mommsen and H.-G. Husung. London: George Allen and Unwin 1985.

Report of the Cambridge Juvenile Employment Agency for 1911. Cambridge: 1912.

Report of the Cambridge Juvenile Employment Exchange for 1913. Cambridge: 1914.

Report of the Committee on Wage Earning Children. London: 1900.

Richards, E. "Women in the British Economy since about 1700: An Interpretation." *History* 59 (1974): 337–57.

Roberts, E. *A Woman's Place: An Oral History of Working Class Women 1890–1940*. Oxford: Basil Blackwell 1984.

– "Working Class Barrow and Lancaster 1890 to 1930." Centre for North-West Regional Studies, *University of Lancaster Occasional Paper* No. 2, 1976.

Roberts, R. *The Classic Slum: Salford Life in the First Quarter of the Century*. Harmondsworth: Penguin Books 1973.

– *A Ragged Schooling: Growing Up in the Classic Slum*. Manchester: Manchester University Press 1976.

Rook, C. "Concerning Hooligans." In *Working Class Stories of the 1890s*, edited by P.J. Keating. London: Routledge and Kegan Paul 1971.

Ross, E. "'Fierce Questions and Taunts': Married Life in Working Class London 1870–1914." *Feminist Studies* 8, (1982): 575–602.

Rowntree, B.S. *Poverty: A Study of Town Life*. 3d ed. London: Macmillan and Co. 1902.

Rubinstein, D. *School Attendance in London 1870–1904: A Social History*. New York: Augustus M. Kelley 1969.

– "Socialization and the London School Board 1870–1904: Aims, Methods and Public Opinion." In *Popular Education and Socialization in the Nineteenth Century*, edited by P. McCann. London: Methuen and Co. 1977.

Russell, C.E.B. *Manchester Boys: Sketches of Manchester Lads at Work and Play*. Manchester: Manchester University Press 1905.

– *The Problem of Juvenile Crime*. Oxford: Oxford University Press 1917.

– *Young Goal-Birds*. London: Macmillan and Co. 1910.

Russell, C.E.B., and L. Rigby. *The Making of the Criminal*. London: Macmillan and Co. 1906.

– *Working Lads' Clubs*. London: A.C. Black Ltd. 1908.

Russell, C.E.B., and L. Russell. *Lads' Clubs: Their History, Organization and Management*. London: A.C. Black Ltd. 1932.

Ryder, J., and H. Silver. *Modern English Society: History and Structure 1850–1970*. London: Methuen and Co. 1970.

Sadler, M.E. *Report on Secondary Education in Birkenhead*. London: G. Philip and Son 1904.

– "Compulsory Attendance at Continuation Schools in Germany." In *Continuation Schools in England and Elsewhere*, edited by M.E. Sadler. Manchester: Manchester University Press 1908.

– ed. *Continuation Schools in England and Elsewhere*. Manchester: Manchester University Press 1908.

Sadler, M.E., and M.S. Beard. "English Employers and the Education of their Workpeople." In *Continuation Schools in England and Elsewhere*, edited by M.E. Sadler. Manchester: Manchester University Press 1908.

Sadler, M.E., and M.S. Beard. "English Employers and the Education of their Workpeople." In *Continuation Schools in England and Elsewhere*, edited by M.E. Sadler. Manchester: Manchester University Press 1908.

Sanders, W.B., ed. *Juvenile Offenders for 1000 Years*. Chapel Hill: University of North Carolina Press 1970.

Searle, G.R. *The Quest for National Efficiency*. Berkeley and Los Angeles: University of California Press 1971.

Second Annual Report of the Lads' Employment Committee. London: 1908.

Senelick, L. "Politics as Entertainment: Victorian Music Hall Songs." *Victorian Studies* 19 (1975–6): 149–60.

Shadwell, A. *Industrial Inefficiency*. London: Longmans, Green and Co. 1909.

Silver, H. "Aspects of Neglect: The Strange Case of Victorian Popular Education." *Oxford Review of Education* 3 (1977): 57–69.

Simon, B. *Education and the Labour Movement 1870–1920*. London: Lawrence and Wishart 1965.

– *Studies in the History of Education 1780–1870*. London: Lawrence and Wishart 1960.

– "Systematisation and Segmentation in Education: The Case of England." In *The Rise of the Modern Educational System*, edited by D.K. Muller, F. Ringer, and B. Simon. Cambridge: Cambridge University Press 1987.

Sims, G. "How the Poor Live." In *Into Unknown England 1866–1913: Sections from the Social Explorers*, edited by P.J. Keating. Manchester: Manchester University Press 1976.

– *How the Poor Live*. London: Chatto and Windus, 1883.

Smith, F.B. "Sexuality in Britain 1800–1900: Some Suggested Revisions." In *A Widening Sphere: Changing Roles of Victorian Women*, edited by M. Vicunus. Bloomington: Indiana University Press 1977.

The Spectator, London: 1889–1898.

Springhall, J.O. "The Boy Scouts, Class and Militarism in Relation to British Youth Movements 1908–1930." *International Review of Social History* 16

(1971), Part 2: 125–58.

– *Coming of Age: Adolescence in Britain 1860–1960*. Dublin: Gill and Macmillan 1986.

– "'A Life Story for the People'?: Edwin J. Brett and the London 'Low-life' Penny Dreadfuls of the 1860s." *Victorian Studies* 33 (1990): 223–46.

– *Youth, Empire and Society*. London: Croom Helm 1977.

Stanley, M. *Work About the Five Dials*. London: Macmillan and Co. 1878.

Stedman Jones, G. "Class Expression versus Social Control? A Critique of Recent Trends in the Social History of Leisure." *History Workshop* 4, (1977): 162–70.

– *Outcast London: A Study in the Relationship Between Classes in Victorian Society*. Oxford: Clarendon Press 1971 and Harmondsworth: Penguin Books 1984.

– "Working Class Culture and Working Class Politics in London 1870–1900: Notes on the Remaking of a Working Class." *Journal of Social History* 7, (1973–4): 460–508.

Tawney, R.H. "The Economics of Boy Labour." *Economic Journal* 19 (1909): 517–37.

Thomas, E. *The Childhood of Edward Thomas: A Fragment of Autobiography*. London: Faber and Faber 1938.

Thompson, E.P. *The Making of the English Working Class*. Harmondsworth: Penguin Books 1968.

Thompson, P. *The Edwardians: The Remaking of British Society*. London: Paladin Books 1977.

– *The Voice of the Past: Oral History*. Oxford: Oxford University Press 1978.

Thompson, T. *Edwardian Childhoods*. London: Routledge and Kegan Paul 1981.

Tobias, J.J. *Crime and Industrial Society in the Nineteenth Century*. London: B.T. Batsford 1967.

Traies, J. "Jones and the Working Girl: Class Marginality in Music Hall Song 1860–1900." In *Music Hall: Performance and Style*, edited by J.S. Bratton. Milton Keynes: Open University Press 1986.

Turner, B. *About Myself: 1863–1930*. London: Humphrey Toulmain 1930.

Vincent, D. *Bread, Knowledge and Freedom: A Study of Nineteenth-Century Working Class Autobiography*. London: Europa Publications 1981.

Walvin, J. *A Child's World: A Social History of English Childhood 1800–1914*. Harmondsworth: Penguin Books 1982.

Ware, F. *Educational Reform*. London: Methuen and Co. 1900.

Webb, B., and S. Webb. *Industrial Democracy*. London: Amalgamated Society of Engineers 1898.

Wedmore, F. "The Music Halls." *Nineteenth Century* 40 (1896): 129–30.

Wilkinson, P. "English Youth Movements 1908–1930." *Journal of Contemporary History* 4 (1969): 3–23.

Williams, A. *Life in a Railway Factory.* [1915]. Newton Abbott: David and Charles Reprints 1969.

Williams, R. *The Long Revolution.* London: Chatto and Windus 1961.

Willis, F. *A Book of London Yesterdays.* London: Phoenix House 1960.

White, J. *Rothschild Buildings: Life in an East End Tenement Block 1887–1920.* London: Routledge and Kegan Paul 1980.

Wohl, A.S. "Sex and the Single Room: Incest among the Victorian Working Classes." In *The Victorian Family: Structure and Stresses,* edited by A.S. Wohl. London: Croom Helm 1978.

Wright, T. ("A Journeyman Engineer"). *The Great Unwashed.* London: Tinsley Bros. 1868.

– *Our New Masters.* London: Strahan and Co. 1873.

– *Some Habits and Customs of the Working Classes.* London: Tinsley Bros. 1867.

Yeo, S. "A New Life: The Religion of Socialism in Britain 1883–1896." *History Workshop* 4 (1977): 5–56.

Zeitlin, J. "Industrial Structure, Employer Strategy and the Diffusion of Job Control in Britain, 1880–1920." In *The Development of Trade Unionism in Great Britain and Germany 1880–1914,* edited by W.J. Mommsen and H.-G. Husung. London: G. Allen and Unwin 1985.

Index

secondary, 40; and family, 41–2
Education acts: 1870, 28–9, 52; 1876, 29; 1880, 29; 1902, 29, 30, 41, 44, 158
Elections, 96
Employment of Children Act 1903, 76

Factory acts, 52, 69
Family: size, 8–10; hierarchy and structure, 10–14, 18–25, 159; household tasks, 14–15; income, 16–17; and pocket money, 23–4; and education, 41–2; and industrial discipline, 63–5; and courtship, 102
Feeding: undernourishment, 7–8; division of food, 13–14
Fighting: among adults, 107; among adolescents, 107–9
Football, 64, 98, 104, 134–9, 160; and street life, 135–6; and churches and trade unions, 135; and boys' clubs, 136, 151, 153
Forster, W.E., 28

Gambling and betting, 75, 99–100, 134
Gateshead, 7
Germany, 65, 141
Gillis, J., xiv, 113
Glamorgan, 109, 128
Glasgow, 61, 135, 147
Guildford, 110

Hanley, 90
Home Office, 76, 105
Humphries, S., xiv, 34–5, 48

Incest, 6
Independent Labour Party, 154

Industry: textiles, xv, 52, 61, 62, 65, 80, 86, 88; engineering, 54, 55, 58, 61, 62, 65, 80; boot and shoe, 54, 62, 85; printing, 55, 80; iron and steel, 55; low-skilled factory, 55; docks and transport, 56–8; food processing, 57; gold and silversmithing, 58; table of boys in, 60; metalworking, 61, 86, 89; shipbuilding, 61, 62, 65, 80, 85; clothing, 62; building, 62; chemical, 71; electrical, 71; automotive, 71; plumbing, 79; smithing, 79; boilermaking, 80; mining, 86, 89

Juvenile labour exchanges, 66–7

Keighley, 39, 79
Kitchener's Army, 141, 156

"Labour aristocracy," 6, 54, 69, 84, 161; and mule spinners, 89
Labour Examination, 39, 42, 74
Labour Party, 161–2
Lancashire, 59, 73, 75, 107, 131
Lancaster, 25, 77, 80, 82, 114, 135, 137
"Learners," 84–8; types of, 85
Leeds, 121
Leicester, 57, 69
Liverpool, 16, 17, 38, 57, 73, 75, 76, 90, 91, 107, 148–9, 153
London, 4, 6, 14, 16, 19, 20, 25, 29, 31, 32, 35, 39, 59, 62–3, 65, 66, 73, 74, 78, 86, 88, 91, 92, 97, 101, 102, 103, 104, 107, 108, 110, 113,

120–1, 130, 152, 161; Limehouse, 6; Whitechapel, 6; Finsbury, 7; East End, 37; Lambeth, 41; Tottenham, 95; Canning Town, 109; Hoxton, 127–8; Hackney, 145; Five Dials, 149
London County Council, 121
London Federation of Boys' Clubs, 151
Lowe, R., 28
Lowe Revised Code, 32–3, 36

Manchester, 14, 38, 67, 77, 90, 127, 130, 151, 153
Mansion House Advisory Committee of Associations for Boys, 66
Marriage: market, 26, 101–3; patterns, 62, 102
Meacham, S., xxii
Middlesbrough, 104, 120
Militia and volunteers, xviii
Mines Bill, 59
Music halls, 20, 64, 75, 101, 118–34, 139, 154, 159; programs, 122; songs, 122–7; stars, 124–5, 127, 129, 131; and class consciousness, 127, 131, 138

National Association of Boys' Clubs, 153
"National efficiency," xvii; and physical deterioration, xviii; and youth movements, xxii, 141; and education, 30
National Service League, 149
National Society for the Prevention of Cruelty to Children, 114
Newcastle-upon-Tyne, 7
Northampton, 4, 7, 59, 105